COMPETITION AND MONOPOLY
IN THE
BRITISH SOAP INDUSTRY

COMPETITION AND MONOPOLY IN THE BRITISH SOAP INDUSTRY

BY

H. R. EDWARDS

SENIOR LECTURER IN ECONOMICS
UNIVERSITY OF SYDNEY

CLARENDON PRESS · OXFORD
1962

Oxford University Press, Amen House, London E.C.4

GLASGOW NEW YORK TORONTO MELBOURNE WELLINGTON
BOMBAY CALCUTTA MADRAS KARACHI LAHORE DACCA
CAPE TOWN SALISBURY NAIROBI IBADAN ACCRA
KUALA LUMPUR HONG KONG

© *Oxford University Press* 1962

Printed in Great Britain by
The Camelot Press Ltd., London and Southampton

PREFACE

THIS book is essentially a study of oligopoly and is thus concerned with a specialist branch of the theory of value (although one of wide application in the modern economy). It is a contribution to that branch of the subject which is concerned with the variety of structure and results in particular market situations. Over and against this there is the broad analysis of the economy as a whole embodied in the 'competitive model'. The critique of Perfect Competition as ideal in the first chapter of this book should not be understood to suggest that this model is unimportant. It is, in fact, and particularly in aggregative analyses (e.g. the Samuelson-Stolper theorem), the basis of the economists' short-hand of 'assuming perfect competition' —referring thereby to certain results (as e.g. that wages tend to approximate the marginal productivity of labour), rather than to a particular structure, of markets. Specialist enquiry into the effects of different market structures are then important, among other purposes, in assessing the manner and extent to which the results of the broad analysis may require modification.

My greatest personal debt is to Mr. P. W. S. Andrews, under whose early guidance this work developed. Many of his ideas are here adopted, and presented without proper acknowledgement as my own.

My thanks are also due to Professor J. R. Hicks for comment on the Oxford thesis of 1957 from which the book derives, and for encouragement to persevere in the subsequent revision.

Among published work I am particularly indebted to the writings of Professor J. S. Bain, Mr. Charles Wilson, Sir Roy Harrod, Professor E. H. Chamberlin, Professor J. M. Clark and Mr. N. Kaldor. Acknowledgement is due to the Harvard University Press for permission to reproduce in Table 1 some of Professor Bain's results from his important work *Barriers to New Competition*. In the early chapters of Part II I have drawn freely on Mr. Wilson's authoritative *History of Unilever* (Cassell, London). My objective, if Mr. Wilson will forgive this manner of expressing it, has been to recast parts of his story from the point of view of an industrial economist and in particular Part I of this book. Mr. P. A. R. Puplett's *Synthetic Detergents* became available after my own account of the soap industry was substantially completed. However where Mr. Puplett's estimates of production, sales, etc. from trade sources differed only fractionally from my own, I have bowed to his precedence in time and accepted his.

My thanks are also due to Unilever Ltd., Thomas Hedley & Co. Ltd., the Co-operative Wholesale Society Ltd., and Shell Petroleum Ltd. for kindly supplying information when requested, and for some helpful discussions during the early stages of the work. None of these firms, however, is in any way responsible for the substance or drift of the argument.

It should be noted that my account of the soap and detergents industry does not go beyond 1957-8, at which date I left the United Kingdom. This accounts for the lack of reference to the television medium in the important context of advertising.

Finally, I am grateful to my wife for her typing and secretarial assistance, but mainly for her long and unvarying forbearance during the writing of the book.

H. R. EDWARDS

Sydney, Australia
June 1961

CONTENTS

LIST OF TABLES

LIST OF FIGURES

PART I

PRICE AND OUTPUT FORMATION IN MANUFACTURING INDUSTRY

CHAPTER 1

'COMPETITION' AND 'MONOPOLY' AND THE THEORY OF THE FIRM

THIS book consists of two Parts. In the first the object is to attempt some reformulation of the theory of price and output formation in manufacturing industry—a sphere of so-called 'Imperfect' or 'Monopolistic Competition'. The second Part contains a detailed study of the structure and working of the British soap and detergents industry. This exemplifies many of the theoretical issues raised in the first Part.

The book is at the same time a study of 'competition' and 'monopoly' in manufacturing industry generally and the soap industry in particular. For, of course, the forces of competition and monopoly in a market are bound up with the process of price and output formation—part and parcel of it. But for most people reference to competition and monopoly as in our title has this further significance, that it points beyond mere positive analysis of just how prices and outputs are determined, to evaluation of the process in welfare terms: it is at once suggestive of the issue of assessing the 'goodness' or otherwise of a situation, in terms of the net balance of competition and monopoly in the market. The problem is indeed a real one, of much interest and practical importance. And the purpose (and ultimate justification) of this study is to shed such light on it as one is able—and hence the title of the book.

The fact is, however, that both the terms 'competition' and 'monopoly' lack precise meaning, and (no doubt, in part because of this) both have acquired a considerable emotive significance not entirely justifiable. Thus 'competitive' applied to a particular market action, or market situation as a whole, frequently means little more than 'good'—in the opinion of the particular investigator. 'Monopolistic', correspondingly, means 'bad'—a term of opprobrium bound to arouse hostility against any activity, firm, or industry so labelled.

With these overtones of meaning reference to competition and monopoly tends only to cloud discussion. And the truth is that one can very well say what one has to say without explicit reference to competition or monopoly at all. One ought therefore to do so—our title notwithstanding! The issue is not merely a semantic one, but involves the large question of the proper procedure of study in the theory of the firm generally. In my opinion, the now-traditional textbook approach to the analysis of the whole range of pricing phenomena, which proceeds from the category of Perfect Competition, through various forms of Imperfect (Monopolistic) Competition, to (Perfect?) monopoly, is basically unsound. This pattern of analysis is heavy with welfare implications. It represents, in the thinking of many, a classification of cases in terms of the 'degree of competition' conceived as varying continuously from a maximum in the Perfect Competition polar case to zero in the Monopoly case.[1] But in so far as a high degree of competition is held to be 'good', and a low degree (large degree of monopoly) 'bad', it tends to beg the important question ultimately at issue, which is to arrive at an explicit and considered evaluation of the working of particular market forms. The alternative and surely more proper approach in this field is to determine by observation and analysis just how the process of price and output formation does actually work, in various types of real-world situations distinguished in a genuinely empirical manner; and then explicitly to evaluate the working of the market in terms of stated criteria.[2] The matter is worthy of some further elaboration, which will serve to indicate the method of approach adopted in this book.

MEANING OF COMPETITION AND MONOPOLY

To begin with it is necessary to arrive at an agreed understanding of the terms 'competition' and 'monopoly'.

As to competition, there is little difficulty. An acceptable definition might run as follows:[3] 'Business competition is rivalry in selling among producers acting independently; their efforts to win customers from rivals, to grow, to undersell, to get a larger share of the market—with the effect of reducing prices, inducing variations in the quality of products and associated services, expanding

---

[1] Cf. for example the scheme in P. A. Samuelson, *Economics* (2nd edn., 1951), pp. 496-7. But Professor Samuelson's discussion is carefully qualified.

[2] Cf. P. J. D. Wiles, *Price, Cost and Output* (1956), Ch. 1 and *passim*.

[3] This borrows from a 'definition' of Mrs. Joan Robinson's, in a broadcast talk 'The Control of Monopoly in British Industry', *The Listener*, 21 March 1957. In point of fact there is rarely to be found in the literature of the subject a definition of competition *per se*—as distinct from the qualified, technical concepts such as Perfect Competition. The meaning is apparently held to be self-evident.

output, promoting the development of technique, and limiting profits.'[1]

The noun 'competition' refers in this way to a form of entrepreneurs' behaviour, not to a stated complex of attributes specifying a particular market situation *as a whole*, as for example 'Perfect Competition'. This seems to me the proper usage.[2] The adjective 'competitive' applied to a particular market action then implies no more than that it is a move undertaken independently in the course of rivalry in the market; in particular, it may, or may not, be 'good' according to accepted criteria.[3]

An obvious extension of the definition should be noticed explicitly. The threatened rivalry of additional (new) producers may be no less important a force in a market than the actual rivalry of existing firms. As is customary therefore one may distinguish *actual* and *potential* competition.

Next as to monopoly. The only acceptable meaning of the noun 'monopoly' is the traditional Cournot-Marshall case of a single producer (seller) of the whole supply of a commodity.[4] In contrast to competition as defined above, monopoly in this sense *is* descriptive of a particular market situation as a whole. The case envisaged is that of a single seller who faces a given demand curve which is not significantly influenced either in the short or the long run by his price-output policy.[5] It is apparent that even approximations to this Elizabethan-type case are rarely to be found in practice; indeed outside the field of statutory or Government-sponsored monopolies it is difficult to cite examples at all.

Monopoly so defined is clearly of little interest and is not what is commonly meant by everyday—or, for that matter, most economists'—references to monopoly in industry. In this wider sense (and as used in the title of this book), a measure of monopoly or

[1] We are concerned in this book with competition and monopoly in selling. 'Monopsonistic' phenomena for the most part are not discussed.

[2] As Marshall, *Principles* (8th edn.), p. 341.

[3] As applied to a particular market structure it would similarly imply no more than that the structure promotes competition (e.g. a 'large' market, where there is a simple technique enabling efficient production on a small scale).

[4] This conforms to the typical dictionary sense of the term, as 'exclusive possession of the trade in some commodity' (*Concise Oxford Dictionary*).

[5] As Joseph Schumpeter, *Capitalism, Socialism and Democracy* (New York, 1947), p. 99. The traditional theory of monopoly, Schumpeter goes on to argue, and surely correctly, 'holds only if we define it in this way'; i.e. only if one precludes, as by this specification of the case, the oligopolistic interdependence which is characteristic of virtually all real-world situations (outside the sphere of agriculture), whether the apparent number of producers in an 'industry' is large or small.

market power is said to obtain where there is a significant degree of individual, or concerted, discretionary control over price through control over supply.[1] While this meaning is obviously derivative from the traditional monopoly case (and indeed can embrace that case) a much less singular and exclusive power is, generally speaking, involved.

Monopoly in this sense can be identified with one, or both, of two factors, namely, 'collusion' and 'exclusion'. Collusion, overt or tacit, effects in greater or less degree the unified control of existing capacity and supply[2]—apart, of course, from the comparatively rare cases where one firm does in fact produce the bulk of the supply. The second factor, deriving from obstructions to the free and ready entry of new producers,[3] confers (a degree of) control over potential alternative supply.[4] It might be argued that collusion is of no significance if there is not also a measure of power to exclude. But this is not correct. Collusive pricing even in circumstances of relatively free entry may for long periods result in a significant mis-allocation of resources, with prices too high and excess capacity;[5] while if there is also power to exclude, then the degree to which it is exploited by established sellers will in general be greater if there is collusion than if there is not. Collusion may thus be regarded as a distinct monopoly element. But the power to exclude alternative suppliers—new competition—is doubtless the more important factor; this is, as it has always been, the essence of the monopoly situation.

Now it is at once evident, as of course is generally recognized,

[1] There should be emphasis in this sentence on the word 'significant'. It is included among other things, to counter a tendency among economists to define monopoly negatively, as all that is not Perfect Competition. This is apt to prove both uninformative and mischievous. The identification of 'competition' with 'Perfect Competition' has led to endless misunderstanding between economists and businessmen.

[2] Collusion between sellers may take a great variety of forms, ranging from conscious oligopolistic 'parallelism of action' (so-called) where there is no explicit communication between the sellers, to the tightly organized price and output cartel arrangement.

[3] 'Exclusion', apart from statutory restrictions, may inhere in market actions (e.g. consistent large-scale advertising by established sellers); or a (collective) exclusive dealing agreement between the principal manufacturers and resellers of a commodity with the effect of confining the bulk of the trade to the parties); or it may inhere in the objective characteristics of a market (e.g. where the technique of production necessarily involves production on a large scale). The more important obstructions, or 'barriers', to new entry of the latter type are analysed in detail in Chapter 3 below.

[4] Collusion and exclusion thus parallel the distinction between actual and potential competition. Collusion suppresses competition among established producers; the power to exclude, where it exists, suppresses the competition of new producers. This conforms directly with the everyday understanding of monopoly as the antithesis of competition.

[5] Chapter 3, pp. 96-100 below.

that in most, if not all, market situations in practice there are at once both competitive and monopolistic elements and tendencies. It is rarely, if ever, a matter of competition or monopoly. The point is worth restating, because the tendency to characterize particular situations as the one or the other, does still persist. But of course this proposition was the starting point of Professor Chamberlin's theory of Monopolistic Competition; and it goes back at least to Marshall who throughout *Industry and Trade* constantly emphasized the ubiquitous 'interpermeation of competitive and monopolistic tendencies'.[1]

More important, it is also evident that competitive actions or tendencies in a market are not all, or always 'good', nor are monopolistic tendencies all, or always, 'bad'. Again, the point is widely conceded (as in textbook discussions of the 'wastes' or 'failures' of competition, less frequently of the case *for* monopoly); though it is often lost sight of. But this raises the prior and important issue of the nature of the criterion—or criteria—of 'goodness' or 'badness'.

CRITERIA OF EVALUATION

Explicitly or implicitly the model of Perfect Competition has been almost universally adopted as such a criterion; as the norm or standard, the ideal pattern, of the structure and working of a market. But this position is untenable, as it is now widely agreed. The reasons for this are two. First, in the real world Perfect Competition is both an unrealized, and unrealizable, state of affairs, and hence is irrelevant as a standard of appraisal. The point has been most convincingly argued by the proponents of 'workable competition', and is now generally accepted.[2] It need not be discussed further.

---

[1] *Industry and Trade* (1919), e.g. pp. 395-9, 423-9.

[2] J. M. Clark, 'Towards a Concept of Workable Competition', *A.E.R.*, 1940; E. S. Mason 'The Current Status of the Monopoly Problem in the U.S.', *Harvard Law Review* (1949) and others.

The essential point is that divergences in the real world from the conditions of theoretical Perfect Competition are fundamentally divergences of structure, differences of kind and not merely of degree, and inevitable in the nature of things. Moreover (to anticipate the subsequent argument a little) there is no simple correspondence between particular divergences of structure, and the degree of impairment of (desirable) competition, if any, involved.

All this is true even of the agricultural and some mining industries, in respect of which there is a measure of agreement among economists that the model of Perfect Competition is relevant as a first approximation (e.g. R. F. Harrod, *Economic Essays* (1952), p. 175; P. J. D. Wiles, op. cit., pp. 30 ff. ; K. Galbraith, *American Capitalism* (1951), p. 118 and *passim*).

In the second place, however, the 'ideal' character of Perfect Competition turns out on closer examination to be itself suspect. Now the 'good' results of Perfect Competition in a market which were regarded as ideal and, because held to be exclusive to this form of competition, justified its elevation to a standard or norm, are two: that the price-output behaviour of all firms tends to conform to a single determinate and hence predictable pattern; and that as the sum outcome of all firms acting in this way, the price tends to equal the long-run marginal (and average) cost of production. The latter outcome is 'good' because this is the condition laid down by the static welfare analysis for maximizing consumers' welfare in given conditions. And granted this (on which more presently), the single price-output behaviour pattern excludes cause, or scope, for the exercise of discretionary choice by the perfect competitor as between his own advantage and the social advantage: the two in fact coincide. In this way Perfect Competition was seen as precluding the arbitrary exercise of economic power—a 'desirable' consequence of not merely economic but socio-political significance.

Now the ideal character of these results has itself been questioned (although this is not the main burden of the objection to Perfect Competition as ideal, which is based on dynamic grounds). Thus with respect to the uniform behaviour pattern in Perfect Competition Professor J. M. Clark has contended that

> A world in which conduct is absolutely standardized would be arid, deadly, and intolerable. It would even be destructive of ethics and morality as we understand them. For while they are incompatible with utterly irresponsible pursuit of individual self-interest, they also presuppose some margin of discretion and choice in conduct.[1]

The point is a proper and important one, and in what follows some attempt will be made to define the margins of discretion that firms do have. (On the more important but much more difficult question of the margins they should have, however, little unhappily is said.)

The ideal character of a cost-price adjustment where the price

---

[1] 'Competition and the Objectives of Government Policy', in *Monopoly and Competition and their Regulation* (ed. E. H. Chamberlin), p. 325. Also the same author 'The Orientation of Antitrust Policy', *A.E.R.* Supplement, May 1950, p. 94. One is reminded of Marshall writing in the same sense: 'But indeed a perfect adjustment [of price to the "expenses" of production] is inconceivable. Perhaps even it is undesirable. For after all man is the end of production; and perfectly stable business would be likely to produce men who were little better than machines.' *Industry and Trade*, p. 195.

is equal to (long-run) marginal cost, has also been questioned, notably by Professor Chamberlin who has long advocated 'the scrapping of the theoretical apparatus of perfect competition', mainly on this ground.[1] The main burden of Professor Chamberlin's argument is as follows:[2] that in general consumers demand variety in products ('products are fundamentally heterogeneous'[3]), and 'since what people want—an elaborate system of consumers' preferences—is the starting point in welfare economics, their wants for a heterogeneous product would seem to be as fundamental as anything could be'[4]; then because 'heterogeneity as between producers is synonymous with the presence of monopoly, *therefore* monopoly is necessarily a part of the welfare ideal'.[4] Or to put the conclusion in an alternative form more directly relevant to our present argument: because 'equilibrium for the firm when products are heterogeneous normally takes place under conditions of falling average cost . . .', therefore the welfare ideal involves some divergence of price from (excess of price over) marginal cost[5]—not price equal to marginal cost.

This contention of Chamberlin's is, in my opinion, invalid. This is not to question his view that some degree of heterogeneity of products is proper and cannot be dismissed as merely due to consumer irrationality, or like interpretations. The point at issue is rather the particular proposition that with heterogeneous products, equilibrium necessarily or 'normally' involves 'falling average cost'— which proposition underlies and is crucial to Chamberlin's position. This, the so-called 'tangency theorem', if not actually invalid in strict logic, is at any rate founded on an unreasonable conjunction of assumptions, which reduces it to a theoretical curiosity or at

---

[1] Quotation from *A.E.R.* Supplement, May 1950, p. 101 (in discussion of a group of papers on 'Capitalism and Monopolistic Competition').

[2] The argument is presented most fully in his article 'Product Heterogeneity and Public Policy', *A.E.R.* Supplement, May 1950, pp. 85 ff., which develops the original suggestion in the author's *Theory of Monopolistic Competition* (4th edn., 1941), p. 94. (This work is hereafter cited as *Theory*.) The article is reprinted as Essay 5 in E. H. Chamberlin, *Towards a More General Theory of Value*, 1957 (hereafter cited as *Towards*), pp. 92-102. See the index to that volume under 'Welfare Economics' for further references.

[3] *Towards*, p. 141.

[4] Ibid., p. 94.

[5] The quotation in this sentence is from p. 98 (first para.) of the work cited: the second part of the sentence is a paraphrase of the balance of the argument of that paragraph. The reference is clearly to the famous 'tangency solution' of group equilibrium (Chamberlin, *Theory*, pp. 81-83), described and explained as 'a sort of ideal' on p. 94. Fig. 1, below, illustrates the tangency equilibrium, and points the divergence of price and marginal cost.

most an unlikely special case.[1] It is therefore scarcely an adequate basis on which to construct the welfare ideal.

The upshot of this is that while one joins with Chamberlin in advocating the 'scrapping' of Perfect Competition as the ideal form of the structure and working of a market; yet the static welfare analysis, the chief conclusion of which is that price should equal the (long-run) marginal cost of production, is a different matter. The welfare analysis—albeit hedged about in strict logic by a variety of qualifications which greatly restrict, or complicate, its application in practice—remains essentially valid. Chamberlin tends to identify the two, i.e. the theory of Perfect Competition and the welfare analysis; but this is incorrect. It is true that historically the welfare analysis was developed in intimate connexion with the theory of 'competition' and price determination, essentially the theory of Perfect Competition. But its early application to the problem of economic calculation in a socialist economy indicates its more universal character. Today it stands as a logically-distinct and self-contained body of knowledge.[2] And to appreciate its importance, one has only to reflect that there are no other grounds at all on which to assess the 'goodness' or otherwise of the current (or static) performance in particular market situations, i.e. to evaluate what is being achieved with the existing organization of the market in the prevailing circumstances of demand, applied technique, and supply conditions of the productive factors.

The relation of Perfect Competition to the welfare analysis is, then, no more than that it is one (abstract) economic structure wherein the optimum conditions are fulfilled by the free working of decentralized markets. There may well be other such structures: and in fact, in the following chapters, a model is developed which is

---

[1] There is now a considerable consensus of opinion to this effect. Schumpeter has referred to it as a 'fringe-end case' (*Capitalism, Socialism and Democracy*, 2nd edn., 1947, p. 85 and fn. 4); according to J. M. Clark it is 'unconvincing' (*A.E.R.* Supplement, May 1955, p. 458); and J. S. Bain writes that it is 'extreme, limiting and unlikely . . . a somewhat bizarre case' (*Barriers to New Competition*, 1956, p. 40). R. F. (now Sir Roy) Harrod would argue that as the normal outcome in conditions of 'imperfect competition with free entry', it is 'altogether wrong' (*Economic Essays*, London 1952, pp. 140 ff.); and F. Machlup argues (*Economics of Sellers' Competition*, 1952) that the alleged divergence from optimum size (minimum average cost) in conditions of 'polypoly and pliopoly' 'will not be quantitatively important' (p. 316) and after further exhaustive analysis expresses himself as 'inclined to take the "waste" story [alleged excess capacity] lightly' (p. 330). The theory is examined briefly in the appendix to Chapter 3 below.

[2] On this point see e.g. T. C. Koopmans, *Three Essays on the State of Economic Science* (New York, 1958), pp. 41-42; and P. J. D. Wiles, op. cit., Ch. 14, pp. 276 ff.

structurally quite different from the Perfect Competition model, but for which in conditions not untypical of a variety of industries in practice the presumptive conclusion[1] is similar, namely, that the price tends to equal the (long-run) marginal cost of production.

The crux of the objection to Perfect Competition as ideal, then, goes deeper. It is summed up in the dictum of Schumpeter (to whom the argument is mainly due) that 'the bulk of what we call economic progress is incompatible with Perfect Competition'.[2] Today, at any rate, significant improvements in the kind and quality of products, and in the technique of production, are dependent on systematic scientific research, with the result that development is both costly and as a form of investment exceptionally risky. It is argued then[3] that the atomistic Perfect Competitor would lack both the capacity and the incentive for initiating technical development: the capacity because costly development is dependent on the resources associated with considerable size; and the incentive because even if 'perfection' of competition does not actually imply *instant* imitation and hence elimination of the differential profits of successful innovation, yet the process must be assumed to be prompt and the individual firm being so small the gains to the innovator would scarcely be likely to measure up to the costs of development. Moreover quite apart from the question of costs and returns Perfect Competition would provide no stimulus to product innovation at all, because in the nature of the case so long as his output conforms to the current standard, the perfect competitor can sell all he chooses to produce at the going price. Product variation and improvement with a view to enlarging the one firm's sales at the expense of rivals' sales just does not enter the picture.

On these grounds, Perfect Competition is unacceptable as the ideal form of 'competition' in a market; even if it were attainable, which it is not.

But this does not, of course, mean that a reasonable adjustment of price to the cost of production in an efficient manner (and all that this implies for the allocation of resources and the distribution of income) is not a proper criterion of evaluation, or objective of economic

[1] On the import of 'presumptive', see below, pp. 24, 94.
[2] J. A. Schumpeter, op. cit., p. 105.
[3] Schumpeter, op. cit., pp. 104-5; K. Galbraith, op. cit., pp. 91-93; and J. M. Clark, *A.E.R.* Supplement, May 1955, pp. 456-7.

policy. What it does mean is that this—the *static welfare criterion*—is not the only, or necessarily the most important, criterion; and in particular that a given market situation must also be evaluated, among other possible criteria, in terms of the extent to which it affords a stimulus to continuing technological progress—the *dynamic criterion*. The importance of the dynamic objective of progress scarcely needs to be stressed. It is apparent from the very arithmetic of growth that even a small but cumulative gain over time in the productivity of a given quantum of productive resources may contribute substantially more to increasing economic welfare than any conceivable realloca- tion of given resources with unchanged technique in accordance with the conditions of the static welfare analysis.

Of course these two objectives may conflict: as the preceding discussion suggests, a 'bad' performance in the static sense may in some circumstances be a condition (in part at least) of a 'good' dynamic performance. The continued introduction of new and cost-reducing methods of production might well be feasible *just because* a sufficient degree of market control is present and can be exerted to maintain prices for a time—and accordingly to restrict output short of what it might be—in order to ensure recovering the costs of developing the new processes.[1] In such a case, in so far as the dynamic criterion should be held to outweigh a measure (at least) of static restriction, then the 'ideal'—or at all events, the 'attainable best'—involves some element of monopoly; and we arrive at Professor Chamberlin's position referred to above though in a different sense.[2] In this sort of context the task of evaluation in terms of the above criteria is indeed a complex one; but there is no other way.

THE THEORY OF THE FIRM

We may now revert to the proposition that competitive actions or tendencies in a market are not all, or always, good, nor mono- polistic tendencies all, or always, 'bad'. Without wishing to seem dogmatic, a few brief illustrations should suffice, beginning with forms of competition.

---

[1] In these circumstances the 'bad' static performance consists in a price too *high* relative to costs. A price which is too *low* relative to cost is, of course, also 'bad' according to the static criterion. In such cases (e.g. industries with chronic cut-throat price competition; the administered too-low (?) price of coal in early post-war Britain), a change in accordance with the static criterion would also promote the dynamic objective.

[2] But more recently Chamberlin has endorsed also the present argument: see *Towards*, pp. 63-64.

Thus rival producers in a market may compete for custom by means of price. But unrestrained price competition over a long period may be 'bad' (dynamic criterion) in that it inhibits technical development for want of the resources to undertake it and by removing the incentive of adequate returns. Moreover with the price consistently too low and output too large, there is a measure of misallocation of resources (static criterion).

Rival producers may also compete by product variation. But this can become excessive, as some would say of the frequent showy and expensive but mainly superficial model changes characteristic of the American motor-car industry. In this respect precise standards of what is 'proper' are lacking, but I suspect that reasonable men can arrive at a majority verdict in the particular case. Where it is deemed excessive, then there is a misallocation of resources and it is 'bad' in the static sense.

Again, large-scale advertising must be accepted as a natural weapon of competition in a market—so long as one's view is not confined by the blinkers of Perfect Competition as a standard. Indeed in many industries in the past it has been the principal factor in enabling a sufficient concentration of production to appropriate fully available economies of scale and standardization.[1] But in certain conditions advertising appropriations may 'build up' to excessive levels (albeit, again, precise standards of what is 'normal' are lacking). This involves a waste (misallocation) of real resources and thereby is 'bad' in the static sense. Further, and apart from whether or not expenditures are too high, the attachment of consumers to rival (established) brands created by advertising may obstruct the entry of new competitors to a significant degree. The phenomenon is then at once both competitive and monopolistic in character. It is 'bad' according to the static welfare criterion in that a price too high in relation to costs is thereby made possible; but on balance it may nevertheless be deemed 'good' if (as before) the measure of market control so conferred has demonstrably enabled a more rapid rate of product and technical improvement than would otherwise have been possible (dynamic criterion).[2]

Thus, in turn, monopoly tendencies are not necessarily always

1 Cf. N. Kaldor, 'Economic Aspects of Advertising', *R.E.S.*, 1949-50.
2 The presence or absence of 'excessive' expenditures on advertising would itself be a pointer in this connexion. The dissipation of the fruits of market control in excessive advertising expenditures would suggest too great a measure of static restriction relative to the requirements for desirable product and process development.

'bad'. And on this (dynamic) ground other so-called monopolistic practices—as, for example, 'building ahead of demand', long-term 'tie-in' contracts or exclusive dealing arrangements, discriminatory pricing practices—*may* on balance be deemed 'good' although condemned from the static welfare standpoint. But of course much depends on the circumstances of the particular case.

Again, high concentration in an industry is monopolistic according to the definition, above, in that it promotes collusion. But it may not do so: even where there are only two or three dominant producers, a spirit of independent rivalry may persist for a variety of reasons —as in the case of immediate concern, the British soap industry.[1] On this score, at all events, concentration is then at least 'not bad'. On the other hand, where the number of producers is large and new entry relatively easy, a measure of collusion may itself be more positively 'good' (on the basis of both criteria) in so far as it prevents the 'chiselling' of prices to levels below costs of production.[2]

It is unnecessary to prolong this discussion. Enough has been said to make it clear that the question whether a particular market aspect is competitive or monopolistic, or whether a particular market situation as a whole is on balance competitive or mono-polistic, is not of any particular interest. For even if it were possible to assess the 'degree of competition' (or its inverse the 'degree of monopoly') in a market in terms of some single meaningful index (which is doubtful), the upshot of the foregoing argument is that this would not amount to a net welfare evaluation of the 'goodness' or 'badness' of the case since the 'competition' is not all good, nor the 'monopoly' all bad. Yet to arrive at such an evaluation is the important question really at issue.

The appropriate procedure, therefore, in the present study as in the theory of the firm generally, is more direct, as suggested above. It is to determine just how the process of price and output formation in a market does actually work, by indicating tendencies with respect to the relation of capacity to demand, and prices to costs, with respect to the rate of profit, the level of selling costs, product variation and improvement, technical development, and so on; and then ex-plicitly to evaluate the working of the market in terms of stated

[1] See Chapter 11 below.
[2] On the subject of collusion, reference should also be made to the 'collusion' necessarily involved in organized marketing schemes in agriculture. Most people accept these as a good thing, being necessary to protect farmers from the rigours of unregulated competition in this sphere.

criteria—the static welfare conditions, agreed standards of 'good' dynamic performance, and other criteria. (The task of devising appropriate criteria is of course an integral part of the subject.) In this, the forces of competition and monopoly are embraced as part and parcel of the objective structure and circumstance of particular market situations. But they are not themselves of any further independent interest.

So much for the purpose and method of approach of this book. The plan of subsequent chapters is as follows.

Chapter 2 begins with an analysis of the role of 'business goodwill' in manufacturing industry—or in other words, of the nature and bases of the separation in this sphere of the total 'industry' market into the particular markets of the individual firms. It is now, I think, common ground that the interpretation of the separation of the market in the 'classical' theories of Non-Perfect Competition was partial and incomplete. The upshot of the analysis of this chapter is that all the phenomena of the 'imperfect' market —product differentiation, advertising, and the like; the discretionary power (within limits) of the individual firm to quote its own price; and so on—may be taken into account within the framework of a particular-equilibrium 'industry' analysis, on which basis the argument then proceeds.

In Chapter 3 the basic static model of price and output formation is set out. The analysis is explicitly oligopolistic, i.e. the number of sellers is presumed small. The theory of oligopoly has long been a bugbear of economists in this field, because of the alleged indeterminacy of the case. But this has been very largely a false issue, which arose because the nexus of potential competition—as distinct from the actual competition of established producers—was largely neglected in the early approach to the subject. The threatened rivalry of new producers (potential competition) plays a key role in the present analysis, as in most recent discussions of the subject. In this connexion obstructions (or 'barriers') to new entry are important in creating a potential excess of the industry price, set at the 'no-entry ceiling', over the 'cost of production'.

The second major cause of a divergence between the industry price and the cost of production in an efficient manner, is 'excess capacity'. This is not, as originally argued, a typical outcome of free (albeit

Imperfect, in the technical sense) competition, but rather is due to the partial suspension of competition via effective industry-wide *collusion*. In such event the perverse phenomenon of 'increasing costs and prices with an increase in capacity and potential supply' may emerge over long periods, and indeed is undoubtedly all too widespread in practice.[1]

Then in Chapter 4 the variety of ways in which the dynamic conditions of reality may modify the results of the basic analysis, are discussed. In particular, in other than long-run static conditions it is a separate question whether the *potential* excess of the industry price due to barriers to new entry will in the event be translated into *realized* gains of equivalent magnitude. And it turns out that, quite typically, there are patterns of intra-industry competition which do militate against the joint realization of their maximum advantage by the established firms in an industry. In this, major product innovations are an important factor.

It appears from our study that this has been so in the case of the British soap and detergents industry, at least in the period since 1950.

In Part II the structure and development of the industry from the nineteenth century to the present day is traced.

In Chapter 5 the basic facts as to demand and techniques of production are set out briefly.

Chapter 6 surveys the early development of the industry. Initially the industry structure conformed to the second of the three broad classes of manufacturing industries distinguished below,[2] one in which consumer goods are not distinctively branded by the manufacturer. But with the entry of W. H. Lever in 1885 exploiting a major innovation in marketing method (large-scale final-consumer advertising), the structure of the industry was gradually transformed until in the decade of the nineteen-thirties national competitive oligopoly in the full sense emerged. In 1930 Procter & Gamble, the largest soap manufacturer in the United States of America, entered the British market by purchasing the long-established firm of Thomas Hedley & Co. Ltd. (Chapter 9). In these conditions of renewed competition there was, it appears, a notable increase in efficiency in the industry; as compared with the

[1] The passing of the Restrictive Trade Practices Act of 1956 and the findings of the Court to date, underline its importance.
[2] p. 28, n. 1.

two principal intermediate stages, namely, the fiercely competitive, but unstable, situation during the first decade of the century, and the subsequent period of dominance of the Lever combination (Chapters 7 and 8).

The post-war development of the industry has been dominated by the exploitation of a major innovation, namely, the soapless detergents (Chapter 10 and 11). During this period—at all events to 1957-8, the end point of this study—there has been effective compeition in the 'soap' industry, with reasonable profits, expanded output, a progressive technology and improved products, and prices in reasonable relation to the cost of production. The conclusion suggested by the study is that national competitive oligopoly, in this instance at all events, has served the consumer tolerably well.

CHAPTER 2

PRICE DETERMINATION IN MANUFACTURING INDUSTRY

I. 'GOODWILL', DEMAND, AND THE CONCEPT OF THE 'INDUSTRY'

THE purpose in this and the two following chapters is to present a systematic analysis of the process of price and output formation in manufacturing industry.

The point of departure is essentially the same as that of the classical theories[1] of Imperfect (or Monopolistic) Competition, namely the fact of the separation of the total market for a commodity in this sphere of industry into the particular markets of the individual sellers, associated with the phenomena of product differentiation, brands, advertising, and so on:[2] as against the notion of a unified industry market and the absence of all these latter phenomena, as envisaged in the theory of Perfect Competition. In the initial formulations of Imperfect Competition theory, this separation of the market was taken into account, within the particular equilibrium framework of Marshallian analysis,[3] by introducing the concept of

---

[1] E. H. Chamberlin, *Theory of Monopolistic Competition* (Cambridge, Mass., 1933); Mrs. J. Robinson, *Economics of Imperfect Competition* (London, 1933); R. F. Harrod, 'Doctrines of Imperfect Competition', *Q.J.E.*, 1934 (reprinted as Essay 7 in his volume *Economic Essays*).

It is well known that Professor Chamberlin has always insisted on the difference between Monopolistic (his own theory) and Imperfect Competition. This is appropriate in so far as the reference is to the approach and particular content of the theories as such. But it is evident that both writers addressed themselves, in intent if not in performance, to the explanation of the same range of real-life phenomena, and that in current usage these are regarded indifferently as the province of 'Imperfect' or 'Monopolistic Competition' theory. *Pace* Professor Chamberlin, therefore, the two terms are used synonymously in this book. (At all times we use capitals and this is to indicate that the terms are technical terms, not necessarily literally descriptive.)

[2] It was Piero Sraffa ('The Laws of Returns under Competitive Conditions', *E.J.*, 1926) who insisted on the importance of taking this obvious fact of experience explicitly into account. But of course it would be wrong to suggest that earlier writers, and particularly Marshall, were not aware of it. (Sraffa's famous article was one of a series of contributions to the *Economic Journal* in the decade of the 'twenties, sometimes referred to as the 'Cost Controversy'. It began with Clapham's 'Of Empty Economic Boxes' (1922) and ended, somewhat inclusively, with the 'Symposium' of Messrs. D. H. (now Sir Denis) Robertson, Sraffa and G. F. Shove (1930).

[3] But it was argued subsequently that this approach should be abandoned: below, pp. 24-25.

the down-sloping demand curve for the (differentiated) product of each individual firm—as Sraffa had suggested. This led to the idea of the maximization of profits by equating marginal revenue and marginal cost[1]—the formula of central importance in the modern theory of the firm; and this behaviour pattern, combined with a presumption of free and easy entry, involved the result embodied in the 'tangency theorem' (referred to in the previous chapter), namely, an equilibrium with falling unit costs and prices higher and outputs more restricted (static 'excess capacity') as compared with Perfect Competition. This was the essentially novel contribution of the classical theory of Imperfect Competition.

The analysis was the more readily accepted because the result seemed to accord well with the second important fact of everyday experience which the cost controversy brought to the forefront, namely, the prevalence of internal economies in manufacturing industry.[2] More specifically, it matched the observation that manufacturing firms are normally operating in circumstances of falling unit costs in the short run, with the prospect of even lower, or at the worst, constant, unit costs should the market permit of expanding the firm's scale of operations;[3] whereas 'competitive' theory envisaged an equilibrium, in face of a horizontal individual-firm demand curve, governed by actual or incipient increasing unit costs.

Now the two 'facts' of everyday experience here alluded to are not in question. But the classical analysis constructed to embrace them, baldly summarized above, was inadequate on a number of counts.

Much of the criticism which can be brought against it may be expressed in the dictum—now a commonplace, but not wholly valid for all that—that the Imperfect Competition theories were 'too short-run'. Certainly in the original works on the subject the distinction between the short-period and the long-period, traditional in economics since Marshall, scarcely played any part at all. It was Mr. (now Sir Roy) Harrod in his notable pioneer contribution to the subject in 1934, who first explicitly applied the distinction on

---

[1] Professor Chamberlin, as is well known, did not employ the marginal concepts, but argued directly in terms of maximising the difference between Total Revenue and Total Cost.

[2] D. H. Robertson, 'Those Empty Boxes', *E.J.*, 1924; P. Sraffa, op. cit.; and others.

[3] In particular, Sraffa, op. cit. (reprinted in A.E.A., *Readings in Price Theory*, p. 189).

the cost side.[1] But the full significance of the relation between short and long-period costs is brought into play only when longer-period considerations on the demand side are also taken into account.[2]

In this respect what is important is that the 'separation of the market' is synonymous with the attachment of customers in varying degrees to particular firms or products, i.e. 'business goodwill' as defined hereafter. Goodwill in this sense is an essential structural

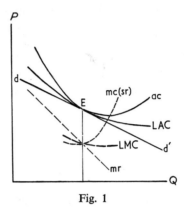

Fig. 1

aspect of the market in manufacturing industry; its role is to channel the going total demand of the market as between the competing manufacturers in the proportions established as the outcome of dynamic processes in the past, and thus to provide the assured (more or less) outlet for the production of each firm which is the *conditio sine qua non* of its continuing and efficient operation.

This I term the positive role of the goodwill factor in manufacturing and commercial business. If it is simple and obvious enough, it was nevertheless not adequately taken into account in the early formulations of Imperfect Competition theory (nor indeed in much of later received theory) where the main preoccupation was with the potential negative aspects of the separation of the market.[3] But emphasis on the positive role of goodwill is important in at least three ways.

[1] *Q.J.E.*, 1934. This had the effect that in equilibrium the down-sloping demand curve was tangent to both the short and the long-period cost curves of the firm, as at E in Figure 1. This suggested 'excess capacity' in two senses: (i) the continued fall of the LAC curve beyond E implies unexhausted economics of scale (long-period sense); and (ii) production at outputs to the left of the minimum point of the ac curve implies that what plant there is is underutilized. (Traditional 'short-period' excess capacity.)

[2] Below, pp. 63-64.   [3] Cf. E. H. Chamberlin, *Theory*, Appendix E.

First, 'goodwill' makes possible a continuity of production and sale comparable to, but different in kind, from that associated with the centralized marketing organization in the sphere of primary industry, and this is significant from the social viewpoint in that it affords a considerable economy in production not otherwise attainable in the circumstances of manufacturing industry.

Second, such a share of the market in terms of 'goodwill' can be built only with difficulty and over a long period of time. Typically therefore the businessman has a high regard for the affiliation of his customers, and will not lightly risk losing this connexion in the pursuit of immediate gain. This is a long-term consideration which is very important in explaining current (or short-term) business behaviour. Firstly, it suggests that the entrepreneur will not normally, systematically, maintain a price out of line with the prices charged for the comparable products of his existing competitors. This is elaborated in the last division of this chapter. Secondly, it is evident that the established manufacturer bent on protecting his acquired market position, is bound to take into account the threat to this position from the intervention of new competition should the price be set too high. The classical analysis did indeed envisage a rapid invasion of the market by new producers in such event; but the idea that the entrepreneur should himself (along with the economist-observer!) foresee this course of events and accordingly, in most cases, charge a lower price so as to forestall new entry and prevent the loss of market, was, so it would seem, overlooked.[1] That the entrepreneur typically has regard to the threat of new competition ('potential competition') in this way is central to the present analysis, as in most recent important discussions of the subject,[2] and is undoubtedly in accordance with everyday experience.

Third, while emphasis on the stability associated with established

[1] Some would hold that the Chamberlin 'large-group' case assumptions (see (iii) (a) and (b), p. 103 below) were designed to preclude such a regard for new competition. This, however, is doubtful. (It was Mr. N. Kaldor, in his important article 'Market Imperfection and Excess Capacity', *Economica*, N.S., 1935, who first emphasized the importance of entrepreneurs having regard to the threat of new competition in this context.) Elsewhere (*O.E.P.* 1955, p. 102, and n. 3) I have suggested Professor Chamberlin took over in his own analysis the broad contours of the neo-Marshallian Perfect Competition model. But in approaching the problem with such 'blinkers', the possibility that the entrepreneur should have regard to potential competitors, since the question does not arise in the Perfect Competition case, was—as it would appear—merely overlooked.

[2] P. W. S. Andrews, *Manufacturing Business* (1949); R. F. Harrod, *Economic Essays*, 8th Essay (1952); H. F. Lydall, 'Conditions of New Entry and the Theory of Price', *O.E.P.*, 1955; J. S. Bain, *Barriers to New Competition* (1956).

goodwill is appropriate, the pattern of a market so determined is, of course, by no means unalterable. Luck, inertia—above all, technical progress—play their parts in this: this is a recurring theme in this book.[1] At this point what is important is that the efforts of each of the firms to cement and extend the 'goodwill' which is the foundation of its continuing and profitable operation, necessarily involves a competitive struggle for the custom of the market. Active competition is thus inherent in the nature of the market structure—in contrast with theoretical Perfect Competition, or situations where the organized exchange obtains which reproduces, approximately, the market conditions of Perfect Competition. The effect of this intra-industry competition is inevitably to reduce the industry price in greater or less degree below the maximum level which the objective circumstances of the market (i.e. conditions of new entry, the extent and elasticity of industry demand, and so on) would otherwise permit.[2]

So much for the positive aspects of the phenomenon of business 'goodwill' which were largely neglected in the early formulations of Imperfect Competition theory. But even in connexion with the negative aspects of the phenomenon, the emphasis in the classical analysis was misplaced. In this respect what is important is that the attachment of buyers to all the established firms in an industry necessarily inhibits to some extent the entry of new producers into the market: the new entrant, to gain a place, must needs effect a permanent alteration in the channels of trade. The primary significance of the down-sloping particular demand curve—the basic new structural element of Imperfect Competition theory, and symptomatic of the separation of the market—is therefore, not that on certain rather unrealistic assumptions it involves with geometrical necessity an equilibrium with falling costs and excess capacity—but rather that it refers to one circumstance, among others, which makes new entry into the market difficult even although it is free.[3] This essentially 'monopolistic' aspect was not systematically taken

---

[1] Below, pp. 38-40, 111-14, and Part II.

[2] Of course, this tendency is often partially restrained by collusive arrangements of varying degrees of effectiveness. Indeed the prevalence of such arrangements in the absence of a Government 'antitrust' division, and the strength of the opposition to them (witness the recent Restrictive Trade Practices Act in the U.K.), is ample testimony to the reality of this effect in conditions of free competition.

[3] 'Free' in the sense of unrestricted by statute, patent or other 'artificial' barriers to the entry of new competitors. (Of course, the distinction between 'artificial' and 'other' restraints is a tenuous one. Cf. F. Machlup, 'Competition, Pliopoly and Profit', *Economica*, 1942, p. 154). The basis for the distinction adopted in this book is whether or not the elements in question are integral structural aspects of the particular industrial

into account in the classical analysis,[1] where free and easy entry was for the most part presumed.[2] Subsequently, however, it was taken up explicitly by Mr. Kaldor[3] and more recently by Mr. J. S. Bain who has investigated it in detail, in the American context, under the heading of the 'product-differentiation barrier' to new entry.[4] We turn to the analysis of this aspect of 'goodwill' in the market in the next chapter.

In fine, then, the element of 'goodwill' has a twofold effect. On the one hand, it enables relatively stable and efficient operation along with a competitive struggle for the custom of the market; but on the other hand, the combined goodwill of the established firms necessarily inhibits to some extent the entry of new competitors into the market. It is evident that the net balance of these opposing

process of production and sale. Thus apart from statutory and patent restrictions 'artificial' barriers would include, e.g. industry-wide collective reciprocal exclusive-dealing agreements; a 'corner' of essential raw material supplies; 'full-line forcing' by a single firm dominant in a industry; and such like. For reasons of space such practices are not discussed in this book.

What is involved at this point in the text is the important distinction, that if entry is 'free' this does not necessarily mean also that it is 'easy'. There has been a tendency to regard the two terms as synonymous, or rather inclusive. But this is an error.

[1] Professor Chamberlin recognizes the point in the following passage: 'In so far as the field in general or particular parts of it are protected from incursion, demand curves will lie to the right of the point of tangency with cost curves, and profits will be correspondingly higher. This is the explanation of all monopoly profits, of whatever sort' (*Theory*, pp. 111-12). But the systematic exposition of his theory (with the emphasis on excess capacity) precedes this: the statement is made along with other afterthoughts in his section on 'The Diversity of Conditions Surrounding Each Producer'. Also, Mrs. Robinson recognized the case of 'trades into which there is no possibility of entry', as e.g. 'the provision of public-houses in a district where a fixed number of licences is granted'. (*Economics of Imperfect Competition*, p. 93). But such cases were regarded as exceptional and there was no further systematic analysis.

[2] We have the high authority of Professor Austin Robinson that '. . . it was of the essence of those theories [Imperfect Competition] that one was dealing with a situation in which entry was assumed to be sufficiently free and competition sufficiently effective to reduce profits to a "normal" level. . . .' (*E.J.*, 1950, p. 773). Chamberlin certainly assumed free (=easy) entry in the basic 'large group' case. It is true that his results in the analysis of 'Pure Oligopoly (Duopoly)' in his Chapter III (particularly the 'monopoly-like' solution of section 4) would require for their validity that there is no possibility of the entry of new competition, i.e. 'closed' entry. But this assumption was not even made explicitly, let alone reasons being given. In the subsequent discussion of the 'small group' case with product differentiation (Chap. V, section 4) he goes on almost immediately (in section 5) to consider the consequences of the proviso that 'the general field may be entered by competitors' (*Theory*, pp. 104-5). The result, in this instance, was that the monopoly price will continue, though profits will be reduced to normal as the DD' curve is driven to a point of tangency with the cost curve—see his Figure 15, p. 92. Entry was thus again presumed 'free'.

[3] 'The Economic Aspects of Advertising', *R.E.S.*, 1949-50 (No. 45), esp. paragraphs 33 ff. The difficulty of entry associated with goodwill in a market is also integral to Mr. P. W. S. Andrews's analysis, *Manufacturing Business*, pp. 148-53 and *passim*.

[4] *Barriers to New Competition* (Cambridge, Mass. 1956), Ch. 4 and *passim*.

tendencies—the former tending to restrain the market price in close relation to 'the cost of production', and the latter tending to permit of its elevation above that cost—cannot be settled by *a priori* analysis, and is ultimately a question of empirical fact.[1] If the former tendency, the price-dampening effect of intra-industry competition, has by and large been neglected in received Imperfect Competition theory with the consequence that net profit margins are held to be typically 'too high', other writers in this field[2] would seem to have assumed rather too readily that the net balance is indeed typically zero. Yet for a wide range (the 'ordinary run') of manufacturing industries, such evidence as there is suggests that that latter judgement is sound; and in other industries (principally the large-scale 'national oligopoly') where the net effect of goodwill is potentially significantly greater than zero, there are often offsetting circumstances. This is to say, in a word, that so far as the relation of prices to costs is concerned, the outcome in conditions of analytical 'Differentiated (Oligopolistic) Competition' is not necessarily greatly different from that of Perfect (i.e. 'Undifferentiated') Competition.

The primary objective in this and the next two chapters then, is to integrate the foregoing aspects of the separation of the market in terms of 'business goodwill' into a systematic model of price and output formation: to serve as a basis for the study of the soap and detergents industry in Part II.

The model, as will be evident from the discussion so far, is a particular equilibrium analysis in terms of the 'industry'.[3] It is well known that Mr. R. Triffin has argued that this sort of approach is invalid and should be abandoned as inconsistent with the notion of 'differentiation' and the unique character of each firm's product.[4] Later, Professor Chamberlin lent the weight of his authority to this view.[5]

---

[1] The outcome of course will vary from case to case, and from time to time in the particular case. The presence or absence of collusive arrangements, previously referred to, will be a factor in this: indeed the essence of the case against such arrangements is precisely that they eliminate, or reduce, the former tendency and permit free reign to the latter.

[2] Sir Roy Harrod, *Economic Essays*, pp. 151, 180-1, and *passim*; P. W. S. Andrews, *Manufacturing Business, passim*.

[3] The significance of the quote marks is that the reference is to the *analytic* concept, as distinct from the connotation of the word in everyday usage.

[4] *Monopolistic Competition and General Equilibrium Theory* (Cambridge, Mass. 1939), pp. 88-89.

[5] 'Monopolistic Competition Revisited', *Economica*, 1951.

On its own premises this position is no doubt logically unexceptionable. In my opinion, however, it is just one further consequence of the one-sided interpretation of the fact of the separation of the market, and is both unnecessary and undesirable from the point of view of the development of the subject. And the truth is that most writers in this field seeking to arrive at definitive results do resort to argument in terms of the 'industry'[1]—or, what is more or less equivalent, in terms of the 'representative firm'.[2] On a different level of argument, the constant preoccupation of businessmen with their 'share of the market' itself points the reality of the phenomenon which the economist would conceptualize by the 'industry'; to throw out the notion of the industry is to ignore this important element of business thinking and behaviour.

The issue of the theoretical justification of the particular equilibrium 'industry' approach is thus an important one. It is taken up in the final division of this chapter, as a necessary preliminary to the formulation of the model structure set out in the next chapter.

'GOODWILL' IN MANUFACTURING BUSINESS

Our model building begins with the analysis of the nature and rational basis of 'business goodwill' in manufacturing business.

In this connexion it is instructive to contrast the structure of production and sale in manufacturing with that in the sphere of primary industry, in particular agriculture. In the latter, central dealing is the characteristic market structure. The development of the organized exchange for the marketing of agricultural products is no doubt a quite natural development. There is first a substantial natural homogeneity of the product; and second, there is a geographical dispersion of many sources of supply (farms), each typically small. (As a theoretical approximation, the long-run cost curve in this sphere is U-shaped, with the minimum point at a scale of production small relative to the total market.)

In manufacturing, on the other hand, central marketing does not obtain. Again this is, no doubt, quite natural. First, manufactured commodities are not naturally homogeneous; but second, and more fundamental as will become evident, the character of costs of production and hence the conditions of individual-firm supply are

---

[1] The recent work of J. S. Bain, referred to in more detail in the next chapter, may be cited, but there is a long tradition including Professor Chamberlin in his initial formulation of the theory of Monopolistic Competition.

[2] e.g. Mr. N. Kaldor in 'The Economic Aspects of Advertising', *R.E.S.*, 1949-50.

typically different from the previous case. And thus in lieu (so to speak) of central marketing, a relatively stable channelling of the going demand for a manufactured commodity as between the particular products of the several firms tends to emerge in terms of 'business goodwill'.

Now where the organized market obtains, the outputs of all the producers are there gathered together, graded and grouped into lots of uniform quality (in general, in terms of objective standards and by independent experts), and then offered for sale, so as to clear the market. The individual producer (farmer) offers an output determined, in principle, by the rising (short-run) marginal cost of production in relation to the prospective market price; and by the very processes of the market he is assured of the sale of this output at a return no lower than that obtained by any other seller of the same grade of the product.

The individual manufacturer is not thus assured of the sale of his output. He can make assured (more or less) sales only to the extent that he has acquired 'goodwill'[1]—to the extent, that is, of the regular demand of the more or less definite group of buyers attached to the firm (or its particular brand of the product) on the basis of the confidence given by previous custom. Beyond this the firm can rely only on the chance purchases of other buyers.

It may be objected that the latter should in any event be sufficient. Suppose, that is to say, that by a natural evolution the total of capacity in an industry (each firm working a normal shift) is just proportioned to total demand: then if, at a going market price mutually recognized and accepted, the orders directed to one firm exceed its particular capacity, will they not be naturally diverted to other firms with a less than full order book? So that even if buyers' inquiries are made entirely at random, demand in this way will be naturally apportioned among the various firms in proportion to their individual capacities.

This objection, however, does not take account of the character of costs and individual-firm supply in manufacturing industry. Whereas in agriculture it is a reasonable approximation to envisage, as above, that rising long and short-period marginal costs define the capacity of the individual productive unit and limit its offering on the market, in manufacturing this is not so. On the contrary,

---

1 'Goodwill' is defined, formally, as 'the attachment of buyers to, and their propensity to purchase, the product of the particular firm'.

long-term expansion of the firm's scale of operations is almost invariably advantageous: this is related to the shape of the long-run cost curve in this sphere (typically L-shaped) and is discussed more fully in the next chapter. And in the short period the capacity of the individual manufacturing firm is in general very flexible: the 'normal', or 'planned' capacity (output) of a plant may be definite enough, but output may be increased substantially beyond this by overtime working, and may be doubled (trebled) by working two (three) shifts instead of one only. And in most cases by virtue of the spreading of overheads, such outputs in excess of the normal capacity of the plant sold at the going market price are very profitable.[1]

In these circumstances it is evident that the process of the natural apportioning of demand as envisaged in the above objection, will not take place. Such an outcome is dependent on the existence of a definitive capacity output for each firm; so that if demand should accrue beyond this it would 'spill over' to other firms with a demand currently less than capacity. But where capacity is flexible and production in excess of planned capacity is both possible and profitable, the tendency is rather for each firm to meet such demand as accrues to it in full. And this tendency to meet demand in full in the pursuit of maximum current profits, is reinforced in that it also serves the objective of expanding the firm's scale of operations on a long-term basis: it both promises a source of finance for expansion, and the demand so met may be permanently 'attached' to the firm. But with the tendency to meet demand in full, the natural apportioning of the demand as between the various sellers will not take place. (The argument presumes that the going price in the market is maintained. Of course, firms for which demand is short may tend to cut the price, and this would indeed work in the direction of an appropriate apportioning of the demand. But a price cut can be easily matched, and will in the end in such a context serve only to bring down the general market price level below the 'cost of production', i.e. 'spoil the market'. This further militates against the workability of such a market structure.)

In the nature of the case, therefore, the development of 'goodwill' is inevitable in manufacturing industry.

First, from the point of view of the seller: in its absence demand would accrue to each firm at random, and would thus be subject

[1] Chapter 3, p. 64 below.

to wide fluctuations from one current period of production to the next. This would carry with it some risk of actual failure—in the event of a chance succession of periods of low demand. More certainly, production to meet such a fluctuating demand would involve a higher unit cost of production than to meet the same average (over time) demand accruing at a steady rate. Thus in the effort to meet such a fluctuating demand without loss of sales, the firm would tend to hold a larger stock of its finished product and/or to invest in enlarged plant facilities towards meeting peak require-ments, as compared with the situation of steady demand. Further, erratic production schedules impair the efficiency of labour, increase wastage in the use of materials (frequently the largest single item in costs), and divert the energies of the management from systematic plant modification and improvement into day-to-day improvisation. All these causes tend to elevate costs. In these conditions the entre-preneur is led naturally to distinguish ('differentiate') his own pro-duct and to seek by advertising and other means to attract the continuing custom of a more or less definite clientele, i.e. to acquire goodwill: this affords the essential stable basis for the firm's con-tinuing efficient operation, and its potential growth affords a measure of security for the firm's large-scale investment in pursuit of long-term expansion. It affords too a measure of (temporary) protection against the competing offers of rival sellers in that the 'attached' buyer will not immediately forsake his customary supplier or brand of the product; this, *contra* the structure envisaged above (compare the parenthesis at the end of the penultimate paragraph), further enhances the stability and workability of the market structure.

In the second place, in rationalizing the inevitability of goodwill in manufacturing industry, there is its significance from the point of view of the buyer. The goodwill relation between seller and buyer is reciprocal, as its considerable stability in practice would suggest. This is more particularly evident in the case of manufac-tured intermediate products.[1] In this sort of case,[2] the product of a

---

[1] Cf. Andrews, *Manufacturing Business*, pp. 146 ff.

[2] It is convenient in this and other contexts in this book, to distinguish three broad classes of manufacturing industries for separate discussion. (The classification excludes durable-use producer goods). There is of course a great diversity of conditions surrounding particular industries within each class. The classes are:

(I) *Manufactured intermediate goods:* for example, paper, leather, rayon, steel, etc. The product of the individual manufacturer is sold direct, or sometimes through intermediate traders, to other manufacturers.

(II) *'Unbranded' consumer goods.* This class is taken to include goods with brands or trademarks which have not been so popularized as systematically to influence over

particular manufacturer will be bought on the basis of a written specification, or the buyer's own judgement of the product in the first instance. The qualities embodied in the product, however, in terms of workmanship, class of materials used, etc., are in most cases not obvious, even to the most discerning of buyers. Further the buyer has not—as in the case of primary products purchased on an organized exchange—a market consensus of opinion as to the quality of the product before him; he has only the guarantee of the individual manufacturer. The essential quality of such a manufactured product, therefore, can be assessed only by experience. But the buyer's need for the commodity is, in general, continuous: as with the seller, the fundamental continuity of the economic process is of overriding importance. Accordingly, if the product of a particular manufacturer brings satisfaction it will also bring the habit of purchasing his product. The buyer's attachment to the particular firm thus has this rational basis: that re-purchase on the basis of the confidence given by previous custom eliminates the risk of buying inferior quality, and obviates the necessity of careful assessment of the product at every purchase. (Of course, the buyer's attachment may be fortified by less rational considerations, as for example when A likes dealing with B because he is good company at the club.) Similar considerations apply in the case of unbranded consumer goods, and in somewhat lesser degree to significantly-branded consumer goods.[1] Thus in a word,

time the choice of the final consumer. Of course, such goods, while unbranded by the manufacturer, will often be significantly branded by wholesaler or retailer. Examples of this class: unpackaged flour, cheeses, most stationery goods, much clothing, etc. The immediate and key customers of the individual manufacturer in this sort of case are the wholesale dealers in his product. (Cf. Kaldor's 'Wholesalers' Domination', 'The Economic Aspects of Advertising', *R.E.S.*, 1949-50, sections 28 and 29.)

(III) *'Branded' consumer goods:* i.e. consumer goods sold to final customers under the manufacturers' own brands, and these brands have been so popularized that they do systematically influence over time the choice of the consumer. Large-scale final-consumer advertising is characteristic of this sort of situation. Examples: cigarettes, soaps; 'quality line' shoes, clothing; refrigerators, motor-cars, etc. In this sort of case the 'goodwill' of the individual manufacturer consists primarily in the attachment and willingness to buy of the ordinary consumer: the wholesaler (and/or retailer) must, of course, still be courted, but is subject more directly to the dictates of the final consumer acting, e.g. in response to heavy advertising. (Cf. Kaldor's concept of 'Manufacturers' Domination', op. cit., sections 30 and 31.)

[1] Thus in the former (class II situations) the bulk of the business of the wholesaler-customer will require regular supplies and sustained quality-at-the-price; in time then, he will come to look first to his customary supplier(s) and—so long as there is no disadvantage in doing so—that is where he will ordinarily buy. (However, the attachments of goodwill in this sphere are likely to be not so strong or exclusive as in the case of intermediate products. The individual wholesaler is likely in general to be closer in touch with 'the trade' as a whole than the manufacturer-customer in the latter case, because the essential activity of the wholesaler is buying and selling

'goodwill' in the market serves the buyer's interest as well as the seller's.

We conclude then that business 'goodwill'—the systematic pairing of buyers with particular sellers—is inevitable in the circumstances of manufacturing industry. And as stated above, this is significant from the social point of view in that the associated stability of the market enables a considerable overall economy in production and sale—a net gain in the social real product assuming full employment in any event—as compared with a situation where a total demand of the same dimension is met in the substantial[1] absence of goodwill. Thus first, production to meet a fluctuating demand involves (as already argued) a significantly higher unit cost of production, reflecting the involvement of more real resources and their less efficient use, than production to meet the same average demand recurring at a steady rate. (Moreover in the unstable situation the quality of products over the whole field will tend to be inferior.)[2]

Of course, this gain must be assessed net of the costs of acquiring and maintaining the stable connexion in the market; which is related to the second factor in the situation, namely, that there will

products of this general type, whereas the main preoccupation of the latter is with manufacture.)

Again, in the case of branded consumer goods (class III) the manufacturer's brand facilitates the repurchase of the same tried and acceptable quality of product—or equally, enables a product found unsatisfactory in use to be avoided. The strength of final-consumer brand-preferences, and of their buying 'habits' in according with these preferences, often surprises one. (Cf. Mr. N. Kaldor, *R.E.S.* 1949-50, p. 18.) Such a buying habit may be engendered almost solely by large-scale advertising. It is a matter first of the consumer, as the result of the impact of a particular advertising line in relation to his own individual psychological make-up and particular circumstances, become the more aware of one manufacturer's product as against the others; and then in terms of its maintained quality, the ease of repurchasing that quality, and the associations of this particular product and its brand-name with all the other factors in the highly individual process of the particular consumer's use of the commodity, a more or less definite buying habit is formed.

It is an important proposition that where buyer-preferences are thus built mainly on advertising (and particularly in case of the national oligopoly, such as the soap industry), there is in general some *necessary minimum* of advertising expenditure which must be undertaken if the firm is to remain effectively 'in the market'—a sum which is thus independent in the main of any particular firm's volume of sales, and which is large in absolute amount. This proposition is elaborated in the Appendix to this chapter.

[1] In practice it could never be completely absent. Any firm has a 'habitat and a name'. Again the location of firms may determine buyer preferences to some extent in a market geographically distributed.

[2] There is a greater opportunity for experimentation with inferior quality of product open to a 'semi-anonymous' firm in an unstable market, not open to the firm with a well-established goodwill. In practice this is one way in which the reality of higher costs with unstable operation may be partially offset.

be additional economies in the costs of distribution.[1] Realistically the development of definitive goodwill connexions is bound to be associated with an increased degree of concentration of the market, with fewer brands of the 'product' and more predictable consumer attachments to them. As compared with a situation in which there is some measure of brand-preference for the variety of products of a larger number of firms, distributors' stocks would be lower (faster rate of stock turnover), storage space smaller, book-keeping less complicated, a smaller proportion of deliveries would be made in small lots ('broken' cases), there would be less duplication overall in visitation by traveller-salesmen, and so on. All these factors serve to reduce the real costs of distribution.

Third, where goodwill is undeveloped there would tend to be a fairly rapid turnover of firms. On the one hand, with buyers largely unattached it is easy for would-be producers to make a start in the field. Also, this circumstance is likely to be attractive to entrepreneurial ability of a lesser order. On the other hand, in the conditions of fluctuating demand chance runs of periods of low demand can occur resulting in business failure. In Perfect Competition, of course, complete mobility of the factors of production means that no costs are involved in entering or leaving an industry. But in fact resources are not perfectly mobile, and those which are applied fruitlessly represent a waste both to the individuals incurring the loss and to the economy as a whole.

Goodwill then orders the market, and makes possible a considerable overall economy in production and sale in the circumstances of manufacturing business. It is indeed as essential a structural characteristic of the case as the centralized selling organization in the case of primary products. And the overtone of suggestion—as for example in Professor Chamberlin's Appendix E in the *Theory of Monopolistic Competition*, previously referred to—that it is inherently and wholly undesirable is, therefore, beside the point. But there are degrees of goodwill, and it is indeed proper to notice the other side of the coin: in particular, that where goodwill is 'strong' it may so obstruct the entry of new competitors (negative

[1] For example, the appropriation (and holding) of the connexion may involve a significant increase in advertising expenditure by the firm. But this contributes (in part) to the realization of the economies of distribution noted in the next sentences in the text, and from the social point of view the latter must be set against the increased advertising expenditure within the firm. Other elements in the sales overhead of the firm may be reduced, however (e.g. increased efficiency in despatch department), and may thus provide a partial offset even within the firm.

aspect) that the net socal gain in real product accrues only to firms as excess profits; or is dissipated in whole or in part by excessive expenditures on advertising and other forms of sales promotion, or by reduced efficiency in production ('the monopolist grows fat and lazy') behind the protection the entrenched position affords. These matters are discussed in due sequence in following chapters.

If a share of the market in terms of goodwill is the necessary basis of the manufacturing firm's continuing efficient operation, it is evident next that it can be built only with difficulty and over a long period of time.

Of course in the early stages of the development of a new industry, it is relatively easy to make sales; and the market positions of the principal firms in many industries owe much to the advantages of an early start. Thereafter if a firm survives the initial 'mushroom' of producers characteristic of a new process of production, it acquires goodwill gradually on the basis of its success in devising a product to meet the requirements of the market; its ability to produce at minimum costs and so to meet (and on its day, to 'beat') the prices of competitors while maintaining the quality and reliability of its product; and its skill in persuading customers to buy. Time is of the essence of the process, and the mere luck of the game plays a significant part.

When in due course conditions in an industry have become more 'settled',[1] the task of increasing the firm's share of the market—and *a fortiori* of acquiring a connexion in the market *de novo*—is indeed difficult. This is evident from a consideration of the three main ways in which the firm may seek to achieve an increase in its market share.

First, it may cut its price. In this way the firm may gain a temporary advantage. But in oligopolistic conditions it is normally very short-lived because rival firms can match the cut almost instantaneously and this neutralizes the advantage. The scope for increasing the firm's market share by price competition is thus severely circumscribed. In some measure, secret discriminatory price

---

[1] The import of 'settled' is that there is an approach to static conditions in the traditional sense, that is, the aggregate demand, design and specification of the product in the large, the supply conditions of the productive services, and the state of technique, are 'given'—have remained substantially unaltered for a considerable time, and the latent possibilities have been more or less fully exploited. But minor variations in product design in the course of competition in the market should not be thought of as inconsistent with 'settled conditions'. (The term is Mr Andrews's.)

concessions to particular buyers may overcome this, and this is a not unimportant source of price flexibility in oligopolistic markets. Again, where significant product variation is characteristic of an industry a price cut can be partially disguised by an associated variation in the product, thereby encouraging some measure of price competition. Of course, too, in so far as a price cut is based on a notable reduction in costs, then the price-cutting firm and other firms which can match its efficiency may increase their shares of the market to the extent that higher-cost firms, constrained to match the new low price but unable to reduce costs, are driven out of business; indeed this is the ultimate process by which efficient capacity is proportioned to demand and supply-price attuned to the cost of efficient production. But this is itself a gradual process, and often costly to both victor and vanquished. And as the stage is reached when all the incurably inefficient (so to speak) have been eliminated and a more even balance of competitive strength has emerged, manufacturers normally eschew price competition: this not only because it is ineffective in the large as a means of altering relative market position, but also because it is mutually damaging and, being ineffective, all to no purpose.[1]

In the second place, a firm may seek to increase its share of the market by increasing its advertising expenditure at the same price (or by some combination of increased advertising and price cut). This possibility is relevant in the main only in the third broad class of situation distinguished above, namely, consumer goods with direct final-consumer advertising by the manufacturers. Like the simple price-cut, however, the effectiveness of persuasion *per se* is also severely circumscribed because of the relative ease and speed with which rival firms can step up their own advertising and so restore the established balance of persuasions brought to bear on the consumer (albeit at a higher level of advertising expenditure all round). To the extent that advertising easily persuades—this

---

[1] The characteristic tendency is thus for established manufacturers to attempt—by a formal Agreement, or informally—to regulate prices in the sense of undertaking to observe quoted price lists and to take common action to alter them, when conditions warrant it. Such a minimal degree of collusion is virtually inevitable, granted the lack of the (more or less) impersonal processes which 'make' prices in the organized exchange and the character of costs of production in manufacturing (as discussed above); and in so far as the individual firm's price quotations are arrived at in competition albeit this regulated, the effects of competition are not necessarily annulled, but rather its excesses avoided. The difficulty, of course, is that in practice the mere regulation of prices tends all too frequently to harden into a collective effort to fix and maintain prices which are 'too high'.

depends in the main on the particular product—the impact effect in terms of the immediate increase in sales might be considerable. But just because advertising easily persuades, this can only be a temporary effect because the firms' competitors can restore the *status quo ante bellum* by similar onslaughts.[1]

Of course with unrestricted competition, advertising 'wars', like price 'wars', do develop; but the outcome, if the contestants are at all evenly matched (and in the absence of innovation), is to leave the relative pattern of the market very much as before. For the most part I think it is correct to say that in practice most firms recognize the ineffectiveness of persuasion *per se*[2] as a means of appropriating a permanent increase in their share of the market, and in consequence seek to limit their expenditure on advertising by some such device as, for example, fixing an upper limit for the advertising appropriation at some predetermined percentage of the turnover.[3]

A further point of some importance for our subsequent argument must be noticed here. It may be argued with reference to the third broad class of case that if as an industry becomes more settled the emergent division of the market is, for whatever reason, very unequal, then the mere passage of time will tend to reduce this inequality; so that the unequal pattern of relative market shares will not remain constant (or approximately so) over longish periods.

This possibility would seem to arise, first, because of the admitted instability of final-consumer choices, already referred to. Thus we have spoken of the continuing 'preference' or buying 'habit' of the ordinary consumer. But these terms suggest too rigid and exclusive buying behaviour. The proper conception is of a less inflexible attachment to a particular brand of the commodity; an incomplete attachment, varying widely in degree from consumer to consumer; a general tendency or propensity to name and buy a particular brand, but yet not such as to preclude the purchase of some other product according to the whim or chance persuasion of the moment.

Reality is very complex; but as an approximation we may suppose that this instability of consumer preferences expresses itself in that say, 20 per cent. of consumers in each buying period (not necessarily all different in each period) purchase other than their customary

---

[1] Andrews, op. cit., p. 193.

[2] Heavy advertising used to 'promote' a new product or an innovation in product design (or as itself innovation; see pp. 146-8 below) is a quite different kettle of fish.

[3] As reported by R. W. Jastram, 'Advertising Outlays Under Oligopoly', *Rev. of Ecs. & Stats.* 1949, pp. 106-9.

brands. Now suppose for simplicity that there are only two rival advertised products, A and B, say, and that A has the larger share of the total demand. Then a progressive reduction in the inequality of the relative market shares of the two products would occur if some more or less constant proportion of all those consumers who purchase a product other than their customary brand were led thereby to transfer their allegiance more or less permanently to that product.[1]

But this result is unlikely. Some consumers might be so won over as a result of chance 'magic' effects at the first trial.[2] But in settled conditions two products of the same commodity sub-class, as here envisaged, will be substantially similar, and by hypothesis both are distinctively packaged and widely advertised; the possibility of such effects at this stage is therefore very small. For the most part the position is rather that while indeed the buying 'habit' of the consumer does not preclude the purchase of another product according to the whim or chance persuasion of the moment; yet it is such that in the absence of these chance stimuli, and while each of the manufacturers continues so to 'match' the advertising of his rival(s) as to maintain the prevailing overall balance of persuasive pressure (the normal tendency in this sort of situation) the consumer will tend to revert to the brand of his customary choice. Thus the continued advertising of the manufacturers (and the maintained equivalence in quality of product) is the constant factor in the situation; whereas the chance circumstances which may dictate a different choice are infrequent and irregular. Despite the admitted instability of consumers' choices, therefore, the unequal division of the market will tend to be maintained, and a considerable stability of the established market shares over longish periods will obtain.

---

[1] Thus, if this constant proportion were 50 per cent.; if total sales were 100 units; and if the initial product allegiance of the consumers was 60 per cent. in favour of product A and 40 per cent. in favour of product B, then the actual sales of the manufacturers would be 56 (i.e. 60 minus 20 per cent. of 60 plus 20 per cent. of 40), and 44 (40 minus 20 per cent. of 40 plus 20 per cent. of 60), units respectively. (This assumes that the consumption of the product takes the form of the same quantity per period per consumer.) In the next period, 50 per cent. of the consumers who purchased B instead of A return to A, and similarly 50 per cent. of those who purchased A instead of B return to B; while again 20 per cent. of all consumers purchase the alternative product as before. Hence in this period the sales of the manufacturers are 54·8 and 45·2 units, respectively, And so on.

[2] i.e. it may happen that a product at the first trial is utilized in a chance combination of favourable circumstances which produces singularly good effects (and would have done so if it were any other comparable product). With this the consumer is likely to become at once a confirmed buyer of that product.

There is a second factor which has a bearing on this point, namely, the normal turnover in the buying population. Some consumers die; others, and particularly young persons beginning life on their own account, enter the market as independent buyers for the first time. Again, in the case of a regional market, some consumers will be leaving for other parts of the country, and others moving to this region. And so on. The magnitude of this component of the 'floating' element of the total potential demand of the market is difficult to judge: certainly its incidence is likely to be more definite for some commodities[1] than others.

Now it might be argued that with the (two) manufacturers advertising prominently, the demand of these consumers entering will tend to be divided more or less equally between the two products. If this were so, then in time the initial inequality in the respective shares of the market would be progressively eliminated.

This argument, however, is not valid. The situation is one in which the preferences of the great body of established consumers have already been formed. In such circumstances it is difficult to think of cases in which the 'new' buyer does not enter the market with some disposition to purchase the one product or the other. For example, the preferences of the newly-married housewife for a wide range of commodities will be influenced, if they have not been moulded, by her experience in the home of her upbringing. The new smoker will be influenced by the customary brand(s) of his parents, or friends. The consumer removing to a new region will tend to be influenced as much by the views of the neighbours and others he (or she) meets there, as by the advertising itself. In all these cases and in these ways, the new consumers will be influenced in their choices; and overall this influence will be roughly proportionate to the established pattern of preferences;[2] so that the unequal division, once established, will tend to be maintained over longish periods. Again, the continued advertising of the manufacturers is the important constant element; both directly in terms of its impact on the

---

[1] As, perhaps, the case of cigarettes, where for the industry as a whole, customers will be lost mainly because of deaths; whereas in this day and age, new smokers will for the most part be recruited among young persons approaching adulthood.

[2] Thus to continue the above examples: the proportions of new housewives favouring different products will correspond roughly to the proportions of old; the proportions of new smokers favouring particular brands will, in the case of parental influence, correspond roughly to the proportions among the parents, or otherwise the probability that the new smoker will adopt a particular brand will correspond roughly to the relative frequency of that brand among his friends; and so on.

new buyers, and also indirectly in maintaining the continuing preferences of the great body of established consumers.

To return to the thread of the argument: there is yet a third means by which the individual firm may seek to increase its share of the market, namely, by actual variations in the quality and specification of its product—very often in combination with increased advertising to publicize the change and, less frequently, a price reduction. This is undoubtedly the most promising weapon of the three; because if the price cut can be matched virtually instantaneously, and if effective counter-advertisement can be devised almost overnight, it necessarily takes some time to perfect and get into production even the simplest variation in the design or quality of the product: during this interval, the change, if successful, will win over buyers at the maintained price. The length of this interval, however, obviously depends on the order of the change involved. But so far as they are characteristically of a minor character, then just because of the tendency to eschew price competition as ineffective and mutually damaging, the attention of *all* firms is directed to such product variation as the most effective weapon of market strategy. And with this, the probability is that if it should be firm X which initiates a change and gains the advantage today, it will be firm Y which does so tomorrow and firm Z (or firm X again) the time after that. Thus even by this means it is difficult in the long period to effect a significant alteration in the established channels of trade.

Yet if it is proper to emphasize the inherent difficulty of acquiring (and extending) 'goodwill', in the dynamic conditions of reality the pattern of a market is, of course, not unalterable.

Thus, first, it is assumed in the preceding discussion that all the established firms seek actively and continuously to maintain their position in the market—that in the third class of case, for example, a renewed burst of advertising by one firm is promptly countered by similar bursts from its competitors. That this is the normal tendency is, I think, the correct view. Nevertheless, circumstances do sometimes arise in practice in which this condition ceases to hold. For example, a large dominant firm, just because of the strength of its position, may move only sluggishly—or even, for a long period, not at all—to counter an aggressive move by a smaller rival and this may enable the latter significantly to increase its share of the market.

Second, it will sometimes occur—gratuitously in the pursuit of immediate gains, or because of errors of judgement—that the market price should be set too high in relation to the cost of production in an efficient manner and other objective circumstances of the case.[1] This affords an opportunity to the aggressive non-conformist among established firms, or to a new entrant firm, to effect a significant alteration in shares of the market. It is thereby enabled to quote a lower price which can be maintained in the long run. Such a new low price provides a compelling focal point for an initial sales campaign. Albeit the price is quickly matched, there is apt to remain a reservoir of ill-will at the high price now revealed to have been not warranted by costs, which properly exploited may ensure a significant increase in sales. Again, a price which is too high in the present sense enhances the prospects of new product developments offered at a price in closer relation to costs.

This brings us (third) to the effect of innovations—in product design or in the methods of production and marketing. With innovation the established pattern of shares of the market may, and in general will, be decisively altered.

INNOVATION IN THE CONTEXT OF INDUSTRIAL ANALYSIS[2]

In this we envisage innovation of a 'major' character. The distinction between a 'major' and a 'minor' innovation, like all such distinctions in economics, is somewhat arbitrary and the one category tends to shade into the other. Nevertheless it is sufficiently clear in practice to serve for the articulation of a theory. That a major advance should be achieved in a single step is essential. Thus the initial development of the internal-combustion engine and the motor-car was a major innovation; and so was Henry Ford's development of mass production methods which made possible the cheap motor-car for the mass market. On the other hand, the advance in design from the typical motor-car of the late 'twenties to that of the late 'forties was also striking enough. But this was achieved stage by stage in relatively small steps, with now one firm and now another showing the way: the effects of this sort of process, discussed at the end of the preceding section, are different

---

[1] That is, in the terms of the analysis of the next chapter, should be set in excess of the 'no-entry ceiling'.

[2] The concept of 'innovation' is due, of course, to Joseph Schumpeter. Schumpeter's main interest in developing the concept was the explanation of the business cycle. But the concept has important applications in the context of industrial analysis, which it is our purpose to develop.

from the major innovation (save in the unlikely event that the same firm consistently initiates the change at each stage).

I would contend that if one reflects on the life-histories of particular industries, one can readily distinguish the relatively infrequent 'big' step and 'big' change (Schumpeter) of the major innovation and, between each such innovation and the next, longish periods of comparative stability, i.e. settled conditions, characterized by frequent but relatively minor changes in product design and production and marketing methods.[1] This pattern of development can readily be traced in the soap and detergents industry.

Apart from institutional factors (such as the patent laws) there are two main reasons why the effects of major innovation are different from an advance by a succession of small changes. In the first place,[2] to carry through a major innovation is, in effect, to change the 'givens' of the industrial situation, and it is in exploiting the possibilities opened up by this change that the opportunity consists. But in general the 'big' opportunity which the major innovation thus affords can be apprehended and carried through against all resistances by entrepreneurial ability of a high order. And typically other entrepreneurs, albeit efficient enough in their management of day-to-day affairs, yet inevitably tend to regard the situation through the 'blinkers' of established modes of thought and customary ways of doing things; so that very often they perceive the significance of the innovation only when they 'behold the thing done'. But (and in the second place) even when—and if—the decision is taken to emulate or otherwise counter the pioneer, it takes time (e.g.) to develop and tool-up to produce an equivalent variant of the new product; or to perfect, independently, the new process of production; or whatever the case may be; this phase is, of course, past for the innovator. In some cases the lag on this account may be as long as several years. For these reasons then (and cumulatively) there is a necessary and substantial lag between the initial innovation and effective counter-action.

It is this lag which creates the possibility of a decisive alteration in the established channels of trade. There is a conjunction of entrepreneurial ability of a rare order, of the 'big' opportunity which the

---

[1] It is not to be thought that there is some unexplained periodicity in the coming about of the possibility of major innovations. It is rather that the exploitation of the next innovation must needs await to some extent at least the 'digestion', so to speak, of the current one.

[2] Cf. J. A. Schumpeter, *Business Cycles*, i. 72 ff.

major innovation affords, and of an inevitable lag in the counter-competition of rivals which enables the pioneer to exploit the situation for a season relatively uncontested. In these circumstances a decisive alteration in relative shares of the market in favour of the innovator is the normal outcome.

In dynamic conditions, then, and particularly in the event of major innovation, the pattern of shares of the market (in terms of goodwill) is not unalterable; we return to this in Chapter 4, and it is a recurring theme in Part II of this book. But for our immediate purpose, which is to formulate the basic model of price determination in manufacturing industry, the existing pattern of goodwill relations is taken as a datum of the analysis.

DEMAND AND THE CONCEPT OF THE 'INDUSTRY'

This model is a particular-equilibrium analysis in terms of the 'industry'. As already stated above this procedure, despite its obvious correspondence with real-world conditions, requires theoretical justification.

The first step is to formulate an appropriate theoretical counterpart of the sort of real-world situation referred to by Professor Chamberlin in his own original formulation of the theory of Monopolistic Competition, namely, a situation where

. . . The differences between [the varieties of products] are not such as to give rise to differences in cost. This might be approximately true where say similar products are differentiated by trade marks.[1]

It is significant that in his process analysis at this point Chamberlin envisages that all the different varieties of the 'product' sell at the same price:[2] significant, because as L. M. Frazer has argued, that one price should prevail for the same physical quality of product is the ultimate criterion of a commodity class, and *ipso facto* of the 'industry'.[3]

Now in the commodity class of Perfect Competition it is assumed that there is perfect and instantaneous substitutability as between the various units of the commodity: this precludes altogether the possibility of divergence in the prices of the various producers' output, and the one price is established (exists) instantaneously and continuously. This condition of things is realized

---

[1] *Theory*, p. 83.   [2] *Idem.*
[3] *Economic Thought and Language*, p. 133.

in practice approximately where the centralized marketing organization obtains, in many such cases the output of the separate producers being merged quite anonymously in the aggregate supply.

In manufacturing industry, however, the organized market does not obtain. Let us postulate a process of manufacture (similar to Professor Chamberlin's) in which a number of manufacturers are marketing products which are in fact (i.e. objectively) identical in all respects, save for the particular identification and sales message of each. It might seem that this would preclude the very phenomenon of goodwill which we have argued is the essential structural characteristic of the market in manufacturing industry. But this is not so. We have already referred above to the manner in which, in the case of advertised consumer goods, more or less stable brand-preferences for essentially similar products emerge with differences in the situation and attitudes of the individual consumer. (In the case of a manufactured intermediate product, one can imagine an entrepreneur setting up business in that trade ordering the product from one manufacturer, or at most several—so as not to have 'all his eggs in one basket'—but not from all. The initial choice of the buyer may have no particular rational basis; but subsequently, from his point of view, the product and its associated services—including the regularity of the supply—of the one manufacturer, or several, from whom he is buying, has been, and is being, proven; which is not true of the products and associated services of the other manufacturers, even when the latter are in fact identical with the former.) In a word, in either type of situation the products of the various sellers, while not significantly differentiated objectively, are thus differentiated subjectively.

Now the existence of goodwill in this situation precludes the instantaneous substitutability which defines the commodity class in Perfect Competition. Nevertheless, an analogous concept of the commodity class and 'industry' can be formulated, granted certain assumptions. These assumptions are two:

(i) that consumers—or at least a sufficient proportion of consumers, as argued presently—are rational in the sense that they will not continue to pay more for the same size/quality of product than they need pay elsewhere. This implies that over time, on the basis of their continuing and accumulating experience, they can and do recognize equivalence in size/quality of product when it exists.

(ii) that the 'demand-transfer' period, i.e. the period during which the typical consumer would act in this wise, transferring his custom in the event of a price differential, is short relative to the 'investment period' of the firm, i.e. the period during which the entrepreneur aims to stay in business in order to recoup his initial capital outlays.

The effect of these assumptions is that one price will tend to prevail for the products of the various producers as the systematic outcome (equilibrium tendency). For let us assume that the one price does in fact prevail, but then one manufacturer raises his price above this going level. Then because of the attachment to his product (goodwill) of those who customarily purchase it (i.e. preferences which are admittedly irrational in the sense of not being related to real differences in specification), he will be enabled to maintain the higher price for a time. That is, it is readily granted that the customers of such a business will not immediately transfer their custom elsewhere. This, it may be noted, was precisely Mrs. Robinson's position: she has written referring to a price cut by a rival firm, that

... not all the customers, who are attached in varying degrees to a particular firm by the advantages which it offers them, will immediately forsake it for a rival who offers similar goods at a smaller price.[1]

But while this is granted, the import of assumption (i) above is that the buyers will not *continue* to purchase the product of the firm at the higher price; that after some interval (the 'demand-transfer' period[2]) their preference for the particular product of this firm, which can well be indulged at the one price previously prevailing, will in face of the price differential be overcome, and they—or at least a sufficient proportion of them—will transfer their allegiance in whole or in part to alternative suppliers who are offering (by hypothesis) the same product at a lower price. This assumption envisages, not (it is true) the instantaneous substitutability which defines the commodity class in the Perfect Competition case, but a similarly complete (more or less) substitutability occurring *with a lag*.

But this means the loss of market connexion, of goodwill. It is not so much that at the higher price the same customers all buy less;

---

[1] *Economics of Imperfect Competition*, p. 90.
[2] This is an average concept; some buyers will move more quickly (and more completely) than others.

it is rather, or predominantly, that customers are lost.[1] But once they are lost, the original position cannot readily be restored: as argued above, the connexion has been and can again be, acquired only

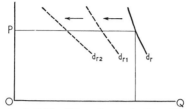

Fig. 2: Individual Firm Demand: Short Period

with difficulty and over long periods of time. It follows then, granted assumption (ii) above, that the individual manufacturer will not systematically quote a price which is higher than rival producers for the same size/quality of product; for in so far as the demand-transfer period *is* short relative to the investment period, that would be fatally to prejudice the security of his investment. The entrepreneur might raise his price relatively to his competitors' for a brief season—to exploit the possibilities indicated by the (possibly inelastic) d_r curve—and then lower it again, and while risking much remain substantially unaffected; but he obviously cannot do that every successive (or alternative) period without loss of custom.[2]

[1] The situation may be represented graphically as in Fig. 2, where OP is the prevailing price level, and d_r the demand curve of the firm in these circumstances. The subscript r is to indicate that the curve is a temporary reaction curve only, relevant in the short term immediately following a price variation. With the increase in the one firm's price, the curve will shift (and quite apart from new entry)—to positions d_{r1} d_{r2}, . . ., according to the magnitude of the increase and the length of time the higher price is maintained.

The d_r curve is analogous to, but not identical with, Professor Chamberlin's dd′ curve (*Theory*, p. 90). Chamberlin, in correspondence relating to an earlier version of the present argument, has asked: 'Why not say that your curve, instead of shifting, becomes more elastic with time?' The answer as is apparent from the above, is precisely because it is the shift—representing the loss of connexion, which cannot after any longish interval be easily regained even by a restoration of the price—to which we would direct attention, and not any associated change in elasticity. (However, in the above figure, the curve is depicted in its successive positions as becoming more elastic.)

A detailed discussion of just such a price increase by one firm out of line with rivals' prices, is to be found in R. B. Tennant, *The American Cigarette Industry* (Yale, 1950), pp. 160-1 ff. In September 1918 the American Tobacco Company increased the price of its 'Lucky Strike' cigarettes by about 15 per cent. By 11 November, when price parity was restored, sales had fallen by some 30 per cent., and continued to fall to January when the loss of sales exceeded 50 per cent. It was many years before American succeeded in recovering its relative position in the market.

[2] And see on this, the further discussion, pp. 51-52 below.

By similar argument *mutatis mutandis*, if the one producer cuts his price, then his competitors (in general, few in number) will be obliged after some interval to match it.

We conclude then that as the systematic outcome, i.e. as the equilibrium tendency in such an established continuing process of production, and notwithstanding the element of goodwill, one price will prevail for the products of several manufacturers. And surely this is the economic criterion of the 'identity' of a number of particular products; as distinct from the letter of the meaning of that word which the argument from the spatial analogy[1] would emphasize.

It is worth emphasizing again that the typical situation in manufacturing industry differs structurally from the situation in much of primary industry (to which the Perfect Competition analysis relates as a first approximation), but it is not necessarily less competitive —at least so far as 'competitive' refers to the substantial identity of prices for the same size/quality of product. Perfect Competition, to repeat, envisages an instantaneous transfer of demand from the higher-priced to the lower-priced source of supply; in point of fact, it is scarcely within the purview of that theory to consider a price higher than the going market price at all. The element of goodwill, on the other hand, does enable a divergence of price; but unlike the case of Perfect Competition, the subsequent loss of demand is not readily regained. It is most important that this latter consideration should be set against the instantaneous substitution of the Perfect Competition case, in passing judgement on the relative 'competitiveness' of the two types of situation.

All this is but the bare bones of a formal analysis. It must now be elaborated in a number of ways.

(1) First, the question at issue in adopting the 'industry' approach is essentially whether the above assumptions (i) and (ii)—which emphasize the preponderating similarity of the competing products in the sort of real world situations which correspond to the abstract case envisaged, and the basic rationality of consumers acting as a body—are more realistic and relevant to the analysis of price determination in manufacturing industry than the alternative Triffin-Chamberlin (1951) viewpoint which emphasizes the unique character of each firm's product and, accordingly, advocates a

---

[1] In contending that the 'industry' approach should be abandoned increasing recourse was had to spatial models. See particularly E. H. Chamberlin, 'Monop. Comp. Revisited', *Economica*, Nov. 1951.

general equilibrium approach. This is not a question of a 'right' (valid) theory versus a 'wrong' (invalid) theory. And as with most of the basic premises of economics, the question cannot be settled definitively; in the last analysis, the relative merits of the two viewpoints is a matter for the judgement of the individual investigator. It will suffice to consider briefly the realism of the present assumptions with respect to the three broad classes of situations distinguished above.

In doing so the general point stated parenthetically in assumption (i) must be borne in mind: it is not necessary to assume that all buyers are thus rational, but only the much less restrictive condition that a sufficient proportion should be.[1] What constitutes a 'sufficient proportion', however, will vary from case to case, and in particular according to the fixity and the incidence of overhead costs in the line of production in question.

Thus consider the position of a firm where the prevailing price for its product is p, its current volume of output x, direct costs per unit βp, and overhead costs per unit αp. Then the net profits of the firm are

$$xp - (\alpha px + \beta px).$$

Suppose now that the firm increases the price for its product by the fraction θ, and as a result (the prices of competing products remaining constant) sales after some interval fall off by γ. The firm's net profits per period will then be

$$p(1 + \theta). \, x(1 - \gamma) \, - \alpha px - \beta px \, (1 - \gamma)$$
$$= px \, \{(1 + \theta). \, (1 - \gamma) - \, \alpha - \beta(1 - \gamma)\},$$

assuming that overhead costs are strictly invariant with changing output, and direct costs per unit are constant. Then the net profits will be reduced to zero if

$$(1 + \theta). \, (1 - \gamma) - \alpha - \beta \, (1 - \gamma) = 0,$$

i.e. if $\gamma = 1 - \dfrac{\alpha}{1 + \theta - \beta}.$

Thus the larger α (the smaller β), the smaller the reduction in sales which will eliminate the net profits altogether. If for example $\alpha = \cdot 4$, $\beta = \cdot 5$ and $\theta = \cdot 1$, then $\gamma = \frac{1}{3}$; i.e. if in the initial position, overheads represent 40 per cent. of the unit price, materials, etc., 50 per cent., and net profits 10 per cent., then with a 10 per cent.

[1] The point is attributed to the late Mr. C. N. Ward-Perkins of Oxford.

increase in the price net profits would be reduced to zero by a $33\frac{1}{3}$ per cent. reduction in sales.

Of course, long before sales fell off to this extent, the firm would cut back the price to its former level, to arrest the decline in sales. In this case, then, a 'sufficient proportion' of consumers would be appreciably less than $33\frac{1}{3}$ per cent.

The analysis is over-simplied, but it is, I think, indicative of significant tendencies in reality. While there are doubtless a good number of us who are rather careless in our shopping (and rarely bother to check the change!), yet there are others, more keen and cautious, who though perhaps a minority control prices for the benefit of all.

(a) Now with respect to the first broad class of manufacturing industries distinguished above, namely, those manufacturing intermediate products, the two assumptions of the abstract analysis are amply justified. The buyers are themselves businessmen, other manufacturers at higher stages of production. This means, in the first place, that it is entirely reasonable to assume that the buyers *are* good judges of quality, and that they will not be ignorant of the opportunities of buying elsewhere. Second, such a manufacturer-buyer has his own competitive position to consider *vis-à-vis* his rivals in his own trade. He may pay a higher price for a time—because of the risks and inconvenience of a change in his customary source of supply (thus imparting some considerable short-term inelasticity to the supplier's d_r curve). But these considerations would not long outweigh the pecuniary advantages of buying more cheaply elsewhere: that is, the business-consumer's own competitive position is certain to override the goodwill relation after some (relatively short) interval. Nor, I think, can there be any reasonable doubt that the demand transfer period is short relative to the investment period of the established firm in this sphere of production (second assumption).

(b) In the second broad class of industries, those concerned with 'unbranded' consumer goods (manufacturer anonymous, more or less, so far as the final consumer is concerned), the immediate customers of the manufacturers are again other businessmen—wholesale dealers in the trade in question. Again both assumptions are amply justified; indeed more so. It has already been suggested above that the attachments of goodwill in this sphere are not so strong or exclusive as in the previous class of case. The individual wholesaler is in general closer in touch with 'the trade' as a whole than is the manufacturer-buyer in the latter context, because the essential activity of the wholesaler is buying and selling products of this general type, whereas the main preoccupation of the manufacturer is with his own line of production. The market in this sort of case then would tend to be even more 'competitive', in that the judgement of quality and the knowledge of opportunities is likely to be greater, and the reaction to a price-quality differential the more prompt.

(c) There remains the third class of cases, namely, that of consumer goods sold under the manufacturers' own brands, often with heavy advertising directed to the final consumers. In this case, the 'buyer' referred to in the assumptions in question is the private individual—the typical 'consumer' of economic theory; and the tendency would be, I think, to deny that the first assumption in particular can be realistically applied to such a buyer. Indeed considerable emphasis has always been placed on the alleged 'irrationality' of the ordinary consumer. There would appear to be two main reasons for this.

First, it is argued that the ordinary consumer's expenditure on the typical consumer good constitutes but a small proportion of his total income. He has, therefore, little to lose in indulging an 'irrational' preference by paying more for a particular product than he need pay for the same quality under a different, less-favoured brand.[1] In the second place, it is argued that in any event the ordinary consumer is not an adequate judge of quality—and particularly when it comes to complex durable products of high unit price.

These arguments have a considerable plausability *a priori*. I would contend, nevertheless, that they misrepresent the case as it typically works out in practice.

Thus, as regards the first, while it is true that the consumer's expenditure on any one product is typically only a small proportion of his total income (and also that it is entirely appropriate for some problems to draw attention to this circumstance), yet the consumer's total expenditure is made up of such outlays on a number of such goods, and he has always to contend with the problem of maintaining a customary standard of living (and saving) with a limited income. It is this aspect of the matter which should be

[1] Cf. e.g. J. K. Galbraith, *Modern Capitalism*, Ch. VIII, pp. 101 ff. This view also underlies Professor Chamberlin's basic 'large group' analysis.

emphasized in the present connexion. In these circumstances, an extravagance in the purchase of one commodity must needs be compensated by niggardliness in another—or in the purchase of the same commodity next time round. For any one consumer over time, these tendencies will average out; and we are left with the general picture of a pretty penny-wise approach to all items of expenditure, however small, at least on the part of the proportion of consumers previously referred to.

The second argument—the charge that the ordinary consumer is no judge of quality—is obviously crucial. The assumption in question requires that consumers in the large can recognize the substantial equivalence of two products when it is in fact present. The issue cannot be resolved definitively; but it is important to make clear just what our assumption implies.

The argument in the opposite sense most germane to this matter is, that by persuasive advertising the ordinary consumer can be led to imagine that the one advertised product possesses superior qualities to another product, strictly equivalent, but differently advertised, and therefore that he will be prepared to pay a higher price for it. Now it is not denied that the consumer may be induced by persuasive advertising to pay such a higher price once, twice or even more; it is granted that the consumer has little to lose by experimenting with different products in this way. Nor is it denied that some consumers may continue to pay the higher price indefinitely. The contention is, however, that other consumers—and in general, a sufficient proportion in the sense indicated—will base their continuing buying habits, not on the claims of the advertisers, but on the actual performance of the product when they try it. Such a consumer, e.g. will not continue to live in hope (and buy expensively) if a higher-priced soap, which it is claimed will beautify the complexion, does not have the desired effect when put to the test. In this way then, on the basis of the continuing and accumulating experience of their day-to-day living, it is claimed that by and large consumers can, and do, pass effective judgement on quality. Evidently this judgement on the part of any individual consumer cannot be effected immediately or outright, but only in time. What is important here is to take due account of the essentially continuing and long-run character of most economic activity.

All this is quite consistent with the obvious and admitted fact of definitive and largely irrational preferences as between different

brands of otherwise similar products *at the same price*. Such preferences, it has already been argued, are sufficiently strong to sustain
for long periods an unequal division of the market at the one price,
should it once emerge for whatever reasons. But the point of the
argument is that this does not necessarily preclude rational behaviour in the foregoing sense in face of a price differential: with the
higher-priced product in such event being bound to lose ground
more or less rapidly according to the relative strength of established
preferences and other factors including, of course, the magnitude
of the price differential. Granted that the 'investment period' is
normally very long—indeed indefinitely so—in the main stream of
legitimate business activity, then the one price for the same size/
quality of product is the characteristic equilibrium tendency.

It is to be noted too that the kind of judgement here required of
the consumer, that he can assess the substantial equivalence or
otherwise of two products, is sufficient for forms of differentiation
other than that at present in view. In the event, for example, that
a product of inferior quality than some currently accepted standard
type is offered to consumers at a lower price, it is not suggested
that the ordinary consumer can judge whether the difference in
price is a proper measure of the difference in actual costs of production. And indeed those consumers for whom the utility of the
money saved is greater than the decrease in utility from consuming
the inferior rather than the standard quality product, will purchase
the former, whatever its price in relation to the cost of production.
But in the event that the price *is* in excess of a 'reasonable' cost of
production (albeit lower than that of the standard product), the
tendency will be for some other producer(s), perceiving the situation,
to offer an equivalent product(s) at a still lower price. The judgement
required of the consumer is then reduced to the above form, i.e.
the recognizing of equivalent qualities.

The foregoing argument may be granted for commodities of
relatively low unit price and subject to repeated purchase at short
intervals (as e.g. most food products, soap, cigarettes, and such
like). But what of commodities of complex structure and relatively
high unit price, and purchased at long and frequently irregular
intervals—as, e.g. clothing (a borderline case), furniture, radio
sets, and so on? For this class of product, the proponents of the
'irrational' consumer may argue that the preceding discussion is
clearly irrelevant; because the individual consumer will buy this

class of product only once in a year, or once in five, or ten years—
perhaps (in some cases) only once in a lifetime. If therefore he is
once induced by persuasive advertising to pay more for a particular
quality of product than he need have paid (or to purchase an inferior
product at the price of a better-class article), he has no redress, at
least not until he again enters the market for the product in question,
which may be years; bygones are bygones for some considerable
time in this context.

This argument, however, overlooks the very important point
that the radio set, the refrigerator and the motor car are not bought
as a rule on the basis of impersonal persuasion (advertising);
though this doubtless gives direction to the consumer's inquiries, and
also the assurance of guaranteed quality which goes with a well-
known brand name. On the contrary, they are bought only after
much thought and deliberation, and with particular regard to the
counsel of friends and others, who have already acquired these
articles and speak from experience. This latter point is significant
in two ways.

First, since the experience of friends provides the consumer with
what amounts to extended trials of the products in question before
the event, his judgement is to that extent informed and he is much
less likely to buy unwisely in the first instance. But in the second
place, should he nevertheless do so, then just as he has discussed
his purchase with persons who have already acquired this and rival
products, now in turn he will pass on his own unsatisfactory experience to others. (Contrariwise if the product pleases him, he will
pass on its praises.) Manufacturers exhibit a lively appreciation of
the efficacy of this grapevine. They should do so. They have invested large sums in plant and factory; and if they have sold to this
consumer and many others in this production period, the life of the
business depends on selling to many more in the next production
period. The unsatisfied consumer, therefore, will influence the course
of events long before he himself needs (or can afford) to re-enter the
market; it is required only that a proportion of wary buyers in
succeeding periods should heed the counsel of unsatisfied customers
and avoid the product in question, in order to enforce the necessary
adjustment of price and quality.

It is in this way that 'the consumers' as a collective body pass
effective judgement on quality with this class of goods. It is true
that the identity of the buyers actually in the market in any

period is different from the preceding period, and different again in the succeeding period; yet the attitudes of the present buyers are sufficiently dependent overall on the attitudes and experience of previous buyers as to realize (approximately) the continuity of discriminating judgement in buying which we envisaged in the first assumption.

On such grounds then the basic assumptions of the abstract analysis may be accepted; at the least, they are approximations equally as close to a very complex reality as most other abstractions in economic analysis.

(2) However, a caution is necessary lest the (equilibrium) tendency for one price to prevail for the same size/quality of product be interpreted too rigidly. Of course, divergences of price will occur and sometimes for longish periods. Particularly where the product is such as to admit of significant variations in design and quality, a price cut may be partially disguised by an associated variation in the product, and this is likely to retard the normal consumer reaction to the cut, and (thereby) to create divergent entrepreneurial expectations, with the result that there is some uncertainty (at least not certainty) that the cut will be either fully or instantly met. In such circumstances, a price differential may be ventured and maintained for a much longer period and in the event with a smaller change in market positions than would otherwise be the case. Another circumstance which may contribute to the tardy matching by one firm of the price cut of a rival is pressure on the firm's financial resources which increases the subjective 'weight' of the immediate (relative) gains from the maintained higher price, as against the prospective loss of future profits from some inevitable recession in the firm's share of the market.[1] (It is perhaps notable that most examples in practice of a price differential with seemingly identical products have, in my experience, been of the present type, i.e. have arisen from failure to match fully the price cut of a rival(s), rather than from an increase in its price by one firm with rivals holding prices constant.)

In view of these possibilities the analysis may be qualified as follows. It must be accepted that at any time there will be variations

---

[1] Professor J. R. Hicks has schematized this process of balancing short against long-term profits (weights 'l' and 'm' respectively) in his model proposed in 'The Process of Imperfect Competition', *O.E.P.*, 1954, p. 45.

as between the established firms in an industry in the degree of their market control, i.e. in the strength of their 'goodwill', and hence in their command over the custom of their own particular 'markets'. This is not to be interpreted, however, (*contra* the theory of Monopolistic Competition) as involving systematic differences in the prices charged for substantially identical products in equilibrium. Rather it involves as an extension of the foregoing analysis that the length of the demand-transfer period will vary as between firms in proportion to the strength of their acquired goodwill, and this implies differences in the degree of freedom of action of each firm in the short run and in the magnitude of the potential (short-term) gains from price variations. But the systematic equilibrium tendency is for one price to prevail for the same size/quality of product; and at this price the aggregate demand of the market will be divided between the competing manufacturers in terms of the goodwill each commands. This is the justification of the particular equilibrium approach, and the starting point of the formal model structure outlined in the next chapter.

In concluding this discussion it is worth emphasizing that all those phenomena which Imperfect Competition theory sought initially to take into account *vis-à-vis* the then current theory of 'competition', find a place in the foregoing conception. These are (1) the separation of the market, represented by the (short-run) down-sloping demand curve; (2) brands and trade-marks as the vehicles (so to speak) of this separation; (3) relatively stable and irrational consumer brand-preferences—'irrational' in the sense of not being related to real differences in the products, but which for some, even a majority, of consumers may well be irrational also in the sense that they will be maintained in face of a price differential; and (4) the power of the individual producer, not shared by the perfect competitor, to quote his own price and a price diverging from his rivals' (though normally on the present view, only for short periods).

(3) There remains finally the problem of enlarging the concept of the 'industry' beyond the confines of the sort of situation hitherto envisaged, that is, a situation where substantially similar products are differentiated only by the particular identification of each (including distinctive trade-mark and sales message).

This situation may be referred to as the 'standard case'. The justification for concentrating attention on this type of situation is that all modes of differentiation can in the last analysis be reduced to it.

In this connexion a distinction is sometimes drawn between 'deceptive' and 'non-deceptive' (or 'legitimate') product differentiation. The differentiation of otherwise very similar products by the distinctive brand name and sales-line, together with other aspects of the conditions surrounding the sale of the product (as, e.g. 'courteous service', attractive shop assistants, and so on), come under the former heading. These modes of differentiation have been the principal targets for economists' strictures against product differentiation; they are the 'monopoly' elements in Monopolistic Competition, as is clear from Professor Chamberlin's arguments in support of those practices which businessmen and the courts have always regarded as 'unfair trading' in his well-known Appendix E, previously referred to. By the same token, the differentiation (separation) of products (markets) based on real differences in the qualities and/or specifications of products is regarded as 'legitimate'.

Now 'real' differences may be of two kinds, according to whether they do or do not involve associated differences in cost when produced in an equally efficient manner. Within the general demand for motor-cars, for example, there are distinct sectional demands. Thus some consumers require a small, economical vehicle; others a larger and more powerful one; and so on. The difference in specification as between a typical vehicle of these types would be such as to involve a difference in cost. Within either class, however—say among vehicles of a given engine horsepower—one make (e.g.) may be highly-geared for greater speed or petrol economy, and another low-geared to reduce the need for gear-changes; but such a (real) difference might not involve any difference in cost.

Now as regards this latter form of quality-differentiation, the tendency in the event that the different qualities do not in fact involve differences in cost, will be for one price to prevail for the various products, as before. It is true that a buyer with a definite preference for a particular attribute might well be prepared to pay something more to obtain it; nor would such a buyer be able to judge whether there was any associated difference in cost or not. But assuming a large number of buyers desiring each of a few such variants of the product,[1] then in the event that one producer should

[1] Of course, if the 'market', for a particular variant is limited, it would more likely be offered as an 'optional extra' by most producers at additional cost.

attempt to exploit the preference for a particular product variant by charging a higher price, we should expect other producers to offer the same variant at a lower price. And in the end then, one would expect competition to enforce the 'one price' in this sort of case, as in the case where the products are substantially identical (the 'standard' case); though the quality variants will of course provide an effective basis for the separation of the market as between a number of producers.

Where quality differences do involve differences in cost, this reduces to the form envisaged above, in so far as the situation within any one sub-class approaches the 'standard' case. As previously argued, in the effort to appropriate and to hold a share of the going demand within any such sub-class, each of the competing manufacturers will be seeking constantly to initiate and to exploit (minor) variations in the design and quality of the product, in the details of sales service, and so on. But any such variation which one manufacturer may introduce and which does prove successful (i.e. wins over demand at the going price) must needs be promptly imitated by rivals; so that as the result of competition, the tendency within any sub-class of a broad commodity group will be towards the situation envisaged in the 'standard case'.

In the formal model-building of the next chapter then, our procedure in arguing in terms of a number of manufacturers producing substantially identical products amounts to this.

First, we abstract, provisionally, from the constant thrust and parry in terms of (minor) innovations in the design and quality of the product, which is the dynamic essence of competition in practice, in order to concentrate attention on the static longer-run tendencies of the system. This applies within any sub-class of a commodity group.

Second, we abstract from the complex itself of product classes within the sort of broad commodity group which is characterized as a distinct 'industry' in practice. In fact, there is a tendency for the pattern of production within such a broad commodity group to stabilize in settled conditions into a conventional product-pattern with a corresponding conventional price pattern—in the British motor-car industry, for example, into the 8-10, 14-16, and 21-23 horse-power 'popular' models, and the general classes of larger and/or 'luxury' models and 'sports' models. This oversimplifies the case, but is meant only to be illustrative.[1] (Competition in practice may then take either of the forms of adjusting price to conventional quality, or quality to the conventional price. The latter is the more common form in the late stages of the development of an industry, particularly in the context of consumer goods). Now in so far as a strictly stable relative price-quality pattern emerges, then as Professor Hicks and Samuelson have shown[2] the group of products can be treated as one, for demand purposes. This is the basic justification for the analytical device of imagining the complex of commodities produced by an actual manufacturing industry as 'reducible to a cost-equivalent standard commodity'—which, it can well be argued, was what Marshall was doing when he spoke of the demand for the product of a manufacturing industry, and drew his well-known market demand curve.[3] To be sure the price-quality pattern will not in fact remain strictly stable; but to proceed in analysis as if it did is scarcely less valid an abstraction, as a sufficient approximation, than most other abstractions in economic analysis.

On these understandings then, we shall in the next chapter continue to speak of the 'industry'; to think thereby in terms of the 'standard case'; and to draw a market demand curve for the 'product' of this industry.

APPENDIX (Chapter 2)

THE 'NECESSARY MINIMUM' OF ADVERTISING EXPENDITURE

THE proposition is advanced above (p. 29, n. 1), that relative to a given market area (we may think in terms of the 'national market') there is a certain minimum level of advertising expenditure, varying widely of course from industry to industry, which each firm must necessarily make if it is

---

[1] It is to be emphasized that the tendency for the conventional pattern to emerge facilitates the task of the consumer by reducing the number of price-quality comparisons to be made. The number of quality-price combinations, in the absence of a conventional pattern, is theoretically infinite in view of the possibilities of variation in the combinations of features. (Cf. P. W. S. Andrews, 'Some Aspects of Competition in Retail Trade', *O.E.P.*, 1950, p. 153.)

[2] J. R. Hicks, *Value and Capital*, Math. App., pp. 311-12; P. A. Samuelson, *Foundations of Economic Analysis*, pp. 141-3.

[3] P. W. S. Andrews, 'Industrial Analysis in Economics', in Andrews and Wilson (eds.), *Oxford Studies in the Price Mechanism* (1951), p. 144.

to keep its product before the attention of the public at all and so remain effectively 'in the market'; and that the magnitude of this expenditure for minimum effectiveness is large in absolute amount, and *to a considerable extent independent of any one firm's actual volume of sales*. In practice the advertising expenditure of firms (as each seeks to match the expenditure of its rivals to maintain the established overall balance) will fluctuate at levels above this necessary minimum; it is clear that a minor variation in product design introduced by one firm might at any time set off a round of competitive advertising which will carry the expenditure of each far above the minimum.

This necessary minimum of advertising expenditure is determined by a variety of factors. It will depend in the first place (and primarily) on the nature of the product. It will be less, *ceteris paribus*, the greater the unit expense and complexity of the product. Thus motor-cars and radio sets are not bought as a rule on the basis of impersonal persuasion (advertising) but only after much thought and deliberation and with due regard to the counsel of satisfied customers; though advertising doubtless will often give a direction to the consumer's inquiries. Soaps and cigarettes, on the other hand, i.e. products of low unit price and of simple and substantially standard (as between various brands) structure, require concentrated and less rational persuasion to establish definite consumer preferences. Again, the necessary minimum of expenditure will be less, *ceteris paribus*, the more frequently the product is purchased (the shorter the period of consumption). The degree of instability in consumer's preferences, referred to above, probably varies directly with the length of this period. This bears on the necessary number of repetitions of advertisements, and thus, *ceteris paribus*, on the total expenditure. Possibly from this cause the advertising of soaps would tend to exceed that of cigarettes. And so on.

In the second place, the turnover in the buying population (discussed above) will necessitate continued advertisement, and the greater the magnitude of this component of the total demand together with any substantial net increase in the population (as, e.g. in the event of large-scale immigration) the larger the necessary minimum of advertising expenditure. To some extent this will vary with the nature of the product, because the relevent buying 'populations' for various products and the rates of turnover, will differ. But whatever the product, new buyers in the market will always necessitate more concentrated persuasion (notwithstanding indirect influences bearing on the new buyer, discussed above). The larger this element in the total demand then, the greater the necessary minimum of advertising expenditure.

In the third place, the necessary expenditure on advertising will depend on the concentration pattern of consumers throughout the market area, as it affects the 'accessibility' of the market. To the extent that the majority of potential consumers are concentrated in closely knit urban areas, a higher 'degree' of persuasion may be effected with a given expenditure on advertising than if the same majority of consumers are situated in smaller, more widely scattered rural communities. In practice, different sections of the one market differ widely in the degree of accessibility;

this is particularly true of the 'national' market. In this latter case, it is often true in practice that of several firms claiming a 'national' distribution of a particular product, the largest (often the longest established) will have a considerably higher expenditure on advertising than its smaller competitors because, for reasons of prestige, it has sought to penetrate all parts of the market, whereas the latter have confined themselves to the more readily accessible only. These may well contain the great majority of potential consumers of the product; so that in the less accessible market areas, there is likely to be rapidly diminishing returns to increased selling expenditure. This goes beyond the complexities which may be introduced into a basic abstract analysis, but the point must be borne in mind in practical cases when weighing the actual (as against the theoretical) advantages of the very large firm.

A fourth determinant of the necessary expenditure on advertising is, of course, the prevailing structure of prices for advertising space and talent. Thus the relative costs of the various media will influence the choice between them; and the price-structure as a whole will finally determine the absolute level of expenditure.

There are doubtless other factors which bear on the determination of this necessary minimum of expenditure on advertising; the foregoing analysis is admittedly rudimentary. The hypothesis is nevertheless maintained (*a*) that such a minimum exists, as some complex compound of the determinants indicated and, hence, independent in the main of any particular firm's actual volume of sales, and (*b*) that in general it is large in absolute amount.

CHAPTER 3

PRICE DETERMINATION IN MANUFACTURING INDUSTRY

II. THE STATIC MODEL

WE are now in a position to set out the formal framework of the basic model of price and output formation in manufacturing industry. The construction in this chapter is still, however, very incomplete: in particular, it is essentially static in character, and thereby neglects some more dynamic aspects of the process which are in fact inherent in this form of market structure. But in analysis it is always necessary to approach the complexities of real life in stages, and accordingly these dynamic aspects are reserved for separate discussion in the next chapter.

In terms of the argument of the preceding chapter, we envisage a process of production—the 'industry'—in which a number of manufacturers market products which are in fact (i.e. objectively) substantially identical save for the particular identification of each. The phenomenon of goodwill, it has been argued, is not inconsistent with this assumption. As to the number of firms, while this is frequently 'large' (say, upwards of ten to twenty), there is typically with respect to any well-defined 'market' a small number of dominant firms (say, from three to nine), and this is presumed here.[1] Further it is assumed provisionally that there is no collusion between them save, perhaps, some minimal 'regulation' of prices in the sense referred to in the preceding chapter.

We begin with a statement of the assumptions of the model with respect to demand, based on the argument of the preceding chapter. In the next division of the chapter some aspects of the theory of costs are discussed. The balance of the chapter is then concerned with the equilibrium of the model. The formal result is that in most

---

[1] The size distribution, of course, is to be thought of in terms of the characteristic reverse-J shape. Mr. P. W. S. Andrews has examined some of the influences determining the character of this distribution in his article 'Limites economiques à la dimension et à la croissance des enterprises individuelles' ('Some Economic Limits to the Size and Growth of Individual Manufacturing Businesses'), *Revue Economique*, January 1956.

cases the industry price will be set at that level which will just suffice to deter the entry of new competition (pp. 70-72). But this leaves unresolved the crucial question of price theory, namely, the relation of the price thus indicated to the 'cost of production'. Next, therefore, some of the more important objective circumstances which bear on this question are examined, namely, the conditions of new entry ('barriers' to entry), and the development of excess productive capacity. The outcome, particularly in connexion with barriers to new entry, will be conditioned by the pressures of actual intra-industry competition; but this is associated with the dynamic aspects already referred to, and is discussed more fully in the next chapter.

DEMAND

On the basis of the argument of the preceding chapter, the following elements represent the conditions of demand in the model.

First, there is the 'market (or industry) demand curve', depicted in the right-hand part of Fig. 4 below.[1] It is contended that this concept is a sufficiently valid representation of the facts for the articulation of a theory. There can be no doubt that producers do see their essential task as being to compete for a share of a going aggregate demand for their type of product; and that if they fail to appropriate a demand, that is because it has been appropriated by rivals. To postulate a market demand curve is the only way to make sense of this preoccupation of entrepreneurs in practice with their 'share of the market'. Such a market demand curve is often relatively inelastic, though more elastic in the long run. (There are some well-known propositions in elementary demand theory which bear on this.[2] The significance of the elasticity of the market demand curve will be discussed further in Chapter 4 below.)

As to the individual firm, there is, first, the particular-market 'reaction' curve d_r as in Fig. 2 above, determined by the extent of the 'goodwill' the firm commands in the market. In the neighbourhood of equilibrium, the primary significance of this curve is that it indicates the 'stop' to sales, so far as the one firm is concerned, at the prevailing industry-wide price. (Its further relevance to policy is, as we have seen, that it represents one dimension of the firm's

[1] p. 71.
[2] See, e.g. G. J. Stigler, *Theory of Price* (revised edn., 1952), pp. 44-47.

discretionary power in price-fixing.[1] This is excluded from view for the purposes of the present basic equilibrium model.)

Second, we draw in the left-hand side of Fig. 4, below, the curve labelled d, which is a fractional representation of the market demand curve DD'. That is, the curve shows against each price a volume of sales which is a constant fraction, equal to the firm's current 'share of the market', of the total demand at each price; it is thus at every point of the same elasticity as the market curve. (This is identical with Professor Chamberlin's DD' curve.[2] He uses the capital 'D' because of the relation to the market demand curve; but the latter is not actually drawn. Here it is drawn, and the capitals are reserved for it.)

This curve reflects the result that the equilibrium tendency is for one price to prevail, and hence is the appropriate representation of the conditions of individual-firm demand in the model. Observe, first, that it involves as a 'solution' to the 'problem of oligopolistic interdependence' that the reaction of rivals to a price change will be to follow suit, and that each firm knows this.[3] The acceptability of this hypothesis in respect of a price cut is attested by the widespread acceptance of the 'kinked demand curve' analysis.[4] But price increases in pursuit of joint long-term advantage (in the event, for example, of a general increase in the prices of raw materials) are also likely to be followed. In any case, if there were any doubt on the part of the initiating firm(s), the concurrence of the market can always be tested by announcing the price increase in advance and abandoning it if rivals do not announce a similar increase. (Of course, if a firm should increase its price gratuitously above a recognized market level in the pursuit of short-term gains, then it is the d_r curve which would be relevant. This is analogous to the upper segment in the 'kinked demand curve' analysis.)

In the second place, it should be observed that it is entirely reasonable to assume that the entrepreneur can apprehend the objective d-curve here envisaged. It is required only that he can know (a) the proportion of the aggregate demand he at present commands (i.e. his current 'share of the market'), and (b) the elasticity of the market demand curve. It is evident that these data are 'knowable' in a sense that a curve like the d_r curve, above, or

[1] Above, pp. 8, 52.   [2] *Theory*, p. 90.   [3] As Chamberlin, *Theory*, pp. 100-1.
[4] R. L. Hall and C. J. Hitch, 'Price Theory and Business Behaviour', *O.E.P.* (O.S.), No. 2; P. M. Sweezy, 'Demand Under Conditions of Oligopoly', *J.P.E.*, 1939.

the analogous Chamberlin dd' curve is not. The old problem of the 'subjective' versus the 'objective' demand curve thus does not arise as an important issue.[1]

It is necessary next to consider certain propositions in the field of costs, as foreshadowed in the previous chapter.

(a) *Costs in the Short Period*. In the upper diagram of Fig. 3 the curve ac is a 'particular plant' cost curve depicting the fall of short-period average full costs with the spreading of overheads as output increases. The curve is not drawn (in continuous-line) beyond the point where it reaches its minimum. Typically, for a manufacturing firm, the continuous application of a variable factor to the complex of fixed factors (the 'plant'), as envisaged in elementary textbooks on economics with the example in mind of employing more and more labourers on a given acreage of land, is not possible. The plant being given, there is a maximum number of workmen required for full working: up to the corresponding output (maximum capacity of the plant with normal working—ox_c in the figure), entrepreneurs attest that average (full) cost falls continuously. The vertical rise of short-period marginal cost shown in the figure at this output (mc) is virtual only.

Up to this point average direct cost—which is here identified with short-period marginal cost, as a sufficient approximation for all practical purposes—is typically constant over a considerable range of output, as drawn in the figure. Raw materials cost per unit, in many cases the major component of unit direct cost, is of course essentially constant; but direct labour costs also vary substantially in proportion to output because in general there are reserves in the 'fixed factors' (basic plant and process machinery) which are taken up as output is increased.

In the figure Ox indicates the projected or 'planned' throughput of the plant. This volume of output is to the left of the minimum-cost point because in setting up the plant the entrepreneur will normally plan to have an overall reserve of capacity for a number of reasons.[2] Thus first, even when goodwill in the market is well developed, he will still anticipate fluctuations in output including

---

[1] Cf. Professor Machlup's emphasis that the relevant magnitudes in the 'marginal' theory of the individual firm are 'subjective' only. *A.E.R.*, 1946, pp. 521-2.
[2] See P. W. S. Andrews, *Manufacturing Business*, pp. 87-93.

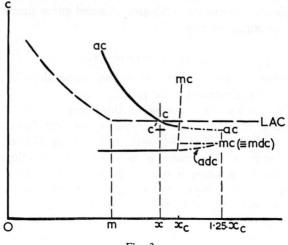

Fig. 3a

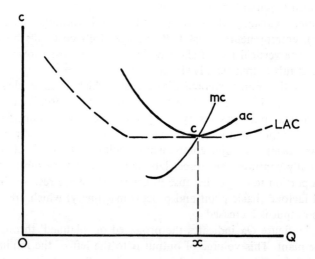

Fig. 3b

Fig. 3: Short- and Long-period Average Cost

sustained periods of peak production in the upward phase of the business cycle. Second, in view of the overriding importance of maintaining and extending the firm's goodwill, a reserve is necessary in case of partial breakdowns, or in any event to enable normal repairs and maintenance, without loss of output. And so on. Now the unit cost xc shown on ac against the output Ox, is higher than would be the cost (xc') with the smaller plant whose ac-curve attains its minimum point at that output. Then if output were constant over time, breakdowns did not occur, etc., the use of such a plant would indeed enable an average (over time) cost per unit of the lesser magnitude xc'. But in fact such ideally stable and uneventful conditions of working do not occur; and the defining characteristic of the plant ac, as against a smaller or larger plant, is precisely that with respect to the output Ox it yields the unit cost xc as the minimum cost attainable on the average over time given fluctuations in output about Ox as mean, and the cussedness of things in practice.[1] In this way xc is the 'true' long-period unit cost of the output Ox, and c is thus a point on the long-period cost curve (LAC in the figure, to be discussed in (b) foll.). The implication of this is that in so far as the ac curve is drawn to show actual short-period costs in function of output solely, it intersects, rather than is tangent to, the long-period average cost curve.[2]

This view of the short-period cost situation of the typical manufacturing firm may be contrasted with that depicted in Fig. 3b, which is the characteristic textbook representation. The difference is of critical importance in explaining actual competitive behaviour.[3] Fig. 3b suggests an altogether too inflexible and unrealistic short-period behaviour pattern of the manufacturing firm. Assuming a ruling market price equal to xc (and sales Ox), it would suggest no reason for the firm to be concerned at all to increase sales; while if nevertheless there were an increase in demand for its particular product, it suggests either an increase in the firm's price, or—if it abides by the ruling market price—that customers are turned away. Competition is indeed dulled as compared with the behaviour suggested by the cost pattern of Fig. 3a where, at normal throughput and beyond, short-period marginal cost is

[1] Loss of revenue due to breakdown is properly regarded as a 'cost' in this connexion.

[2] The same view, based on similar reasoning, has been advanced by Professor J. M. Clark, 'Concepts of Competition and Monopoly', *A.E.R.* Supplement, 1955, p. 458.

[3] And cf. above, pp. 25-27.

significantly below average cost, so that at a ruling price equal to the latter the firm is eager to make additional sales and to appropriate any new orders as may come its way.

And of course short-period output is even more flexible than the analysis so far would suggest. For longish periods, although not indefinitely, output can be increased beyond Ox_c—and this profitably at a going market price in the vicinity of xc—by overtime and multiple-shift working. The effect of overtime working in a typical case is indicated by the extensions in dotted lines, of the ac and direct cost (average and marginal) curves of the firm in Fig. 3a. In this illustration, assuming direct labour is paid 'time-and-one-half' for overtime work, short-period average cost is virtually unchanged (fractionally less) for an increase in output to 25 per cent. beyond 'capacity' (x_c).[1]

But overtime working can scarcely be continued indefinitely because of the difficulties of carrying out normal maintenance and the increasing likelihood of breakdowns. In the long period, however, the firm can enlarge its plant—which brings us to the long-period cost function, or 'scale curve', of the firm.

(b) *Costs in the Long Period.* Assuming a given state of technical knowledge and given factor prices, the long-period average cost curve of the firm will tend to be of the general shape indicated by the LAC curve in Fig. 3a: that is, it tends to fall relatively steeply in the initial stages, and then to flatten out for a more or less indefinite range.

It is useful in this connexion to distinguish, following Mr. Andrews, the 'technical' and 'managerial' costs of production.[2] As regards the character and variation of the technical costs of production, it is broadly correct as Miss Brunner has argued that

... all economies of scale . . ., other than those of management proper will lie in the technical unit cost curve. This must be seen as falling continuously [in function of output], sharply at first, then more and more gently, for once the major economies of flow production are open to the firm, the extension of large-scale mechanization will be confined to ancillary

---

[1] In the figure the (constant) unit direct cost at output x_c is drawn as amounting to 70 per cent. of the unit full cost (c, say) at this output. Of this 70 per cent., assume 20 percentage points is direct labour cost per unit, and 50 percentage points materials cost per unit. Then beyond x_c, time-and-one-half for direct labour will raise direct cost per additional unit of output (i.e. marginal direct cost—'mdc') to $\cdot 8c$. Thus average full cost at output x_c plus 25 per cent.
$= \{ \cdot 3c. \ x_c \ [\text{i.e. overhead inc. normal profit}] + \cdot 7c.x_c + \cdot 8c \ \cdot 25 \ x_c \} / 1 \cdot 25 \ x_c$
$= c\{ \cdot 3 + \cdot 7 + \cdot 2 \} / 1 \cdot 25 = \cdot 96c < c.$
[2] *Manufacturing Business*, Ch. IV.

processes, such as handling and transport, and further economies in the main manufacturing processes will probably be confined to the improvement of particular machines or parts of the process. Some further technical economies of scale will always be open to the firm, but they will become relatively less important.[1]

Thus so far as the trend of (unit) costs of the technical factors are concerned, there is no limit to the continued expansion of the firm. Underlying this is the obvious condition, that the basic factor of production in manufacturing—namely, machines, and machines of whatever efficiency—can be readily duplicated:[2] in contrast to the situation in agriculture where the best land (most fertile, in closest proximity to the marketing centre), and similarly lesser 'grades' of land, are for all practical purposes limited in supply by nature.

Next as to 'managerial costs'. It has been usual to assume that management costs per unit necessarily rise after some point, because of the increasing difficulties of co-ordination and control with an 'ultimate management' factor of limited capacity. This proposition is now widely challenged. Mr. Kaldor in particular argued that apart from risk-bearing (which really rests with the ownership, and can be spread over as many persons as there are shareholders) the functions of management are two, namely, supervision and co-ordination: and that it is only the latter which is fixed and lends uniqueness and determinateness to the firm as such.[3] He went on to argue that in proportion as the firm approaches the equilibrium of a going concern, the number of 'co-ordinating' tasks becomes less and less and the volume of business which the 'unit' of co-ordinating ability can manage larger and larger.

Again there is an obvious contrast between manufacturing industry generally, and agriculture. In the latter sphere, the nature of the tasks to be performed changes with the seasons and—more frequently—with every variation in the weather from day to day.[4] Here then 'the frequency and magnitude of the adjustments to be undertaken' (Kaldor) at successive points of time are considerable; so that we should expect, and indeed we find, a relatively small and more or less determinate 'optimum' size. In manufacture, on the other hand, where to a very large degree there is in a going

---

[1] Elizabeth Brunner, 'Competition and the Theory of the Firm', *Economia Internazionale*, v, No. 4 (1952), pp. 13-14.

[2] Subject, of course to patent rights in new machines, adequate 'knowhow', etc.

[3] 'The Equilibrium of the Firm', *E.J.*, 1934, pp. 69 ff.

[4] Cf. T. N. Carver, *Principles of Rural Economics*, pp. 239 ff., especially pp. 244-5.

concern a repetition day-in and day-out of the same set tasks and processes, the task of the co-ordinating factor is of a quite different order. In any case it is wrong to argue that the capacity of the entrepreneur is 'fixed'.

In fact, ever more complex aids to, and systems of, management become economical in function with size: this is the essential point of Mr. Andrews's argument as to 'levels' of management.[1] There are appropriate management techniques available for different ranges of output, and in this way the 'capacity' of the ultimate manager is extended with the growth of the business. There may indeed be a sudden sharp rise as the firm gets too big for personal supervision by one man. But '. . . there seems little reason to suppose that each succeeding level of management will be progressively less efficient than the preceding one',[2] the business having settled down at the new high level of output; and

. . . once the step has been made to more impersonal management one would expect the decrease in efficiency to slow down. Moreover with each level of management, over the appropriate range of output, managerial costs will not be rising, and each succeeding level will extend over a progressively wider range of output.[2]

(In point of fact rising unit costs associated with management are more likely to arise in practice in function of the rate of increase of output, rather than in function of output as such.)

Typically, then, taking managerial and technical costs of production together,

. . . we may expect costs to fall sharply at first, and then more slowly, until at [some] scale they can be taken as approximately constant.[2]

Thus the curve of long-period costs per unit in manufacturing industry of the general shape of the LAC curve in Fig. 3a—the 'law of the L-shaped cost curve', according to Mr. P. Wiles.[3]

Three points require to be noticed in connexion with the long-period cost curve.

First, it is necessary to definite the 'minimum optimum' scale of production. In traditional analysis where the long-period cost curve of the firm was seen as U-shaped, it was possible to speak unambiguously of 'the' optimum scale of production, as that scale of production where the unit cost is at a minimum. But if the cost

[1] op. cit., Ch. IV.   [2] E. Brunner, op. cit., p. 14.   [3] Op. cit., Ch. 12.

curve is L-shaped, then there is no such unique optimum scale of production. Rather we speak of the 'minimum optimum scale', as the smallest scale of production at which the major economies of production open to the individual firm in the line of production in question can be appropriated. This scale of production would be *Om* (approximately) in Fig. 3*a*.

Second, in Fig. 3 and succeeding figures, the long-period curve is represented by a dashed line. This is to indicate that it is a curve of potential, not actual, positions—a sort of 'shadow' control behind the actual (short-period) cost curve of the existing plant; apprehended more or less clearly from entrepreneur to entrepreneur; a curve 'locating', as it were, the present position of the firm relative to the whole range of possibilities. The cost curve relating to the existing plant (as *ac*, in Fig. 3) on the other hand, is drawn in continuous line, as showing the variation in cost per unit of explicit and immediate relevance to the policy of the firm.

What is important in this connexion is that, starting from his ascertained average cost as from the existing plant, the expectation of the entrepreneur as to the course of costs with an expansion in his scale of operations will be influenced by the curve of (unit) 'technical' costs which tends to fall continuously with increasing scale. This is so because the entrepreneur will not expect that he himself, or the management generally, will become less efficient just because the firm grows—albeit in the event this turns out to be so (i.e. the LAC curve rises because of an actual decline in managerial efficiency). In general, therefore, the expectation of the entrepreneur is, that if he can but expand sales permanently at the going market price, then with the appropriate enlargement of the plant the firm will be able to produce at a lower unit cost, and hence at a higher margin of net profit in the long run. Thus the pattern of long-period costs reinforces the short in encouraging active competition for the custom of the market.[1]

Third, the long-period cost curve as viewed by the individual entrepreneur will (granted its shape) be positioned higher or lower with respect to the horizontal axis according to the firm's current efficiency, i.e. according as the firm is currently a high- or low-cost producer. In practice the unit full costs of different firms in the same line of production vary widely: this is a well-attested fact of experience which an adequate theory of price determination must needs

[1] Above, pp. 27, 63.

take explicitly into account.[1] Such variations in realized unit costs arise in part from differences in managerial skill operating essentially the same productive apparatus; but more importantly they arise dynamically from the uneven exploitation of developments in productive technique. What is important is that this is no mere random circumstance, but part and parcel of the process—among other reasons because innovation necessarily implies leaders and followers. And in turn the resulting pressures affect the relation of prices to costs, keeping rivalry alive and undermining the collusive pursuit of maximum joint advantage.

But at this stage we abstract from these dynamic aspects of the case, which are taken up in the next chapter. And for the purposes of the present basic static model it is assumed initially that all the firms in the 'industry' have equal unit costs at the planned throughput of their plants: that is, they are 'on' the (flat stretch of the) identical long-period cost curve—though not of course all with the same size of plant (ac curve).

POTENTIAL COMPETITION, THE 'NO ENTRY CEILING', AND THE EQUILIBRIUM OF THE MODEL

The equilibrium of the model may now be indicated as follows.

The key factor in the situation is potential competition, that is, the threatened intervention of new competitors if prices are set too high. In practice, apart from statutory or other Government-sponsored monopoly, it is rarely (if ever) the case that a firm, or

---

[1] Many practical inquiries witness to the reality of such wide variations in costs. It will suffice here to notice some examples taken at random from *Reports* of the British Monopolies Commission:

'Industry'	Range of inter-firm variation in manufacturing costs expressed as a percentage of lowest cost: i.e. $\dfrac{c\ max - c\ min}{c\ min} \times 100$
Cables, all products	25%
Ditto, particular products:	
Smallest Variation	4
Largest Variation	200
General-service Lamps	10
Fluorescent Lamps	90
Matches (3 plants)	17
Cathode Ray Tubes: 14 inch	98
17 inch	81

Of course special factors account for some of the larger of these ranges, but it is not possible to discuss these in detail here.

collective of firms, is free from the threat of the intervention of new competitors at *some* level of price. This is as true of the large-scale national oligopoly as it is of the semi-anonymous producers of chain-store mousetraps. The implicit presumption at the back of much of the traditional analysis of duopoly (oligopoly), namely, that the market is, and will remain a closed preserve whatever price policy the sellers adopt (on the analogy with Cournot's mineral springs, where two producers had appropriated the only available sources of supply), is quite inappropriate. Of course, in either of the situations referred to (but more importantly in the large-scale oligopoly), there are indeed obstacles to the entry of would-be new producers: these are analysed in detail in the following pages. Nevertheless experience attests that in all such cases there is some level of the market price at which, should the established producers quote persistently above it, new competitors will appear and promptly, and will as often as not succeed ultimately in appropriating a not insignificant share of the market.[1]

Moreover, established entrepreneurs are in the main aware of this, i.e. are aware that at some level of price they are vulnerable to new competition. In the classical theory of Imperfect Competition it would seem, on the face of it, that this was denied. But this is a question of fact concerning which the testimony of entrepreneurs is conclusive. And the testimony is unambiguous. Sir Roy Harrod has reported the replies to this effect of entrepreneurs interviewed by the Oxford Research Group,[2] and many other investigators have found similarly.

It is this awareness of the threat of new competition if prices are set too high which governs the equilibrium tendency of the system. The controlling factor is the long-term consideration on the demand side elaborated in the previous chapter, that a share of the market in terms of acquired 'goodwill' is the very foundation of the firm's continuing profitable operation and this is built only with difficulty and over a long period of time. But new producers, once attracted and established in the market, threaten to undermine this foundation to an indeterminate degree, depending on their skill and tenacity (and financial strength) and the unpredictable play of events in the market: the danger is not less—rather it is more— compulsive because the ultimate effect is thus shrouded in uncertainty. It is then held that, aware of this threat and bent on

---

[1] Above, pp. 37-38. [2] *Economic Essays*, pp. 143-4.

protecting the firm's established connexion in the market, the dominant objective of the entrepreneur in setting his price is, typically, to forestall the emergence of such new competition.

In Fig. 4 then, which illustrates the equilibrium of the model,[1] let OP be the critical level of price referred to, that is, the minimum industry price at which the threat of the intervention of new competition will become actual, or, alternatively, the maximum price which will just suffice to deter such entry. This may be termed the 'no-entry ceiling' price, to adopt Mr. H. F. Lydall's felicitous phrase,[2] and is represented by the heavy line drawn across the figure through OP. To view it thus as objectively uniquely-valued is a simplification, because, as discussed below, it depends in part on the expectations (optimistic or otherwise) and subjective discount factors of potential entrants.[3] Nevertheless it is a sufficiently valid first approximation like most other concepts in economics.

Then the objective of the individual entrepreneur, aware of the threat of new competition and bent on protecting the firm's established position in the market, is to fix on this level of price—and by charging just less than this, to deter new entry and so preserve the firm's connexion intact. It is readily granted that the subjective apprehending of this critical level of price by the individual entrepreneur is bound to be blurred, and of course errors do occur.[4] Nevertheless entrepreneurs attest that in practice they can form very good ideas about it, and that they are in fact concerned to do so.[5]

Thus from the point of view of the individual firm, the 'no-entry ceiling' becomes what Miss Brunner has called the firm's 'price-policy line'[6]. Alternatively, that part of the line to the left of p may

---

[1] In the figure, the right-hand diagram refers to the 'industry', with D the aggregate demand curve and OX the industry output at price OP. The left-hand figure refers to the individual firm. LAC is the long-period average cost curve assumed common to all firms (as above), and c the (presumed) 'equal' unit full cost of production. (This presumes that all firms are operating at, or beyond, the 'minimum optimum' scale. This is a result of the model: see below). The 'plant curve' ac will vary in position along LAC according to each firm's planned scale of operations, in the light of its share of the market represented by the d-curve, as explained above.

[2] 'Conditions of New Entry and the Theory of Price', *O.E.P.*, October 1955, p. 301.

[3] A belt or range about such a price as OP, with varying probabilities of attracting new competition, would be more appropriate.

[4] A well-documented example was the notorious 1931 increase in the prices of the 'standard' brands of cigarettes in the U.S.A. (R. B. Tennant, *The American Cigarette Industry*, New Haven, 1950, pp. 88 ff., and W. H. Nichols, *Price Policies in the Cigarette Industry*, Nashville, 1951, pp. 85 ff.). Mr. Tennant does in fact entitle his discussion of this episode 'a pricing error'.

[5] See Sir Roy Harrod, *Economic Essays*, pp. 155-7.

[6] op. cit., p. 11.

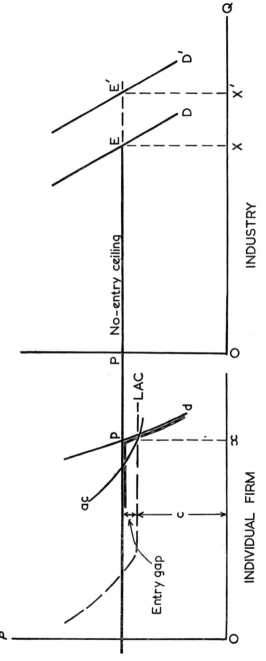

Fig. 4: Static Equilibrium of the Model

be viewed as a segment of the firm's (objective, long-period) demand curve, which is thus 'kinked' at p—the enclosed-dashed line in the figure. The corresponding marginal revenue curve, discontinuous at p, runs down the vertical line px; and providing the market demand—and hence the firm's d-curve—is not too elastic in the neighbourhood of the ceiling price,[1] then (long-period) marginal revenue is 'equal'[2] to marginal cost (long- or short-period) at the price and output combination, xp and Ox, respectively. In this way the equilibrium of the individual firm may be depicted in terms of the orthodox marginal revenue-marginal cost condition for maximum profits.

But this adds scarcely at all to the understanding of the situation, and indeed stated on its own would leave us as much up in the air as to why the demand and marginal revenue schedules are where they are, as in the traditional 'kinked demand curve' analysis. A more direct and informative statement of the equilibrium tendency would run as follows: that in static conditions* and on the assumptions (i) that the market demand is 'not too elastic' in the neighbourhood of the equilibrium price and (ii) that the firms seek the maximum profits that can be maintained in the long run, then in most cases** the industrial process envisaged in the model will tend to a stable equilibrium of price *defined by the condition that the industry price is just such as to deter the entry of new competitors*; each firm producing the maximum output it can sell at this price as determined by the extent of the buyer allegiance (goodwill) it commands in the market.

The following qualifications as indicated by the asterisks are noted immediately:

* First, the import of the phrase 'in static conditions' is that the equilibrium we have envisaged, with the price at (just below) the 'no-entry ceiling', abstracts from growth in the aggregate demand of the market and the dynamic process of actual intra-industry competition (as referred to above, p. 68) which is bound up with technical progress. The effect of these factors is in general to lower the price somewhat below the maximum imposed by the 'ceiling', that is, in a final analysis going beyond the confines of the present static model there is a price-dampening effect which may be

---

[1] 'Not too elastic' would imply an elasticity $< |1/1 - adc/p|$ (identifying adc with short-period mc). If adc/p is typically of the order of $\cdot 6$, this would involve an elasticity not greater than $|2\cdot5|$. See Chapter 4, p. 119 below.

[2] i.e. $mr > mc$ 'to the left', and $< mc$ 'to the right'.

conceived as a third component of the ultimate (equilibrium) industry price in addition to the 'cost of production' and the 'entry gap' distinguished almost immediately in what follows, and to which attention is confined in this chapter. What is important is that this component, being in the negative sense, may offset in part or in whole the 'entry gap': or in other words, that notwithstanding obstructions to new entry, the price may quite typically approximate to the cost of production.[1] This qualification, which (as previously indicated) is taken up in the next chapter, should be borne in mind throughout the following analysis.

** Second, the qualification 'in most cases' is added, because important exceptions may arise in circumstances where new entry is comparatively easy, but there is either effective industry-wide collusion between a large number of sellers or the market has become highly concentrated as the outcome of the particular historical development of the industry. In these circumstances the price may be set for long periods, or from time to time, at a level above the no-entry ceiling, and excess capacity tends to emerge as new entry is attracted (or periodically attracted and reattracted). Situations of this sort are discussed in detail in the last division of this chapter.

Subject to these qualifications, then, the formal result of the model is that in general the industry will tend to a stable equilibrium of price governed by the threat (or the fact) of the intervention of new competition. Three points should be noticed in elaborating on the character of this equilibrium.[2]

First, for the individual firm it is evident that the price is the thing: output takes care of itself (so to speak). To fix on this price—the maximum which is such as to deter the entry of new competition —the entrepreneur will proceed in the only manner possible. First, he will look to his own full cost; for this is some guide to the unit cost of a new entrant, which is obviously a factor governing the critical level of price. (Typically this takes the form of applying some costing 'rule of thumb'. The concern of entrepreneurs in practice with average, as against marginal, costs—emphasis on

---

[1] Above, p. 24.
[2] A fourth important aspect of the equilibrium, namely, that in the absence of collusion the tendency is for the most efficient firm at the time to set the price, is discussed in the next chapter where the consequences of relaxing the assumption of equal costs are examined.

which fact was the essential contribution of so-called 'full cost' theory—is thus readily explicable.) But the unit cost of a new entrant is not the only relevant factor; moreover in practice, as emphasized above, the unit full costs of established firms vary widely. Secondly then, and overriding the firm's own costing, the entrepreneur will look to what rivals are doing in both his own and adjacent lines of production (potential competitors), and adjust his policy accordingly. Oligopolistic behaviour in this sense is thus inherent in the present approach, and this irrespective of whether the number of actual competitors is large or small. Again this is in accord with experience. In manufacturing and commercial business it is well known that entrepreneurs are concerned constantly with the activities of rivals. To preclude such behaviour from the analysis[1] is both unrealistic and, as it now turns out, unnecessary.

As to output, the best the firm can do is to supply to the full the custom it commands at the price thus set—while striving always to increase its share of the aggregate demand for the reasons indicated above. The position may be expressed by saying that for the individual firm there is an equilibrium of price, but not a determinate price-output equilibrium in the usual sense. Or in other words: the 'right' (i.e. the equilibrium) price for the firm's product is independent in the large of its planned, or achieved, output, being governed by conditions 'outside' the firm (so to speak)—by the overall competition of the market and in particular the threat of the intervention of new competition.[2] (It follows, referring to the right-hand diagram of Fig. 4, that in the event of an increase in aggregate demand to D' with industry output OX', the locus of the points of long-period industry equilibrium (E, E') represented by the heavy dashed line is not a long-period supply curve in the traditional sense. For in the equilibrium at E, each firm could supply more, and would do so, and at the going price in both the short and the long period, if the additional demand were there; so that such an increase in demand will in general be wholly supplied by the

---

[1] The assumptions of Chamberlin's 'large group' case were designed to this end (*Theory*, p. 83). Harrod apparently, also would proceed this way (*Economic Essays*, p. 151).

[2] Hence the invariance of the 'oncost percentage' for fluctuations in output about the planned throughput of the firm. No *ad hoc* extension of the so-called full-cost pricing 'ritual', such as Harrod has suggested (*Economic Essays*, p. 168), is needed to explain this.

existing firms, and the new long-period equilibrium at E' will be attained without any rise in the price. The contrast is with a Perfect Competition industry model of 'constant returns' (individual-firm LAC curve U-shaped), where in the event of an increase in aggregate demand the price rises initially, yielding excess profits, while finally the whole of the increased demand is supplied by new firms at the previous price).

The second point in connexion with the above equilibrium is, that in so far as in most cases (apart from pricing errors) the equilibrium is governed by the threat, and not the actual, intervention of new competitors, the emergence of 'excess capacity' is not a necessary outcome of conditions of Non-Perfect Competition— except in so far as the strategic reserve capacity referred to above might be so regarded. In particular, significant unexhausted economies of scale are properly to be regarded as incompatible with equilibrium in the absence of collusion. A situation of unrestrained competition in which for the typical firm there were yet such unexhausted economies of scale would require that the competing firms were all more or less equally matched in financial strength so that the outcome of a price war would be in doubt; more or less equally efficient so that no firm(s) would accumulate larger profits at the going price and so gain financial dominance; more or less equally matched in vision, business acumen, and daring (or the lack of it); and so on.[1] This array of assumptions is inappropriate to a general theory. Accordingly it is presumed in the model that each of the extant firms in equilibrium is producing at or beyond the minimum optimum scale of production, as in the left-hand diagram of Fig. 4, i.e. (as stated above) is 'on' the flat stretch of the long-period cost curve.

One hastens to add, however, that this is not to say that excess capacity in either the 'short-period' (established plants systematically constrained to outputs short of planned throughput) or 'long-period' (firms systematically constrained to scales of operation too small fully to appropriate available economies of scale) sense never, or only very infrequently, occurs. It is denied only that it is characteristic of conditions of free but Non-Perfect Competition, as suggested

[1] T. Wilson, 'Inadequacy of the Theory of the Firm as a Branch of Welfare Economics', O.E.P., Feb. 1952. Also P. Sraffa in the 'Symposium' (E.J., 1930, p. 90), where he contends that internal economies 'are one of the forces which make for equilibrium', and the implication of this is that 'they cease to act *at* the point of equilibrium'.

by the tangency theorem of classical Imperfect Competition theory. Where, however, there is effective industry-wide collusion, the case is quite different, as already foreshadowed in the second qualification, above, to the statement of the equilibrium tendency in the model, and analysed in detail in the last section of the present chapter.

Finally (the third point we would make), it is necessary to emphasize that an equilibrium of price at (just below) the no-entry ceiling as here envisaged is independent of the number of actual competitors in the market, be it large or small, inasmuch as each of the firms is subject to the same threat of the intervention of new competition.[1] The long-standing difficulty of the alleged indeterminacy of oligopoly has been greatly exaggerated, and indeed is very largely a false issue. It arose because attention was concentrated on hypothetical situations of the Cournot mineral-spring type where the intervention of new competition whatever the level of price is precluded by the nature of the case (as in traditional single-firm monopoly). Such a case is indeed indeterminate in terms of the 'givens'—i.e. market demand curve, and the cost curves of individual firms—which suffice in the Perfect Competition and single-firm Monopoly cases.[2] But the great majority of real-world oligopoly cases, as already stated above, are not of that type—albeit there are obstructions to new entry (which we now proceed to analyse) that effectively preclude new competition at some (lower) levels of price. Of course, the pattern of actual intra-industry competition in oligopoly situations may assume a great variety of forms in practice, and generalization is more difficult: this is the subject of the next chapter. But such strategic market manœuvring, which has been the main concern of traditional oligopoly analysis, can take place in the long run only within the limits imposed by the nexus of potential new competition which in this sense is of primary importance.

BARRIERS TO NEW COMPETITION

The outcome of the discussion to this point—that the industry will tend to an equilibrium of price which is just such as to deter

---

[1] The level of the price, however, will not be independent of that complex of objective factors (as e.g. substantial economies of scale) which may itself have ordained in the particular case that there should be only a few firms (oligopoly *stricto sensu*) in the industry.

[2] Presuming ready entry and exit of firms, in the former.

the entry of new competition—is yet purely formal, the beginning rather than the end of analysis. It has been concerned with the mechanics of the equilibrium, so to speak. But this of itself does not answer the basic question really at issue, namely, what are the fundamental objective factors which govern the level of the equilibrium price?

The first answer to this question, and in the last analysis, the dominant factor in the situation, is 'the cost of production'. It is assumed at this stage (as above) that all the established firms have equal unit costs at the planned throughputs of their plants: this defines a unique unit 'cost of production', c in Fig. 4. If now it were further assumed that new entrant firms, when established, can produce at the same unit cost, then *if* there were nothing to obstruct the ready entry of new firms into the industry, the established firms could not for long (systematically) charge a price different from this cost of production. That is, in these circumstances the cost of production, c, is the objective determinant of the 'no-entry ceiling' of the formal analysis. (This result would correspond to the assumed circumstances of Perfect Competition.)

In manufacturing industry, however, there are in the nature of the case obstructions, 'barriers', to the ready entry of new competitors. Goodwill in the market, as previously indicated, is itself one such barrier, since it involves that the new entrant to attain a place must needs effect a permanent alteration in the established channels of trade, which is normally very difficult. The very existence of goodwill then and other factors make it difficult for new competitors to effect an entry into the market; and it is evident that in proportion (more or less) to this difficulty of access, the firms already established in the market may be able to elevate the industry price somewhat above the cost of production without attracting new competition. With this the level of the ceiling may be viewed as consisting of two (objective) components, namely, the cost of production c, and a margin above this—sometimes referred to as the 'entry gap' (see Fig. 4)—determined by the extent of the barriers to the entry of new competitors in the particular trade.

What are these factors which, singly or in combination according to the particular case, obstruct the access of would-be new competitors to the market?

Apart from 'artificial' restraints[1] they are principally four-fold:[2]

(1) the acquired goodwill of established firms and associated factors;

(2) the presence of substantial economies of scale;

(3) a systematic cost differential in favour of established, as against potential new entrant, firms, because of patents and other factors preventing equal access to current knowhow and production technique;

(4) large initial capital requirements.

(The last may, or may not, be a factor independent of the others: thus, if goodwill is strong, the prospective new entrant will have to finance heavy initial promotional expenses, or substantial break-in losses. This would greatly increase the initial capital requirements of the new entrant. On the other hand, the absolute magnitude of the capital required may be large even where goodwill is not strong, and even if the minimum optimum scale of production relative to the total market is small.)[3]

We now discuss each of these 'barriers' in turn, beginning with the last.

With respect to capital requirements, it is no doubt true that the necessity to raise capital sums which are large in absolute amount restricts in some measure the field of potential new competitors. The difficulty is not only the magnitude of the initial capital *per se*, but the advantage of the established firm in terms of its standing in, and access to, the capital market. In this connexion, however, it is necessary to stress Mr. Andrews's point that the 'new entrant' is often, indeed usually, an established firm in a related trade where the technical processes of production are similar. Such a firm, limited in the markets for its existing products (in terms of the goodwill it commands), is always looking around for profitable ways of expanding its operations. (Apart from mere limitation of its primary

---

[1] Above, p. 22, n. 3.

[2] Mr. J. S. Bain, to whose work every writer in this field is heavily indebted, would characterize the first of the following categories as the 'product differentiation barrier', and the third as the barrier due to 'absolute-cost differences'. (*Barriers to New Competition*, Chs. 4, 5, respectively.)

[3] To these objective market and technological circumstances one might add:

(5) the potential retaliatory power of strong oligopolistic firms, as a partially independent factor. This introduces a measure of indeterminacy into this context of analysis somewhat analogous to that in the traditional oligopoly analysis of the equilibrium of a given small number of actual competitors. But in comparison to the other factors listed, the (net) effect is likely to be small. Reference is made to this element in appropriate contexts in the following analysis.

markets, another and not unimportant reason for this is the desire to extend the bases of a business wide in order to 'spread the risk'.) Now so long as one thinks in terms of the brand-new business, as is perhaps customary, heavy initial capital requirements (aggravated by the inevitable 'break-in' losses the new entrant must incur —see below) must indeed appear a problem. But the new entrant which is an established, and often a large, firm in an adjacent line of production itself has standing in the capital market; and granted the profitability of its primary markets, it is able to meet initial losses, and to persist in its endeavour to enter the 'new' market so long as there is any reasonable prospect that time will justify its efforts, for a much longer period than the limited resources of the brand-new firm would permit. (One offset to these losses, of course, would be the virtual tax rebate it will gain in so far as the losses so incurred will be consolidated with—and thus will reduce—the taxable profits earned in its customary business.)

There is too the growing tendency for co-operative ventures in 'new' fields by firms from industries of a diverse character.[1] In such case, the new firm is backed not by one, but by a combination of firms in the 'competitive field'.

Where then the initial capital requirements of new entry are large, there are ways of circumventing the difficulty in practice. It is doubtful therefore whether, in the absence of other impediments to entry, capital requirements alone would involve any systematic divergence of the no-entry ceiling from the cost of production in the great majority of cases.[2]

Next as to systematic cost differences between established and potential new competitors. Assuming for simplicity that potential new entrants are alike in business acumen and skill (parallel to the assumption of equal costs for established firms), this element involves in the terms of the model that new entrants have access only to a (long-period) cost curve LAC' which is 'higher' at every scale of production than that of established producers (Fig. 5). In this event, and if other barriers are not significant, the no-entry ceiling —i.e. formally, the maximum price which will deter new competitors—is evidently (just short of) the unit cost c' of potential new entrants, as in the figure.

[1] For example, Forth Chemicals Ltd., set up by the Distillers' Union, Monsanto Chemicals, and British Petroleum in 1952. Part II, p. 215 below.
[2] Cf. J. S. Bain, op. cit., pp. 156-66.

The underlying causes of such a systematic divergence as between the costs of established and potential new firms are principally threefold: patents; superior knowhow embodied in key personnel, secret production processes, and the like; and the pre-emption by established firms of available sources of key raw materials. In manufacturing industry, it would appear that only the last of these is important as a cause of persistent cost differences in practice.[1]

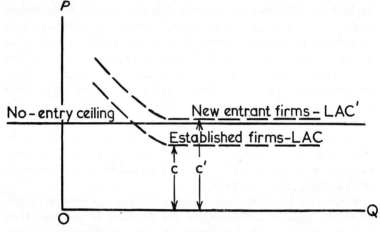

Fig. 5: Systematic Cost Difference and New Entry.

This is a large subject but the following must suffice in this place. As to patents, there is of course much said and written in some circles about their alleged effects, or more particularly the so-called 'fence of patents', in excluding or handicapping new competition. But so far as there is substance in these allegations, this sort of effect as a continuing factor in the situation would appear to be confined to relatively few, and those rather exceptional, cases.[2] As regards 'knowhow' embodied in the experience of particular managers, technicians, and other personnel, this can normally be acquired by hiring such persons. The salaries and other inducements it might be necessary to offer may be large in absolute terms, but would scarcely amount to more than a fraction of 1 per cent. of the annual sales turnover of the firm when established. Subject to patents and knowhow then, the new firm has in general a positive advantage

---

[1] Cf. Bain, op. cit., Ch. 5.

[2] A reading of the Reports of the British Monopolies Commission to date does, I believe, support this view. Also Bain, op. cit., pp. 155-6.

as against the long-established firm in that it can plan its plant *de novo* to produce the projected throughput most efficiently, and with the most up-to-date machinery. Again the location of the firm, as an element in productive efficiency, may well favour the new firm. If proximity to the final market is advantageous (because, e.g. the product is of great weight, or perishable), then a long-established producer may find himself at a disadvantage in the event of a sustained shift in population away from his original location. The new entrant, however, may locate his factory, as near the centre of population as he deems expedient (save, of course, in so far as he is subject to official restrictions in residential areas, etc.). In general, in modern conditions of production remote from the final consumer, there is surely no site-advantage which the new entrant might not emulate.

Finally there is the question of access to raw materials. So far as supplies purchased on the open market are concerned there is no difficulty. With manufactured materials the new entrant may suffer some initial disadvantage by way of a smaller discount on his restricted purchases while establishing his position in the market, but this is overcome as his scale of operations grows. There remain those industries where typically the production process is integrated back to original ore supplies (e.g. iron and steel, gypsum), and available deposits have been appropriated by the established firms. Such cases afford the principal instances of a significant entry gap under the present head.

In fine, what is important is that (with a qualification as to the role of patents in promoting new and risky development) equal access to raw materials and current knowhow and production technique is a precondition of effective competition; and public policy, including constant oversight of the working of the patent law, should be directed to ensuring that this condition obtains.

More important as a barrier to new competition are economies of large-scale production. In the terms of the model, the presence of 'substantial' economies of scale implies that the minimum optimum scale is large relative to the total market (the latter measured in terms of the aggregate demand (industry output) at a price equal to the (common) unit cost of production of the established firms, i.e. $O\bar{X}$ in Fig. 6a).

Analysis of the effect of economies of scale is complex because the outcome turns in part on the character of the reactions of established firms in the event of actual new entry. A first analysis[1] which is useful in bringing out the main issues involved and in providing some indication of orders of magnitude, may proceed on the assumption: that established producers in face of new entry will maintain their outputs unchanged, accepting the necessary

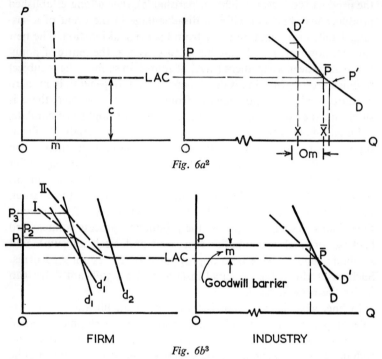

Fig. 6a[2]

Fig. 6b[3]

Fig. 6: Economies of Scale and New Entry

reduction in the (industry) price due to the entrant's additional output on the market, and that potential entrants anticipate this. (Professor Modigliani terms this 'Sylos' postulate'.) Suppose further that technology in the industry is such that it is virtually impossible to produce at less than the minimum optimum scale: thus the LAC curve (left-hand of Fig. 6a) is shown as rising almost vertically at Om.

[1] This analysis follows Bain, op. cit., pp. 98-100 *et seq*, which has been elaborated by Franco Modigliani in his important article 'New Developments on the Oligopoly Front', *J.P.E.*, 1958, pp. 217-20. Professor Modigliani reports that the analysis was developed independently by Paolo Sylos Labini, in his book *Oligopolio e progresso tecnico* (Milan, 1957).

[2] The horizontal scale in both diagrams is the same.

[3] Cf. J. S. Bain's Fig. 1, op. cit., p. 107.

Then a new firm must enter at (or beyond) the minimum optimum scale, or not at all. In these circumstances it is evident that the established firms collectively may restrict the industry output to OX —that is, less than $O\overline{X}$ by just short of the output Om at minimum optimum scale—and so elevate the price to OP, without attracting new entry. For with OX, the minimum addition of Om to the industry output by a new entrant would bring the market price down to (just) below $\overline{P}$,—to P' in the figure, at which price neither the new entrant nor the established firms would cover average costs. At price P, therefore, a (rational) potential new competitor will not enter the industry. This price then indicates the no-entry ceiling, i.e. the level of price which will (just) deter the entry of new competitors.

It is evident by inspection from the figure, that the entry gap— the margin between the ceiling and the (common) unit cost of production—will be the greater

(i) the larger the optimum scale relative to the size of the market, and

(ii) the less the elasticity of the market demand (D', say, Fig. 6a).

To illustrate and indicate orders of magnitude: if the market elasticity of demand were unity, then corresponding to minimum optima at 1, 2, 5 or 10 per cent. of the total 'market' $(O\overline{X})$, the entry gap expressed as a percentage of the unit cost of production would be in each case (approximately) of the same order. If the market elasticity of demand were $|\frac{1}{2}|$, then the gap would be 2, 4, 10 and 20 per cent., respectively, of the unit cost of production.[1] (It will be observed that as $Om/O\overline{X}$ becomes very small, as presumed in Perfect Competition, the entry gap tends to zero, i.e. the price will equal the unit cost of production, as concluded in that analysis.)

But of course the cost curve is not in general vertical at Om, as here envisaged. If the curve rises only gently with progressively smaller scales of production below Om, then it is evident that the

---

[1] As follows: If the elasticity of the market demand curve at $\overline{P}$ is ϵ, then for a (small) change in price to P we have (approx.) that $\epsilon = \dfrac{Om}{O\overline{X}} \Big/ \dfrac{P-\overline{P}}{\overline{P}}$. The denominator on the right is the ratio of the entry gap to the unit cost $c(=\overline{P})$, so that we have

$$\text{Entry gap} = 100. \ \frac{Om}{O\overline{X}} \cdot \frac{1}{\epsilon} \quad \text{per cent. of c.}$$

Substitution in this formula yields the above results. (Similarly the restriction of output below OX corresponding to a given entry gap, m (m for 'margin' above c), less than the maximum (P-c) for whatever reason, would be

$$100 \ \epsilon \cdot \frac{m}{c} \quad \text{per cent. of } O\overline{X}.)$$

entry gap *ceteris paribus* will be smaller. For example, with the minimum optimum scale at 5 per cent. of the total 'market', with $\epsilon = / \frac{1}{2} /$, and with the cost curve vertical, the entry gap would be (approx.) 10 per cent. But an elevation of the price of this order could not be sustained, if at an output equal (say) to 1 per cent. of the total 'market' the unit cost of production was only of the order of (say) 2 per cent. greater than at the optimum scale. For a new competitor entering at this smaller scale with a unit cost thus equal to 102 per cent. of c, would depress the industry price by only about 2 per cent., i.e. to approx. 108 per cent. of $\bar{P}$ (equals c). His entry would thus be profitable, and so would further entries. In fact, the maximum potential elevation of the price above $\bar{P}$ in such a case would in the first instance be rather less than 2 per cent.[1]

A third generalization therefore may be added to the above, namely, that the 'entry gap' will be the greater

(iii) the steeper the slope of the cost curve up to the minimum optimum scale. (The outcome on the assumption that the curve is 'vertical' at the minimum optimum is therefore an upper limit,— the maximum value for the no-entry ceiling in the sort of case in view for given elasticity of the market demand and proportionate minimum optimum scale.)[2]

The foregoing analysis is, I believe, not at all inappropriate to situations approximating to theoretical Homogeneous Oligopoly,[3] of which the large-scale non-ferrous metal extractors would be the principal instances, or to other (so-called) 'heavy' manufacturing industries. In these cases the large incidence of fixed costs tends on the one hand to make for inelastic short-period supply in the event that the intrusion of new competition should upset the orderly temper of the market and initiate a period of all-out competition, thus validating the above reaction assumption (Sylos' postulate); on the other hand, this vulnerability to overproduction and losses

[1] The magnitudes in this illustration would correspond approximately to the circumstances of cigarette production in the U.S.A., if that industry were not (for reasons other than economies of large-scale production) so highly concentrated.

[2] We referred above to the potential retaliatory power of strong oligopolists. The ceiling then could be even higher if, *contra* the assumption of the above analysis that pre-entry outputs would be maintained unchanged (Sylos' postulate), the established firms by their past performance (and financial strength) had created the expectation on the part of potential entrants that they would actually increase their outputs in face of new entry, in order the more rapidly to kill the new entrant.

[3] Sylos' analysis, according to Professor Modigliani, is explicitly concerned with this case.

provides a strong incentive in 'normal' circumstances to collusive action to realize—if not the maximum—then a goodly measure of the joint advantage.

But in other cases, and particularly branded consumer goods (the third broad class of manufacturing industries distinguished in the previous chapter, to which the soap and detergents industry belongs), while the analysis remains suggestive, the particular reaction assumption, which is critical, is inappropriate. In such cases the incidence of overhead costs is frequently relatively small and short-period supply accordingly more elastic. Moreover the prices of branded consumer goods are well-known, and often widely-advertised, as part and parcel of the whole product, as it were.[1] In this sort of context then, it is more appropriate to assume that the established firms will tend to maintain their prices firm (except in so far as to match a lower price quotation by a new entrant, and not always that immediately), and to resist reductions in their sales from the intrusion of the new entrant(s) by increased advertising and other measures of non-price competition. This active resistance is virtually inevitable if the policy of holding prices firm is adopted, so that the present reaction assumption is not in general, from the standpoint of the new entrant, more optimistic than the assumption of the previous analysis.[2]

With this, however, analysis of the effect of economies of scale in this sort of context is even more inconclusive than it is in any case bound to be, because of the variety and complexity of the factors which determine what share of the market a new entrant can appropriate where goodwill in the form of brand-preferences and the like is well developed.[3] In this way the effect of economies of scale is inextricably bound up with the goodwill factor (product-differentiation barrier) as a restriction of new entry, to be discussed in the

[1] 'Sunlight Soap at 3*d*. per carton from Land's End to John O' Groats' was a constant theme of Lever Bros.' advertising in the first twenty years of that firm. (See Part II, p. 147 below.)

[2] Bain (op. cit., p. 105) proposes the assumption (and corresponding entrant expectation) that 'established firms will hold their prices constant permitting the entrant to win such market share away from them as he can', as the 'optimistic extreme' establishing a sort of lower limit to the entry gap (other elements given) as contrasted with the 'pessimistic expectation' (Sylos' postulate) establishing the upper limit. This 'optimistic extreme' envisages a passive acceptance of the reduction in sales due to the output of new entrants, and is thus different from the above assumption in the text. The latter is thus outside, or apart from, the 'limits' referred to—as, indeed, Bain would recognize (op. cit., p. 98).

[3] Above, pp. 32-40.

following sub-division. Experience, however, affords some guide. In Part II of this book, a number of instances of new entry of the character and in the circumstances here envisaged, are examined in detail.[1] On the basis of these and other experiences, I would venture the judgement that, in the absence of significant innovations in product design or in marketing method (which are outside the scope of the present long-run static analysis), new entrants would do well to appropriate a market share in excess of the order of 5 per cent.—hardening more definitively to such a figure where the market is concentrated and vigorous intra-industry competition (via sales promotion and product variation) is characteristic of the market.

With reference to Fig. 6b above, we may now proceed as follows. Since some barrier associated with goodwill in the market (m, in the right-hand diagram) is inevitable, let OP represent the no-entry ceiling as governed by this factor alone (as on p. 90). Then one can say that the presence of significant economies of scale will constitute a net barrier to new entry (i.e. will contribute to an overall entry gap greater than m) if the d-curve representative of the market share likely to be attained by the new entrant (frequently, as suggested, not greater than the order of 5 per cent.) is positioned with respect to the LAC curve as d_1, but not if positioned as d_2. (Here d_2 is representative of d-curves positioned from, and to the right of, that which would pass through the intersection of the ceiling-line and the LAC curve.) And it is evident that such a net barrier due to economies of scale, where it exists, will be greater

(i) the larger the minimum optimum scale relative to the size of the total market;

(ii) the less inelastic the market demand (i.e. the larger $|\epsilon|$); and

(iii) the steeper the slope of the LAC curve up to the minimum optimum scale.

The last condition is apparent from a comparison of the LAC curve segments I and II, given d_1: with the former, established firms could fix the price OP_1 without attracting (rational) new entry, but with the latter the price could be elevated to OP_3.

The second condition, with respect to the elasticity of demand, is evident from a comparison of the result with the less inelastic market demand curve D', as against D (d_1', and d_1 corresponding), given the LAC curve (I, say). With d_1 the maximum price would be OP_1,

1 Part II, pp. 176-8, 192-7 below.

but with d_1' it would be OP_2. It will be observed that the present result is opposite to that in the former analysis.[1] Here it follows, because so long as the price-level *is* maintained, then the more elastic the demand the smaller for a given elevation of price will be the actual volume of sales corresponding to a particular share of the market attained by the new entrant. (But if the entrant should force a 'break' in prices—*contra* the assumed condition of this analysis—then indeed more elastic demand would work in his favour, and against the established producers, reducing the entry gap, as in the former analysis.)

Just how important generally are economies of scale as a barrier to new competition? A detailed answer is beyond the scope of this book. It is, of course, any net barrier over and above the goodwill barrier which is relevant; and if the above judgement as to the size of the new entrant's (maximum) likely attainable share of the market (5 per cent.) is near the mark, then this net effect is likely to be significant only where economies of scale entail a minimum optimum scale greater than 5 per cent. of the market by an amount depending (as analysed) on the shape of the LAC curve and the elasticity of demand.[2] On Mr. Bain's data relating to the large United States' market, a significant net barrier would be likely in only a small proportion of cases.[3] But elsewhere the effects of economies of scale are potentially much more significant. This is so in Australia, for example, where the most advanced technology tends to be introduced quickly, but the size of the market is very much smaller —hence the proportionate minimum optimum scale is much larger. The problem in this case, however, is not so much one of enhanced margins of net profit (distribution problem), but rather of the efficiency of production. For in many industries new entry tends to take place anyway, particularly in the form of overseas firms establishing Australian subsidiaries, among other reasons in order to have a stake in the much-publicized future potential of the country. The effect is to restrict all, or most, firms to scales of

[1] As Bain, op. cit., p. 106.

[2] For example, if the demand were perfectly inelastic, and the scale curve were higher by 3 per cent. at half the minimum optimum, then with a goodwill barrier not less than 3 per cent. there would be no net barrier due to economies of scale for a minimum optimum scale up to 10 per cent. of the market.

[3] His own finding is that there are 'great' entry barriers (i.e. entry gap in excess of 5 per cent. of minimal cost) on account of economies of scale in only two of his twenty industries, namely, motor-cars and typewriters. In both these cases, however, the 'product differentiation' (goodwill) barrier is also found to be 'great', so that the net economies-of-scale barrier is probably small or zero.

production less than the optimum; and with an adequate collusive understanding between the firms (and supported by an accommodating Tariff Board), there is an upward pressure on costs and prices albeit profits are only about normal or reasonable.

There remains the first mentioned of the barriers to ready new entry listed above, namely, the acquired goodwill of the established firms. As argued above, the new entrant has himself to acquire a similar connexion in the market, but this is normally very difficult. Conceptually then the very existence of goodwill in the market involves a potential entry gap analogous to the other barriers, as follows.[1]

It is assumed in order to isolate this factor that new entrants have access to the same long-period cost curve as the established firms, and that economies of scale are insignificant, i.e. the LAC curve is substantially horizontal over the whole range of outputs at the level of the common unit cost of production, c. Now if the (industry) price were set equal to c, new entry could not in general be undertaken; because such a price would return to the new entrant, even if successful in attaining a place in the market, less than a normal profit over the whole period of his operations.[2] Thus, first, the new

[1] Cf. N. Kaldor, 'Economic Aspects of Advertising', *R.E.S.*, 1949-50, section 33, p. 20; and Bain, op. cit., Chapter 4.

[2] Underlying this and the preceding analysis is the notion that there exists for any 'industry', or particular process of production, a 'normal' level of profit—expressed as a rate per cent. of the capital employed—which is determinate in principle in terms of a number of objective factors, and which is to be regarded as a 'cost' to be met by the price in the long run. The cost curves drawn in the analyses therefore are presumed to include this profit (which is a fixed sum in case of the ac curve), as is customary.

It is necessary to emphasize that such a 'normal' rate of profit is a technical concept, and is not to be identified with the rate of profit which may 'normally' prevail in an industry in the sense of 'what is customary'. Where barriers to new competition in an industry are systematic and persistent, the latter rate might be (say) 25 per cent. of the capital employed, whereas a 'normal' profit in the present technical sense might be only (say) 15 per cent. Mrs. Joan Robinson, whatever her present position, appears in her *Economics of Imperfect Competition* to have confused the two senses (p. 93), and perhaps also my good friend and mentor Mr. P. W. S. Andrews (see e.g. *Manufacturing Business*, p. 174).

Again, I emphasize 'determinate . . . in terms of . . . objective factors', because Sir Roy Harrod would define a normal profit as 'the rate of profit which the entrepreneur would himself deem just sufficient in considering whether or not to undertake an extension of his plant' (*Economic Essays*, pp. 143, 103-7). This I believe is unsatisfactory. It raises the old problem of the 'subjective' versus the 'objective' in economic analysis. Thus that a subjective rate of profit such as here envisaged by Sir Roy governs action will be granted; but this must ultimately be brought into line with the objective rate (presuming such exists) which determines equilibrium. And that such does exist is the view here embraced. In fact, however, my own procedure and Sir Roy's reduce to the same thing if it is correct to interpret his procedure as follows: that the above definition relates to the 'representative entrepreneur', and

entrant in the first instance must project some output to which he hopes to attain, and establish his plant accordingly. But it is inevitable that for some period while the connexion is being built up, sales will fall short of the projected 'normal' throughput of the plant, so that the realized average cost of production will exceed c and the entrant will incur 'break-in losses'. Second, in order to attract customers from the established sellers, the new entrant will be obliged for some period to expend more than they in selling costs in proportion to sales, and/or to offer the same quality of product at a lower price (so far as established sellers will permit this). Either or both of these causes will reduce the realized net return of the new entrant for some initial period as compared with the established producers. It is evident then that since in the end (i.e. if and when the entrant firm is finally established) a price equal to c would yield only a normal profit, the net profit over the whole period of the firm's operations would be less than a normal profit: in the expectation of such a net loss, therefore, new entry would not in general take place.

The established firms may thus elevate the price somewhat above the unit cost c without attracting new entry. But there will be some point at which, if the price is set and remains there, the new entrant has a reasonable expectation of earning normal profits over the prospective life of the business; i.e. there is some price at which the

that such an entrepreneur correctly apprehends the objective rate in planning his investment.

What are the elements, governed by objective factors, in a 'normal' rate of profit?

First, there is the element of a rate of interest; because this is the return for parting with capital.

Second, however, the investor in risky business enterprises would require something in excess of a gilt-edged rate of interest; for this rate is the return for parting with capital at no risk. In the long run, if successful business did not yield more than this, then capital funds for such investments would dry up.

The ultimate determinants of this premium, however, are obscure, and would necessitate a separate theoretical and empirical study. It will certainly be related to the rate of technical progress (in both design of product and technique of production) characteristic of the industry. If this is rapid, then not only are the chances of falling behind in the race or even of actual failure greater (i.e. the current, as distinct from the original, risk is large), but the necessary charges on account of obsolescence (which must come out of net profits) will be greater also.

There is a third element, namely, the reward attributable to the efficient direction of a business. However, the correct view, I believe, taking the economy, or an industry, as a whole, is that this is not so much to be thought of as an independent component of a normal profit, but as the circumstance determining the distribution as between the extant firms of the normal returns to business enterprise under the previous two heads. It involves (in the absence of restrictions on new entry) that the most efficient firm 'normally' makes a realized profit considerably in excess of the normal rate, while (at the other extreme) the least efficient firm will realize a negative profit (see next chapter).

net losses incurred during the break-in period can in principle be recouped from the higher-than-normal profits which the new entrant may share with the established firms if and when it is itself finally established. On the one hand, however, there is some risk that this position will never be attained; in this event the super-normal profits of the later period will be taken in at a higher discount factor than their mere remoteness in time would render appropriate. On the other hand, there may be advantages (sometimes of a non-pecuniary nature) to a prospective new entrant which is an established firm in a related line of production, which would cause it to discount somewhat the early losses so long as there was a reasonable prospect of ultimately becoming established. Subject to these qualifications then, at just such a level of price new entry may, or may not, eventuate; while at prices above this level, there would be an expectation of a net profit in excess of normal profits and new entry would in general take place. This indicates the no-entry ceiling in the present instance.

One can say then that the magnitude of the entry gap from this cause will be larger, the longer the break-in period and the greater the disadvantage of the new entrant during this period as the result of higher selling costs and/or a lower price, and higher production costs at sub-optimum throughputs. These in turn will depend on a variety of factors, but fundamentally on the nature of the product and the conditions surrounding its sale.

Thus in the case of manufactured intermediate products (the first broad class of industries distinguished above), the buyers—themselves manufactures at a higher stage of production—are good judges of quality, and sensitive as to price. In the event that the prevailing price is 'too high', therefore, the new entrant can gain relatively ready initial access to the market by quoting a lower price. And this threat of the intervention of new competitors is likely to be systematically effective over time. For while, on the one hand, the businessmen buyers in this type of case evince a considerable loyalty to their customary supplier(s) so long as the price and quality is 'right'; on the other hand, in the event, that this should be exploited—the buyer 'taken for a ride', so to speak—the termination of the relationship is often abrupt and final. In this type of case then, goodwill is likely to prove only a provisional restraint on the entry of new competition.

The case of consumer goods of low unit price and comparatively simple specification is similar where sold in unbranded (or least, not brand-distinctive) form. The immediate customers of the manufacturer of such goods are wholesalers in the trade, who again are well-informed and price conscious. But the result is likely to be quite different, if as the outcome of the particular historical development, large-scale advertising of a few well-known (manufacturers') brands emerges with this same type of consumer good: this emphasizes the role of the 'conditions of sale'. Advertising in this situation is necessarily all the more concentrated and heavy just because the relatively simple and standard character of the product does not admit of effective differentiation in any other way. Moreover, not only is the absolute magnitude of the advertising expenditure of each of the established firms normally very large, but (as in the appendix to the preceding chapter) it is to a considerable degree independent of any one firm's actual volume of sales. Spread over the total sales of the large established firm, this advertising cost per unit is small; but for the new entrant during an extended break-in period, its incidence is severe—and the more so, to the extent that the existing firms step up their own advertising expenditures to counter the new threat to their markets.[1] It is likely therefore that the potential restriction of new competition inherent in the heavy advertising of large oligopolistic firms, is considerable.

In the case of durable and complex consumer goods of high unit price (which are typically brand-distinctive), the good reputations of long-established manufacturers are in themselves a major stumbling block to any new firm seeking to make sales in such a market. For the individual consumer the initial outlay for such a product is large, and he is unable to judge quality save on the basis of his (or

[1] It is important to emphasize, however, that such initial advertising expenditures incurred by a new entrant—or by a firm exploiting a product innovation—are of the character of investment outlays. The money is properly viewed as invested in the creation of a market, in establishing the essential 'connexion' which is the basis of the subsequent activity of the firm.

These expenditures, indeed, exhibit all the attributes of the ordinary internal investment of the firm. In particular, money is expended currently in the expectation of returns (if successful) spread over a period of years in the future. And in the nature of the case, the outcome of the venture is uncertain—highly uncertain; for the business environment in which it takes place cannot be assumed to be even approximately constant, since it is of the essence of the project to alter that environment.

Looked at in this way, the source of these expenditures is properly the capital, or accumulated profit reserves of the business; and theoretically they are chargeable to current production, like other capital costs, only at an appropriate rate of interest (and amortization rate). There is evidence that businessmen do often think of them this way; and the incidence of the current total of such expenditures—which are often spectacular and unduly influence opinion about advertising—is not necessarily wholly on current prices (albeit charged against them for taxation purposes).

his friends') accumulating experience with the product after purchase; he therefore stands to lose a great deal in the event that the untried product of the new entrant should prove inferior. The break-in period thus tends to be long indeed. Advertising, which does occur in this sort of case and sometimes on a considerable scale, probably adds little to the already formidable barrier to new competition and is mainly of intra-industry significance.

Another important factor in this connexion is that some products of this type require frequent service attention, the replacement of worn parts, and so on. But the goodwill of the manufacturer depends on the performance of the product throughout its life, and this may be jeopardized by inexpert repairing and servicing. It is common therefore for the individual manufacturer of such a product to establish an exclusive dealer-organization throughout the market area, thus ensuring the standard of service deemed appropriate (and of course, cementing the attachment of buyers all the more securely). But the necessity to emulate such an organization greatly increases the difficulty and cost of effecting new entry.

These generalizations conform on the whole with Mr. Bain's authoritative findings.[1] His quantitative results for the twenty industries and subdivisions thereof in his sample are indicated in Table 1, where the industries are reclassified into the three broad classes distinguished above.[2] (Bain's final ranking of the 'aggregate'

[1] Op. cit., pp. 130-1, 142-3.

[2] The quantitative estimates are based on data relating to the length of break-in periods and the net disadvantage of a new entrant, derived in the main from expressions of opinion by businessmen in the industries concerned. These data take the form, for example (quoted with some abbreviation from Bain's Table XI, pp. 127-9):

Industry	Rating	Estimated extent of prospective entrant's disadvantage
Copper	I	Slight and transitory.
Steel	I	2 per cent. of price for 1 to 2 years.
Flour (miller's brand)	II	5 to 7 per cent. price disadvantage for an undefined period, partly offset by lower promotional costs.
Motor-cars	III	5 to 15 per cent., in price or extra promotion, for ten years, incurred with substantial risk of failure.

To translate evidence of this character into estimates of entry gaps it is necessary to know the 'typical' discount factors to be applied to both the prospective later gains and the early break-in losses. Mr. Bain admits to 'uncertainty' concerning these (somewhat of an understatement!), but the 'best guesses' of so informed and pains-taking an investigator as to the final entry gaps must nevertheless be accepted as authoritative.

The orders of magnitude indicated in Table 1 are as follows (Bain, pp. 132-3):

I 'Negligible or slight': about 1 per cent. (at most 2 per cent. in a few cases) of c.

II 'Moderate': from 2 to 4 per cent. of c.

III 'Great': from 5, up to 10 or 20 per cent.

THE STATIC MODEL 93

or 'over-all' barrier to entry is also shown.[1]) The concentration of industries with a large entry barrier associated with goodwill in the third broad class is evident, as anticipated. Industries of this type are of primary interest in this book. They are discussed further in the next chapter, and Part II is devoted to the particular case of the British soap and detergents industry.

TABLE 1

Goodwill, or 'Product Differentiation', Barrier to Entry.
J. S. Bain's Findings.

Industry	Goodwill Barrier	Over-all
I. Producer Goods:		
Manufactured Intermediates		
Cement	I	I
Copper	I	III
Flour (Industrial)	I	I
Gypsum	I*	I
Metal Containers	II*	I
Rayon	I	I
Steel	I	II
II. Consumer Goods:—'Unbranded'.		
Canned fruit, etc. (standard)	I	I
Flour (retailer-label sales)	I	I
Fountain pens (low price and ball point)	I	I
Shoes (not brand-distinctive)	I	I
Meat packing (fresh)	I	I
III. Consumer Goods:—'Branded'.		
(i) *Low unit price*		
Canned fruit, etc. (specialities)	II	I
Cigarettes	III	III
Flour (miller's brand)	II	I
Liquor	III	III
Petrol	II	II
Soap	II ? III	II
(ii) *Medium-priced*		
Fountain pens (quality or 'high-priced')	III	III
Shoes ('high-priced' men's and specialities)	II	II
Motor tyres and tubes	II	I
(iii) *High-priced, complex*		
Motor-cars	III	III
Typewriters	III	III
Tractors and complex form machinery†	III	III

* Refers to period since 1950. Before then—and successful anti-trust suits—would have been rated higher.
† Producer durable good.
Source: J. S. Bain, *Barriers to New Competition* (Cambridge Press, 1956), Tables XIV, XV, pp. 169-70, *et passim*.

[1] Note that the magnitudes corresponding to the ranking symbols I, etc., in this column are rather less definite, but apparently higher, than before (Bain, op. cit., pp. 170-1). However, on my reading of Bain's evidence, I would be inclined to suggest that a closer correspondence between the two would perhaps be more apt. One suspects that Bain has underestimated the point made above in connexion with capital requirements, that is, the distinction between barriers to the entry of brand-new firms (to which his estimates primarily relate), and barriers to new competition generally, particularly as from the large established firm with a well known brand of its own which may be applied to the product in the new field.

But the findings with respect to the industries in the other two classes is also significant. The point is central[1] that the net effect of the factor of goodwill in the market cannot be settled by *a priori* analysis. But this evidence would suggest that for these industries, which are representative of the 'ordinary run' of manufacturing industries, the effect is indeed approximately zero. On the one hand, the potential entry gap due to goodwill is in these cases of the order of 1 per cent. (or at most, 2 per cent.). But on the other hand, in the absence of formal collusion the price-dampening effect of active competition for the custom of the market (referred to above, and elaborated in the next chapter) is likely to be of much the same order of magnitude, in the negative sense.[2] The significance of this empirical result is that it permits one to envisage a 'pure' model of Differentiated Competition in which in the absence also of systematic cost differences and significant economies of scale,[3] the price is substantially equal to the average cost of production, as in the model of Perfect (i.e. 'Undifferentiated') Competition.

Barriers to new entry then are essentially 'monopolistic' in terms of the definition of Chapter 1: that is, the effect is to exclude new entry within the price range above the cost of production determined by the over-all entry gap in the particular trade.[4] Within this range established firms have a measure of discretionary power in price fixing (subject to the pressures of intra-industry competition): this is the second—the long term—margin of discretion referred to above.[5] And in so far as this power is exercised, there is a (monopolistic) restriction of the industry output below the norm of the static welfare analysis by an amount dependent on the elasticity of the market demand as in footnote 1, p. 83 above.

[1] Above, p. 24.

[2] Public evidence as to the magnitude of this effect is scanty. The above opinion is based on confidential estimates relating to some industries, prepared by industry representatives, as to the value to the industries as a whole of prevailing industry-wide price-fixing arrangements. Some slender evidence as to this order of magnitude in the circumstances of the soap industry in the latter decades of the nineteenth century is noticed in Chapter 6, p. 138 below.

[3] That the confluence of all three conditions is not infrequent in practice, at all events with respect to markets in the United States, is indicated by the findings as to the over-all barrier recorded in Table 1.

[4] It is evident that the entry gaps due to systematic cost differences (where such obtain), goodwill, and the net gap due to economies of scale (if any) are, as analysed above, simply additive to indicate the over-all barrier to new entry.

[5] pp. 8, 60.

The concomitant of this as envisaged in the analysis so far, are margins of net profits in excess of normal profits. But it is important to notice three other possibilities. First, the gains associated with maximum entry-excluding prices may be dissipated in part or in whole by excessive expenditures on advertising and other forms of sales promotion (including showy, but 'inessential'—in the judgement of reasonable men—variations in products). Second, the protection afforded from new competition may lead to some relaxation in the effort to minimize costs. This inefficiency in production would be represented graphically by an upward rise of the plant and long-period cost curves throughout their length, with the effect that the maximum entry-excluding price yields only a normal profit (or worse).[1] This result of 'monopoly', involving the deployment of more real resources for a given output than need be, is regarded by some writers (including, I believe, Mrs. Joan Robinson) as its worst feature of all, and rightly so, albeit it is outside the scope of the static welfare analysis.

Third, where there are substantial economies of scale the entry barrier may be exploited to permit of a comfortable coexistence at but a normal profit of a number of more or less evenly-matched firms each (or most of them) of less than the minimum optimum size. (This involves, not a shift of the long-period cost curve as in the previous case, but an 'equilibrium' at a non-optimum point on the curve as it obtains at the time. It is most likely to occur where there are a small number of 'strong' competitors, and the development of technology has been such that the minimum optimum scale has grown faster than the size of the market.[2]) Such an 'equilibrium' with unexhausted economies of scale is inherently unstable, as argued above,[3] but may yet persist over long periods where there is this difference as compared with the circumstances envisaged above, that there is a strong measure of effective collusion between the firms—in this case taking the form of a tacit recognition that the price shall be such as to permit the coexistence of all.

This last sort of result, however, which may well be not unimportant in practice, is not further discussed in this book because it

---

[1] The experience of the Lever combination in the nineteen-twenties is ample witness to the reality of this sort of outcome. Below, Chapter 8; also Chapter 9, p. 198.

[2] Or as in the Australian case (p. 87-88 above), where the entry barrier is large but new entry from powerful overseas firms takes place anyway in anticipation of rapid growth of the total market.

[3] p. 75.

is not characteristic of the soap and detergents industry. First, in this industry the minimum optimum scale of production has always been small relative to the size of the market, and even though it has become larger in recent years remains small relative to the size of the principal firms in the industry.[1] Furthermore (second), the product-mix characteristic of the industry has remained comparatively simple, and extensions (into perfumery for example) have been undertaken in the main by means of setting up, or acquiring, specialist firms in such lines of production. The incomplete exploitation of economies of scale ('imperfect specialization') as a result of what Sir Dennis Robertson has called 'commercial joint supply'[2] is thus also not a feature of this industry.

The reference above to the restraint of free competition by effective collusion in an industry brings us to the final section of this chapter, the purpose of which is to examine within the terms of our model the Chamberlin phenomenon of short-period excess capacity. The importance of the phenomenon is this: that it is the second— the first being barriers to new entry—of the two major causes of a divergence between the industry price and the unit cost of production in an efficient manner in circumstances of Non-Perfect Competition.

COLLUSION AND 'EQUILIBRIUM' WITH EXCESS CAPACITY

It has already been suggested at several points above that the received theory of (short-period) excess capacity is essentially invalid. It is examined briefly in the appendix to this chapter. But the reality of the phenomenon itself, and accordingly the vision (so to speak) as distinct from the details of the theoretical argument, remains unimpaired.

With Professor Chamberlin then, we now envisage a situation in which there is a large number of sellers,[3] and goodwill is not 'strong': that is, each of the sellers has some 'connexion' in terms of regular customers, but a large part of the custom of the market is un-attached or at most semi-attached. In these cicumstances new

---

[1] Chapter 5, below.

[2] In his 'Some Recent (1950-5) Writings on the Theory of Pricing', Essay I in *Economic Commentaries* (London, 1956), pp. 32-33.

[3] Economies of scale presumed not significant, and there are no systematic cost differences.

entry is free and easy, as presumed by Professor Chamberlin.[1]

Now what is essential is that one should cease to think of the situation as one of free, unrestricted competition, and introduce as a key condition of the analysis the 'monopolistic' element that there is effective industry-wide collusion between the sellers.[2]

The import of this condition is that the sellers fix their common price collusively. With this, in this analysis where a large number of sellers is envisaged, equally as in the foregoing analysis where the number of producers was presumed small, the relevant demand curve for the individual firm is the fractional market demand curve determined by the firm's share of the market and of the same elasticity as the aggregate demand curve (i.e. it is our d-curve or Professor Chamberlin's DD' curve)—and not the Chamberlin dd' curve of the 'large-group' analysis, analogous to our d_r curve.

In Fig. 7 then let D be the aggregate industry demand curve, which remains unchanged throughout. Let ac in the left-hand figure be the particular-plant cost curve of a typical firm (includes a normal profit), and d its demand curve governed by its (average over time) share of the market. Now suppose that initially there is an 'equilibrium' at the price OP equal to the firm's average cost at the corresponding volume of sales (output) Ox, but that from some cause (e.g. would-be entrepreneurs wish to become service-station proprietors; they observe existing proprietors earning a normal profit; then since entry is easy, why should it not be possible to do likewise?[3]) new firms enter the industry. As these entrants appropriate a share of the 'floating' (i.e. unattached) demand in the market, the share of each of the established firms is reduced—in the figure, to d_1 say. Sales and output thus fall to Ox' (at the maintained price OP), but at this volume the average cost exceeds OP and the firms fail to make normal profits.

---

[1] To fix ideas one may think (e.g.) in terms of the 'industry' of retail petrol service stations. While there is frequently only a relatively small number of stations in any particular locality, and while many motorists of course have their customary service station, motorists also frequently purchase petrol supplies elsewhere in the course of journeys; so that in this sense most of a large number of sellers have at least some access to most of the buyers.

This is the sort of situation to which Professor Chamberlin's analysis has always seemed to be mainly relevant. But while the tendencies to be analysed are perhaps more widely prevalent in the distribution trades, they are not entirely absent from some manufacturing industries proper.

[2] That is, as at the end of the preceding section, we here reverse the provisional assumption of no collusion made at the beginning of this chapter.

[3] Cf. E. H. Chamberlin, *Theory*, p. 105 (bottom).

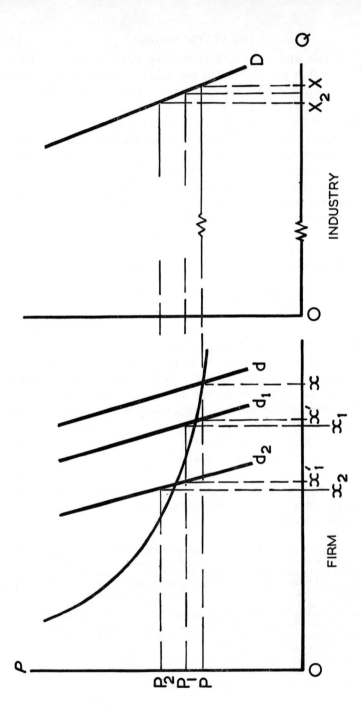

Fig. 7: 'Equilibrium' with Short-period Excess Capacity

With this a cry is raised that 'gross margins are too low to return a reasonable profit': whereupon it is agreed collusively, formally through the medium of the appropriate trade association or informally, that the price be increased—to OP_1 say. Individual-firm sales are reduced initially somewhat further, to Ox_1; but if (as in the figure) the rise is generous enough, i.e. greater than (the higher) ac at this volume, profits are restored to normal and better.

But with this—and for the independent reasons, above—further new entry is encouraged. Again the d-curve is shifted to the left (market demand D unchanged); and should this go as far as d_2, as well it might, the cry that margins are too low is again raised, and the whole process may be repeated.[1]

In this way the phenomenon of increasing costs and prices with an increase in capacity and potential supply, which Mr. Kaldor once described as the most 'intellectually striking [and] significant from a practical point of view . . . of all the doctrines emerging from . . . the economics of imperfect competition'[2], may indeed emerge in practice; and its necessary correlative is excess capacity— an 'equilibrium', or succession of 'equilibria' in which established plants are underutilized.[3] The waste (economic loss) involved in

---

[1] Reference was made above to service stations, because in recent years this sphere in N.S.W., Australia, has provided a striking example of the present phenomenon. During the four years ending June 1958 the retail margin on petrol sales was increased from $3\frac{3}{4}d.$ to $6\frac{3}{4}d.$, an increase of 80 per cent. Over this period wage costs—the main cost element in the margin, and of which the 'fixed' element of the proprietor's return is the dominant component—increased by 12 per cent., but this would largely have been offset *ceteris paribus* by the expansion of 37 per cent. in the overall consumption of petrol during the period. It is evident then that when a further increase of $\frac{1}{2}d.$ (7·5 per cent.) was sought by the Service Stations Association (the S.S.A. Ltd., the relevant trade body in the case) in 1958, it was reduced turnovers due to the phenomenal expansion in the number of stations, in pursuit of the major oil companies' policy of setting up the maximum number of own-brand stations possible, which was the nigger in the woodpile.

[2] 'Market Imperfection and Excess Capacity', *Economica* (N.S.), 1935, p. 44. The phenomenon is 'intellectually striking', because in the framework of the traditional competitive analysis, an increase in capacity and potential supply with the industry demand constant (as here envisaged) would necessarily involve a fall in price. (Graphically, the increase in capacity would involve a shift of the short-period market supply curve, i.e. sum of firms' short-period marginal cost curves, to the right, and hence a new point of intersection with a constant demand curve, at a lower market price.) This traditional analysis is most readily applicable to primary industries. But manufacturers also, in conditions of free competition, are the first to claim that competition in price only really begins when capacity becomes excessive relative to demand.

[3] This excess capacity may take a variety of forms as illustrated by the important example of the Australian butter industry. The collusive monopoly element in this case consists in Government action to reserve the Australian market wholly to Australian producers, and to permit them within certain limits and subject to Government approval to fix, collectively, the Australian-market price of butter

this process is obvious, since a less industry output (OX_2 as against OX, in the figure) is produced by an increased quantum of resources; thus the net marginal social product of the resources deployed is negative. What is important is that this is not an outcome of *free* competition, non-Perfect Competition or otherwise. (The example of the butter industry is sufficient to free the phenomenon from any necessary association with differentiated products, as may derive from its original formulation.) The key condition, in a word, is the collusion of the sellers—a condition absent, at all events explicitly, from Professor Chamberlin's analysis.

Yet while this sort of outcome may persist for long periods, the 'equilibrium' is inherently unstable and hence the inverted commas. For at any time the more enterprising, efficient and/or affluent of the parties to the arrangements may undermine it by cutting the price in an attempt to increase permanently their share of the market by driving out less-advantaged firms. Or new forms of competition —as for example the intrusion of the chain-store branch into the preserve of a group of local retailers—may effect the same result.[1] (If the outcome in such a case as this latter is to bring prices down in closer relation to the cost of efficient production, 'excess capacity' may continue because of the 'net advantage' of independence to the small retailer, but not accompanied by a 'normal' monetary return.)

In concluding this discussion it is necessary to notice that the threat, or the fact, of new entry does not in these circumstances govern the level of the price, as foreshadowed in the second qualification (**) to the statement of the equilibrium condition of the model (above, p. 73).

(supporting this price by appropriate tariff and import controls to exclude competition from foreign supplies). Production in excess of Australian demand at this price is sold for a much lower return at export. The entry of new producers in Australia, however, is not restricted; and with such entry, the additional output is necessarily sold on the (low-price) export market which reduces the average return to the producers. With this there is pressure for an increase in the Australian price, which raises returns and encourages further new entry (and increased production by existing producers). As output expands, with the surplus sold at export, the average return is again depressed, and there is renewed pressure for a further increase in the Australian price. And so on. Thus from the point of view of the Australian consumer, there is increasing costs and prices with the increase in capacity and supply. But in this case the 'excess capacity'—excess in relation to the Australian market—takes the form of uneconomic production for export. (See N. T. Drane and H. R. Edwards (eds.), *The Australian Dairy Industry* (Cheshire, 1961), pp. 197-200 and *passim*.)

[1] In the case of the N.S.W. service stations, this has taken the form of increased installation of industrial pumps, and a substantial increase in drum trading. But of course, while the collusion persists and all the service stations remain in business (or the rate of increase in stations matches the increase in total demand), these measures only aggravate the situation.

Apart from cases of the foregoing type, it is necessary to notice two other types of situation which tend to give rise to excess capacity.

First, consider the case of a consumer good of relatively simple and standard specification, where there is a moderately 'large' number of firms (say, fifteen to twenty) each relying for sales on relatively heavy advertising of its own branded product. In the absence of the advertising, one would expect a relatively stable pattern of the market (i.e. a situation belonging to the second broad class of industries distinguished above); and similarly with advertising, but with a small number of sellers.[1] But with the larger number of sellers, a given measure of instability in consumer preferences (which results because of the more or less standard character of the product envisaged, and the insubstantial character of preferences based only on advertising) is likely to involve some considerable fluctuations over time in the demand to particular firms. In this event there would be a tendency (as suggested above) for some enlargement of the capacity of each firm, relative to that which would obtain if the same (average over time) demand accrued at a more steady rate.[2] In general, then, where goodwill is not strong and there is a large stochastic element in the demand per period to the individual firm, 'static' excess capacity will tend to emerge: this differs perhaps only in degree from the strategic reserve capacity argued to above.

The second type of case is as follows. In a situation where initially there is a large number of producers and new entry is relatively easy (i.e. technique of production comparatively simple; minimum optimum scale of production small; and goodwill, though well-developed, is scarcely 'strong') it may happen that a formal association of a number of the firms controlling between them a very large

[1] In fact, the introduction of large-scale advertising into a situation of the second class typically leads to a considerable concentration of the market (See N. Kaldor, *R.E.S.*, 1949-50, pp. 13ff.) But it may not, in the event that there is initially a number of well-established firms who all succeed in adopting the 'new' method of sales promotion (large-scale advertising).

[2] As previously suggested (p. 28), a fluctuating demand may be met without loss of potential sales in two ways: first, by holding a larger (average) stock of the finished product than would otherwise be necessary, and second, by increased manufacturing facilities (capacity) as required to meet peak production requirements. Some preference towards the latter may be explained in part in terms of the structure of 'capital' in the case of mass-produced consumer goods, where the ratio of the annual turnover to the capital employed is often of the order of 3 or 4 to 1, with a large proportion of the capital (sometimes a half or more) made up of investment in stocks and work-in-progress.

share of the market (say, 70 per cent. or upwards) is formed ('cartel' or outright merger). In this event it remains true, as in the pre-cartel situation, that the industry price cannot diverge for long from the cost of production. Yet it might be profitable for the 'cartel' to exploit its market control for short periods, on occasion, by holding the price above such a level—despite some subsequent reduction in the combined share of the market of the associated firms as new competition becomes actual. In the present connexion, the significance of this is that should this tendency to price above the cost of production recur frequently, excess plant capacity is bound to emerge and to persist as new competition is periodically attracted and reattracted (and particularly if plant is long-lived). (Note that again the threat, or the fact, of the intervention of new competition does not in this event define a stable equilibrium of price in the market, as foreshadowed above.)

It is mainly in the first of these two types of situation (but to some extent in the second) that the existence of excess capacity *per se* will tend to result systematically in a price in excess of the unit cost of production, and this time in the absence of collusion. In such a situation all firms are involved to a more or less equal degree in some enlargement of the plant, and so also would be any new entrant firm. In such event, the tendency would be, I think, for each firm to 'take full cost literally' (so to speak), and thus systematically to base price quotations on an average utilization of the plant significantly below the technical optimum. (If this were of the order of 20 per cent. below, it might involve an elevation of the price of the order of 1 to 2 percentage points.)[1]

This completes the statement of the basic static equilibrium analysis of price and output determination in manufacturing industry.

---

[1] Suppose the average output were 100 units, while the 'normal' utilization of the plant would be an output of 125. If the 'plant overhead' costs represented 5 percentage points of the unit cost (=price) at normal utilization, then they would amount to 6·25 percentage points at the lower (average) output—an increase of 1·25 percentage points. If these 'plant overheads' represented 10 points of the unit cost, the increase would be 2·5 points. (A figure as large as 10 per cent. might be relevant in this connexion, if 'plant overheads' are conceived to include supervisory personnel, etc.).

APPENDIX (Chapter 3)

THE DOCTRINE OF 'EXCESS CAPACITY'

The doctrine of excess capacity as originally propounded has now been largely discredited. (See the references, Chapter 1, p. 10n, above.) The most direct and uncompromising attack has been Sir Roy Harrod's in his 1952 essay 'Theory of Imperfect Competition Revised'.

In its original formulation, the essential conditions of the theory were three (free competition, i.e. no collusion, was presumed throughout[1]):

(i) that the demand curve for the 'product' of the individual firm has a significant downslope;

(ii) that 'entrance to the field in general and to every portion of it in particular'[2] is free and easy; and

(iii) that each firm maximizes its profits by equating marginal cost (as of the given plant) with marginal revenue (as from the curve postulated in (i)) and without regard to the effect of this in stimulating the entry of new competitors. (In fact condition (iii) was taken as following from the prior conditions: (a) that there are a large number of small firms; and (b) that 'consumers' preferences [are] evenly distributed among the different varieties' of the product.[3] This last involved as corollary the notion of 'impact effects' of a price change by one firm being spread over many firms, hence no reaction back on the one firm, hence no oligopolistic difficulties in respect of its demand curve which is, therefore, known and determinate.)

On these assumptions, the doctrine of excess capacity follows with almost geometrical necessity, since the only equilibrium compatible with the assumptions is that where the particular demand curve is tangent to the cost curve—which must needs be to the left of the minimum point of the short-period (particular plant) cost curve.

Now Mr. Harrod directed his attack against condition (iii), arguing in effect that the representative producer would not maximize profits in this way, but rather (as above) would have regard to the threat of new competition if the price were set too high and, accordingly, would so moderate his price policy as to forestall the entry of new competitors. In this event the recession of the firm's market associated with the actual advent of new competitors would not take place, and thus excess capacity would not necessarily emerge.

We have already concurred above in the view that this sort of behaviour must be regarded as typical—typical, that is to say, of manufacturers in a settled process of production; and Mr. Harrod's emphasis on it in such contexts was entirely proper. But it is nevertheless necessary to observe that in the circumstances postulated by Professor Chamberlin,

---

[1] See particularly, Professor E. A. G. Robinson, 'The Pricing of Manufactured Products', *E.J.*, 1950, p. 773.

[2] Chamberlin, *Theory*, p. 111.   [3] Ibid., p. 83.

the assumption that entrepreneurs maximized their (short-run) profits was not entirely inappropriate. A situation of initial disequilibrium[1] with a large number of producers and easy entry was envisaged, and in these circumstances whatever the entrepreneur were to do new competitors would be likely to materialize anyway.

In assessing the theory on its own ground, therefore, criticism should be directed not to condition (iii), but to the conjunction of the assumptions (i) and (ii). This conjunction, I have argued elsewhere[2] is invalid, in that the assumptions are contradictory. The first—that the demand curve of the individual firm has a significant downslope—is indicative of the entrenched market position; but with this so for all firms, it is scarcely compatible with the second assumption, namely, that new entry is easy.[3] On the one hand then, if the latter assumption is maintained, this implies that the downslope of the demand curve is scarcely significant, so that even if firms do maximize profits in the ordinary sense the point of tangency of the demand to the cost curve will only be slightly displaced to the left of the minimum-cost point; i.e. the 'excess capacity' will be negligible. On the other hand, if the former assumption is maintained, then new entry will not be easy, and the doctrine of excess capacity does not necessarily follow: a determinate equilibrium with output at, or beyond, the point of minimum-average cost is quite conceivable—with the price in excess of average cost if profits are maximized by the equation of marginal revenue and marginal cost. (On the present assumption, however, inasmuch as the 'entrenched position' will have been attained only with difficulty and over a long period of time, a pricing policy such as Mr. Harrod envisaged—i.e. aimed to 'protect' the acquired position—is the more likely to be adopted, and the likelihood of excess capacity will be correspondingly further diminished.)

In fine then, the geometry of the 'tangency theorem', despite its elegance and tantalizing simplicity, is scarcely valid in economic terms. This is not to deny, however, that there are circumstances in practice which do give rise to the phenomenon of excess capacity, but merely that they are of rather a different character as argued above in the text.

[1] *Theory*, pp. 90 ff.

[2] *O.E.P.*, Feb. 1955, pp. 100 (bottom)-1.

[3] It might be argued—in line with the notion of impact effects spread over all sellers in the group (accepted for the sake of argument, though in my opinion quite unrealistic)—that a single new entrant would only have to attract from, say, 100 existing sellers about one per cent. of the custom of each; this may be deemed negligible, non-finite; and in this way the two assumptions are compatible. But the role of easy entry in the analysis is to reduce a situation of general excess profits, should it prevail, to one of normal profits, and this would involve, in general, a finite shift of demand curves to the left. For each of the *number* of new contenders necessary to effect such a finite change, the appropriation of a place in the market in face of entrenched sellers would be difficult; and this would become generally known.

CHAPTER 4

PRICE DETERMINATION IN MANUFACTURING INDUSTRY

III. DYNAMIC ASPECTS

THE static framework of analysis set out in the preceding chapter is necessarily incomplete, as foreshadowed in several places above. In particular it does not take into account the wide variation in the unit full costs of different firms, which is characteristic of most industries in practice.[1] Proximately this range of costs is due above all to the uneven exploitation of technical developments, which in turn is due in part to the natural scarcity of entrepreneurial skill of the highest order (with the effect that no practicable degree of competition can ensure all-round maximum efficiency) but is also in part the outcome of the whole process. The point is developed in the following section, as the first step in an analysis of the variety of ways in which the dynamic conditions of reality may modify the results of the preceding chapter, and in particular the effect of barriers to new entry. The latter, as we have seen, create a margin (the entry gap) between the maximum industry price that can be charged without attracting new entry and 'the' cost of production. But in other than long-run static conditions, it is a separate question whether this potential excess of the price will in the event be translated into realized gains of equivalent magnitude. This question is the subject-matter of the present chapter. We will then be in a position to proceed with the study of the British soap and detergents industry in Part II.

'EQUILIBRIUM' WITH UNEQUAL COSTS

We may begin by assuming the condition which is in part a result of the process, that there is a persistent structure or 'ladder' of relative efficiencies in the industry, with the range from the lowest cost (most efficient) to the highest (least efficient) being often of the

---

[1] Above, p. 68.

order of 10 to 20 per cent. or more expressed as a proportion of the former.[1]

It is first necessary to argue that in the equilibrium tendency, the price will be set (either actively or permissively) by the most efficient firm as at the time and at a level which while it yields that firm the premium profits normal to the 'most efficient' rung of the ladder (so to speak), yet bears no necessary relation to the costs of other firms. To this end it is instructive to contrast the situation here in view with the traditional model of Perfect Competition as applied to a primary industry producing under conditions of 'decreasing returns'.

In that analysis it is assumed, first, that there is an efficiency ranking of units of the basic factor land, in terms of relative fertility and/or proximity to the marketing centre, and this is fixed and given. (New discoveries constitute a change in the data, and are excluded from view as external to the process being analysed.) In these circumstances, the first 'firms' in the field will be the most efficient because they will utilize the best units of the basic factor— which, however, are limited in supply. In seeking to expand their capacity at a later stage, they will have to make use of less efficient units of land, as also will new firms entering the industry at that stage.

It is a second assumption of this theory that each firm is subject to decreasing returns because of diseconomies of large-scale management. This assumption (as already suggested above) is indeed appropriate in the context of agricultural industry, where the management function is so detailed and complex. The primary purpose of the assumption as such, however, is to limit the size of the individual firm, including the most efficient firm(s), and so justify the Perfect Competition condition of 'large numbers'.

It follows that in this model, as the aggregate demand expands, the most efficient firms must necessarily make room also for new (from the second assumption) and less efficient (from the first assumption) competitors. Relative to a particular state of aggregate demand, long period equilibrium will obtain when the price is such as to cover the minimum average cost of the least efficient (the marginal) firm necessary if the aggregate demand is to be met at the price. On the

---

[1] This would be represented graphically by a series of long-period average cost (LAC) curves positioned at increasing levels above the horizontal axis. The plant (ac) curves of the various firms would be located on the long-period curves, with the most efficient not necessarily the largest.

assumptions of the case, this is a necessary result if the aggregate demand is to be met at this, and not a higher, price.

But neither of the two assumptions of this case are appropriate in the sphere of manufacturing industry.

As to the first, it is true that there are factors which may cause a systematic difference between the costs of new firms as against established firms (as discussed in the preceding chapter, pp. 79-81). In the majority of cases the evidence there referred to suggests that these are comparatively unimportant. But in any case the effect is not to create the condition of the foregoing model, that each of a succession of new entrants is necessarily higher-cost than its predecessor. Thus with respect to the factor of ultimate business capacity and managerial skill, it is only reasonable to assume that the abilities, including the range and variation of abilities, of potential new producers is roughly similar to that of the existing firms: in particular, that the more efficient of established firms in related trades possess entrepreneurial skill of the same high order as the more efficient in the trade in question. The effect then of a systematic cost difference is (to a sufficient approximation) that the mean long-period cost curve of potential new firms is higher by the cost difference than the mean curve of established firms; but that is all. Such a difference, where it exists, may easily be allowed for, but we shall proceed on the assumption that there is none such. Subject to this then the essential point, in contrast to the foregoing model, is that the basic factor of production in manufacturing, machines, can be duplicated without limit; unique site advantages are unimportant; and so on.

As to the second assumption of the above model, it has been argued that the long-period cost curve of the firm in manufacturing is approximately constant (after some point) over a very large range, even when due account is taken of the management factor.

The effect of this is that there is virtually no limit from the production (cost) side to the continued expansion of an established firm. The more efficient of the established firms in particular, therefore, could (and would) supply the whole market—were they but able to wrest from their less efficient competitors the custom these latter command. The production of the latter, therefore, is in no way 'necessary if the aggregate demand is to be met at the price', as necessarily followed in the above model; so that the price bears no necessary relation to the supply price (cost) of this output.[1] On the contrary, in manufacturing industry it is the efficient firm(s) which will call the tune (so to speak), and the inefficient may hang on if they can.

And indeed, it is a reasonable presumption that the price will tend to be set by the most efficient firm as at the time (on the supposition that this firm is numbered among the larger firms of the group). First, in the neighbourhood of equilibrium it is unlikely that any other, less efficient, firm would tend (or continue) to quote lower than the most efficient. Second, it will itself remain subject to the threat of similarly efficient competition from without. Its own low costs, that is to say, cannot but make the firm aware of the possibility that other firms—and particularly similarly-efficient firms in related trades—might in due course be able to emulate its own superior efficiency. While therefore the price will in general be set so as to return the most efficient firm the premium profits which are 'normal' to the most efficient position,[2] yet this premium will be governed by that which similarly efficient entrepreneurs among potential competitors would deem adequate. And in view of the observed magnitude of the range of variation in the costs of established firms, it is unlikely that this would permit of a price with which the less efficient of established firms would readily acquiesce (i.e. would cover their high costs including normal profits). The likely outcome is a conflict of interests, and the initiative will lie with the more efficient—and, as a reasonable presumption, the *most* efficient— since there can be only one price and the latter will prefer the lower.

(It might be remarked that the result that the initiative in fixing the price will rest with the most efficient firm is arrived at also in the textbook analysis of homogeneous (i.e. so-called 'pure') duopoly, where one of the duopolists has lower costs than the other. In Fig. 8 let mc_1 and mc_2 be the marginal cost curves of the more and the less efficient of the sellers, respectively. Let D be the aggregate

---

[1] In a word, in conditions of Non-Perfect Competition, while it is of course always likely that at any price there will be some firm which is 'marginal' in the sense merely that its unit full cost (including normal profits) happens to be equal to the price, there is no such thing as the Marginal Firm whose average cost is of key price-determining significance as in Perfect Competition.

[2] And other firms only somewhat less efficient, the profit appropriate to their own positions. It is not suggested that the price will be set at such a level that 'only the most efficient can earn a living'—as a distinguished critic has commented (not without justification) about an earlier version of the present argument in the *O.E.P.*, 1955, *passim*.

demand curve for the (homogeneous) product, which at any, and every price will be divided equally between the sellers so that the individual firm demand curve will be d. The curve of marginal revenue is then mr, and this will always cut the (lower) marginal cost curve of the more efficient producer to the right of its intersection with that of the less efficient producer. The former therefore will maximize its profits at—and will thus prefer—the lower price OP, as compared with the price OP' preferred by the latter. But since there can only be one price, that price will be OP—as set by the more efficient producer.)

In elaboration of the equilibrium of the preceding chapter, then, what is now envisaged is an equilibrium in this, as in every, trade *governed by the mutual potential competition of most efficient enterprise in all trades.*

In such an equilibrium in circumstances of normal aggregate demand and capacity, the more efficient firms in each trade will appropriate a premium profit, over and above normal profits plus any 'excess' profit associated with the exploitation of barriers to new entry. For at any given time entrepreneurial skill of the highest

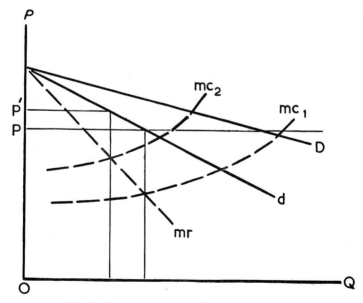

Fig. 8: Homogeneous Duopoly with Unequal Costs

order is scarce in the nature of things.[1] And while the indefinitely horizontal long-period cost curve would indicate that the most efficient in a particular trade *could* supply the whole market, it would be a prolonged and costly undertaking to wrest from established rivals the custom they command in the market, albeit they are less efficient. Some pressure in this direction, in terms of a price set below the full costs of the least efficient firms as the more efficient seek to expand their share of the market in face of the prospective fall in long-period costs,[2] is likely and indeed normal.[3] But beyond a point it is quite evident that the game—very prolonged as it would inevitably be—would not be worth the candle, and particularly (as will be argued shortly) inasmuch as the most efficient firm of today is unlikely to remain so indefinitely and will, therefore, be the more intent to reap the rewards of its attained position while it lasts.

With this the industry price in a market (P) may be analysed ultimately into four components: symbolically

$$P = c_e + p + m - d.$$

In this c_e ('e' for 'efficient') is the unit cost of production in the most efficient manner, which may be taken as in principle given (for all practical purposes, it may be identified with the unit cost of the most efficient, lowest-cost, firm, as at the time); p is the premium profit margin over and above normal profits (included in c_e), governed in the last analysis by the mutual competition of most efficient enterprise in all trades, as just discussed; m is the overall entry gap, as analysed in the preceding chapter; and d indicates the magnitude of the price-dampening effect of unrestricted intra-industry competition, discussed provisionally above[4] and the subject matter of this chapter.

It is reasonable, I would suggest, to identify the sum $(c_e + p)$ with the unit cost of production of a firm of reasonable or average— or better, 'representative'—efficiency. The notion is indeed analogous

---

[1] It is important, however, that the distribution of available entrepreneurial skill as embodied in the managements of particular firms should not be thought of as a 'given'. A management which today is lacking, may be toned up by the infusion of new blood and in other ways, and so come to the forefront tomorrow. (Failure to recognize this was the essence of Mr. (now Lord) Robbins's error in the 'cost controversy' of the nineteen-twenties. 'The Representative Firm" *E.J.*, 1928.)

[2] Above, p. 67.

[3] Many practical inquiries attest that in most industries most of the time, a proportion of the supply (sometimes a surprisingly large proportion) is being produced at a loss.

[4] pp. 24, 94. In the latter context, it was suggested that $m \doteqdot d$.

to Marshall's 'representative firm', and just so is not necessarily the cost of any actual firm.[1] Except in some such terms, to speak of 'the cost of production' is meaningless in view of the fact of wide variations in the costs of established firms in practice.[2] But beyond this one cannot go; and indeed to seek to do so would be to demand a greater precision in this field than in fact is attained in other branches of economics.

The next stage of the argument may be developed by noticing a possible objection to the foregoing equilibrium, namely that it could not persist in the long run. Thus on the one hand (it may be objected), the more efficient firms are accumulating revenues which in time could be brought to bear against the less efficient in a price war, or such-like; while on the other hand, the less efficient may not be appropriating sufficient returns to meet even normal profits regarded as a 'cost' to be met if such firms are to remain in the industry in the long run.

Now this objection serves to focus attention on the characteristic pattern of the actual intra-industry competition of the established firms in a manufacturing industry, as distinct from the nexus of potential competition which has hitherto received the main emphasis. In particular it is necessary to refer to that 'passing to and fro of the industrial leadership' which, as Mr. Andrews has observed, is the dynamic essence of competition in practice.[3] Thus we have envisaged that there is normally a structure or 'ladder' of relative efficiencies in an industry, and a persistent one. But it is important to stress that while *a* structure persists, the actual firms

[1] The (assumed common) unit cost c of the previous chapter should be thought of in this way. Such a cost, as the base of analysis, would relate to scales of production beyond the minimum optimum, and would be conceived to include the margin per unit for normal profits, and the (unit) cost of the minimum sales promotion, in the form current at the time, necessary to maintain the market connexion. (Perhaps there should be some further element by way of a notional component on account of the costs of obtaining—as distinct from maintaining—the connexion? This would be analogous, where the central marketing organization obtains, to the charges (interest and amortization) on account of the original capital expenditure in setting up the market; which charges have to be met by the price charged for commodities marketed in this way.)

[2] Some persons, more conscious than others of this dispersion of costs and of the difficulties arising from common costs and the like, would hold that indeed it is meaningless to speak of the cost of production of a product. This view is altogether too extreme, and is likely to be destructive of all theory of the subject. It is, however, corrective of textbook expositions which postulate too simply given and knowable cost functions.

[3] P. W. S. Andrews, 'Industrial Analysis in Economics', *Oxford Studies in the Price Mechanism*, ed. T. Wilson and P. W. S. Andrews (Oxford, 1951), pp. 145, 171.

which occupy the various positions on the ladder (so to speak) will tend to differ over time.

We are not here making an appeal to Marshall's analogy of the 'trees of the forest'. That envisages 'a population of transitory firms' as Mr. G. F. Shove once put it.[1] This does avoid the above dilemma, in that the firm is presumed to pass through a typical life cycle: when it is young and just struggling to get established, its costs are high; when it has attained its prime, its costs are low (occupies most efficient position); then when old and dying, it once again occupies a high-cost 'rung'. In this way no firm would continue to occupy—and to appropriate the rewards of—the most efficient position.

But the typical situation today is that there is a group of firms in most industries which continue year in year out and in fact comprise the dominant element in the industry. In these circumstances what is important (as Shove argued) is that the relative positions of the firms which make up this permanent cadre, fluctuate over time as the efficiencies of their managements wax and wane, or fashion ebbs and flows, or the trend of good fortune solely is upwards or downwards. The loss of position from these causes can be associated with either a vertical shift of the cost curve, or with a backward movement along a (particular plant) cost curve due to a recession in demand. In either event, the essential point is that different firms among the permanent group will, from time to time, occupy the different positions on the ladder of efficiencies—which itself, however, remains a more or less permanent feature.

Indeed this sort of process would follow from the equilibrium tendency predicated above, and in this sense is part and parcel of the whole process. On the one hand, there is the dispersion of unit full costs, and on the other, the tendency is for the price to be set by the most efficient firm (as at the time) and at a level which bears no necessary relation to the costs of other firms, and may—indeed, as experience attests, very often does—involve for the less efficient of these zero, or even negative profits. In these circumstances then— just because it cannot be assumed that the profits of the inefficient amount to a normal return on the capital employed, as necessarily followed in case of the marginal firm in the Perfect Competition analysis—the less efficient among the firms have all that more incentive to do something above it; they must, or they are on the

1 'Symposium', *E.J.*, 1930, pp. 114-15.

way to elimination from the industry. It is a familiar theme that the greater the challenge, the greater the response—unless the leeway is just so large as to completely overwhelm the resolve to retrieve the situation. At the same time, the tendency for the most efficient firm (the current industry leader) is to grow complacent, to reap the fruits of its current favourable position, and to rest on its laurels. In this way the leader of the one period becomes—often it would appear, almost inevitably—the 'led' of a later period: there is a 'constant passing to and fro' of the active industrial leadership. (But not too readily. It takes time to knock a good man down!)

Another factor in this is that the attempt to 'catch up' and if possible to go ahead of rivals, when once having fallen behind in the competitive struggle, calls for action by way of reorganization and investment of a long-term character: both the periods of gestation and subsequent exploitation of the investment (and of the 'leader' position, if achieved) are relatively long. In the meanwhile, other firms will have embarked (or be embarking) on similar action, and these periods of action inevitably overlap. Thus, for example, in the motor-car industry, the competitive process consists in introducing improved designs, and appropriating a larger share of the market (and reduced costs) on this basis. But to tool up to produce the new design involves not insignificant capital outlays; and it is necessary to hold to the design for some considerable period to recover these sums. Meanwhile other firms, in meeting the challenge, may have gone on to superior designs, thus taking over the active competitive leadership of the industry. (Thus in the British industry, the Standard Company in 1948 introduced the Vanguard, with American-type body styling and overhead-valve engine. The design was maintained substantially unchanged until 1952; but in the meantime the Vauxhall, Ford, Nuffield and Austin Companies in turn came out with improved models along similar lines.)

The upshot of the argument is then: that it is appropriate to envisage a persistent structure of relative efficiencies in the industry; but that different firms among the permanent group (and sometimes new ones) will, from time to time, occupy the different positions in this structure. And in particular, the identity of the most efficient will change over time—A (say) in this period, B in a subsequent period, and C (or A again) yet later; and in this way, one particular firm will not continue to appropriate the premium profits which are 'normal' to the most efficient position. The 'equilibrium' accordingly is one of change and movement, and hence the inverted commas in the title of this section.

In concluding this point it is necessary to remark the possibility that it may turn out in a particular industry that one, or a few, firms might by the sustained vigour and imaginative grasp of the management, sales, and design staff, continue to lead indefinitely, and to appropriate the rewards of the most efficient. In this event it does indeed follow that this (or these) firm(s) will gradually appropriate an increasing share of the total trade in the product in question. (One might cite as an example—at least, until recently—the General-Motors and Ford companies in the American motor-car industry). But I suspect that in practice, it has been rarely the case that a very large share of the market (say in excess of 50 per cent.) has been won in this way alone, i.e. by indefinite occupation of the most-efficient 'rung of the ladder'; more often the voluntary merger of one firm with others (which have not by any means been brought to their knees) has played a significant part in the appropriation of such a share of the market. For a firm in such a position, it is apparent that in the absence of legal restraints there are opportunities for it to maintain its position by mere strategic manœuvre ('unfair competition', and so on) rather than solely by sustained efficiency in technique and product-design, which are not open to the smaller firm. Any such tendencies on the part of very large firms to misuse their market power must indeed be countered by public policy, and continuing and determined Government action to this end is a necessary element in maintaining a proper balance of forces in the quasi-free enterprise system of our times. So far as this is effective, then a large share of the market must needs be held by sustained effort to maintain efficiency, and the mere size of the dominant firm(s) does not necessarily imply the absence of effective competition.

INTRA-INDUSTRY COMPETITION AND THE REALIZED VERSUS THE POTENTIAL ENTRY MARGIN

The importance of the foregoing analysis is that the pressures associated with such a process of intra-industry competition do in general result in a systematic tendency for prices to rule rather below the maximum which the no-entry ceiling would permit (but of course to a greater or lesser extent according to the circumstances of the particular case); i.e. the price-dampening effect represented above by the symbol 'd',

Thus first, it is apparent that a competitive process of the above character is well calculated to keep alive such traditional rivalries and individual preferences for aggresssive independent action as may exist in an industry. The probability that at any one time all the firms should be in such a neutral position (so to speak) as would provide a starting point favourable to subsequent joint action, is slight, and this then militates against a ready acquiescence by all sellers in concerted action to realize the maximum joint advantage. (It is perhaps significant that many of the formal trade associations investigated by the British Monopolies Commission seem to have had their origins in the depressed conditions of the early 'thirties. One might indeed expect that a depression, which reduces all firms in common to a sort of enforced inaction, would generally provide just such a starting point for joint action as here referred to.) In the absence of formal collusion then and particularly in less concentrated industries, the process of actual intra-industry competition involves a significant paring of the price below the level of the no-entry ceiling, as suggested above.

But this requires more elaboration in case of the concentrated 'modern oligopoly',[1] which is of primary interest in this book. In this connexion the circumstances in which a significant potential entry gap is likely to be appropriated more or less in full are the following: (i) that the few dominant firms in the market are all much of a size and fairly evenly matched in efficiency and financial strength; (ii) that the product of the industry is of a relatively simple and standard character little subject to change; and (iii) that the industry demand is not at the time, or potentially, very elastic. The effect of the second condition is that significant product innovations occur very infrequently or not at all (as e.g. with a product such as cigarettes), and with this the overall import of the three conditions is that the circumstances of the case are essentially (long-run) static in character. In the absence of determined Government anti-monopoly policy, effective if tacit collusion[2] to realize the maximum joint advantage—facilitated by the smallness of numbers and amply motivated by the large and apparent mutual interdependence of the evenly-matched sellers—is the likely outcome, with intra-industry rivalry confined to the thrust and parry of competitive advertising. The American cigarette industry in the inter-war period provides an

[1] This embraces most of the industries in Class III above, where as indicated in Table 1, (p. 93) the potential entry gap is significant.
[2] As 'conscious parallel action', in the terminology of U.S. antitrust.

excellent example of this sort of case, where the level of profits combined with heavy advertising expenditures were consistent with the maximum exploitation over a long period of the large 'goodwill' entry barrier in this industry.[1]

In general then it is the absence in varying degrees of the above three conditions which is likely to result in prices significantly below the no-entry ceiling even in the circumstances of the modern oligopoly. In the sort of context where the product is such as to permit of significant variations and advances in design (*contra* condition (ii) above)—particularly so in the case of complex durable products such as refrigerators, motor-cars, and the like—new product development as the main vehicle of intra-industry competition is characteristic of the case. (Similarly innovations in the techniques of production.) This is so, as argued above, because the large oligopolistic firm, as against the perfect competitor, has both

---

[1] The industry was composed of four dominant firms, three—American Tobacco ('Lucky Strikes'), Reynolds ('Camels'), Liggett & Myers ('Chesterfields')—much of a size, and the fourth, Lorillard ('Old Golds'), rather smaller. (This uncharacteristic size distribution resulted from the establishment of firms of more or less equal size following the dissolution of the American Tobacco Trust in 1911).

Now Bain's estimate of the 'goodwill' barrier (equals over-all barrier) in this case is 'at least 6 to 8 percentage points in ratio of profits to sales (including excises)' (op. cit., p. 289)—which at the level of excise tax prevailing at least in the late years of the interwar decade 1930-40, would amount to about 15 to 19 per cent. of sales excluding excises. That in the first year of this decade the cigarette companies 'over-exploited' this advantage is evidenced by the extensive and determined new competition which in fact developed. (In 1931 the ratio of profits net of tax, to sales excluding excises in the case of the American Tobacco Company, was 30 per cent., while for 'all manufacturing corporations' it was about zero. But this is a pretty invidious comparison to make. 'All manufacturing corporations' includes the heavy industries which were deeply depressed at this time. Again, among consumer goods industries the cigarette industry is peculiar in that the ratio of capital to annual sales is about unity, because of the necessity to maintain a three-years stock of tobacco for drying and curing purposes. Nevertheless, if a more reasonable basis of comparison were a ratio of 10 per cent. rather than zero, this is still consistent with the exceeding of a goodwill barrier of 15 per cent. or a few points more.) For an account of the new competition after the notorious 1931 price increase, see Tennant, op. cit., pp. 88 ff.

For the decade as a whole, the net profit as a percentage of the manufacturers' price (excluding excises; data relating to all 'standard' brands) was 24·4 per cent. and advertising expenditures 12·3 per cent. If it were assumed that the latter were consistently as much as 50 per cent. above a reasonable normal, and that a 'reasonable' profit would have been about 15 per cent. on the average (equal to about 10 per cent. net of income taxes on the capital employed), the realized 'excess' margin would appear to be about 13-14 percentage points. This might indicate that the goodwill barrier was not fully exploited, but not conclusively since (quite apart from the limited validity of the data) the level of profits was generally low in this period.

At all events, it is clear that the profits earned over the period were very large.

It is some indication of the effectiveness of the United States antitrust policy that following a successful action against the cigarette companies in 1941, the reported profit rate in the post-war period 1945-9 was 15 per cent. of sales excluding excises, and the same ratio of capital employed—about the same as for 'All manufacturing corporations' during this period. (Profits data from Tennant, op. cit., *passim*.)

the incentive and the capacity for initiating technical development. It is well known that Joseph Schumpeter has argued that the dynamic effects of this kind of continuing development—in the form of significant price-falls over time for the same quality, or substantially improved products at much the same prices—are impressive; and that so-called monopolistic restrictive practices are merely controls which enable an even faster rate of progress (in much the same way as better brakes enable the motorist to travel at a faster average speed). These dynamic effects over long periods must (as we have argued) be weighed against the restrictive static effects as may obtain at any point of time. In this way the dynamic performance of an industry—and the prospect that it will be repeated in future long periods—must always in practice be taken into account.[1] But here our concern is with the question of the effects of the innovation process on the relation of prices to costs.

A first preliminary point is that while competition in this sort of case takes the form in the main of innovations and product variation, yet this in itself facilitates some measure of price competition —or at all events a greater measure of price competition than would otherwise be the case where sellers are few and large. As previously suggested above,[2] a price cut partially disguised by an associated variation in the product (or product-mix) is likely to create divergent expectations with the result that there is some uncertainty that the cut will be either fully or instantly met.[3] In the end it probably— indeed normally—will be. But the cumulative effect is some downward pressure on the price (or price-structure) as compared with the level which would prevail if price competition were more severely circumscribed by virtue of the fact that parity of price is in fact, and is therefore expected to be, instantaneously maintained. And this promotes also a more effective 'tailoring' of the product in accordance with the real wants of consumers, to the extent that it prevents the price-product structure of the industry from becoming so 'conventional' as to be impervious to change.

---

[1] Cf. below, Chapter 11, esp. pp. 242 ff.   [2] p. 51.

[3] A simple example: where the characteristic product of all producers in the industry is of a given weight and quality (standard 'pack'), one firm now offers a pack of twice the weight (same quality) at significantly less than twice the price. The doubling of the quantity (by weight) involves of course much less than a doubling of the size of the pack, consumers may have some suspicions as to maintained quality, they may prefer a smaller unit anyway, etc.; these factors may in fact retard the normal transfer of custom. The initiator of the change, however, may believe (optimistically) that they will not, and his rivals, unwilling to follow the cut, may have some grounds for believing they will.

A second preliminary point is that where the possibility of frequent and significant innovation is admitted, the likelihood of successful new entry—by virtue of the exploitation of such an innovation—is greatly enhanced. For we have already analysed above how in this way an established firm may be enabled decisively to alter the pattern of market shares in an industry;[1] similar considerations apply to the new entrant who is also exploiting such an innovation. Indeed there can be little doubt that, apart from a rapidly growing demand, most new entry in practice takes place in a context of product innovation (less frequently, though there are some important examples, in terms of a major innovation in production technique).[2] The significance of this is that where new product developments tend to occur frequently, the no-entry ceiling is thereby reduced. And inasmuch as the new entrant is frequently an established firm in a related trade, this conclusion is modified only a little by the observation that it is from within the large firm in the particular trade with its developed research facilities and achieved knowhow that important product developments are likely to spring.

To return to the sphere of intra-industry competition, the degree to which product innovation may restrain the price to levels below the no-entry maximum (thus qualified) would appear to be greatest when two further conditions obtain, namely, that the industry demand is potentially relatively elastic or is actually growing rapidly (*contra* condition (iii) above);[3] and there is some disparity in size as between the dominant firms in the industry (*contra* condition (i) above).

If the industry demand is relatively elastic, this may involve directly a price below the no-entry ceiling, if the firm in its current period price and output policy gravitates to a position of maximum profits with respect to short-period marginal cost. It is easy to show that the condition for this, if the marginal cost is approximately

---

[1] pp. 38-40.

[2] e.g. Brunner Mond's in the alkali industry, below, p. 167.

[3] In respect of products which permit of frequent product innovations, it is in fact the case that the demand for complex durable products is relatively price elastic. It is unnecessary to elaborate on the reasons for this which are well known. While statistical estimates are subject to wide margins of error, it is of interest that Mr. Richard Stone on the basis of data relating to the inter-war period, has found a price-elasticity of about $-1 \cdot 8$ for a composite of 'refrigerators, washing-machines, and sewing machines', and -3 to $-3 \cdot 7$ in the case of motor-cars, both for the U.S.A. (The Analysis of Market Demand', *J.R.S.S.*, 1945, pp. 328, 330.)

Also we speak of potentially elastic, articulating a distinction between the immediate and longer-run response to a price change. Industry demands which are relatively inelastic in the short-run are frequently more elastic in time.

constant and equal to $a.c$ (where c is the unit full cost of a firm of 'representative' efficiency), is

$$|\epsilon_D| > \frac{1}{1 - \dfrac{a.c}{c+m}}$$

where m is the overall entry gap.[1] Thus if $a = \cdot7$ and if m were as great as 20 per cent. of c (that is, $c + m = 1\cdot2$), then any elasticity of the market demand greater in absolute value than $2\cdot4$ would involve a price set below the ceiling, i.e. the ceiling would be inoperative in governing the price. (It can be shown further that if the d-curve is a straight line and $|\epsilon_D|$ is now interpreted as its elasticity at a price equal to c, then this profit maximization would determine an output

$$100\left\{\frac{1 - \epsilon_D(1-a)}{2}\right\} \text{ per cent.}$$

below the output corresponding to a price equal to the unit cost c (the 'competitive' output, some would say). Thus if $|\epsilon_D|$ were as great as 3 with $a = \cdot7$, then the indicated output would be 5 per cent. below the latter, and the corresponding elevation of the price approx. $1\cdot7$ per cent. above c; as compared with the potential elevation, and corresponding output restriction, as high as 10-20 per cent. envisaged above.)

Thus if the industry demand is potentially elastic, this in any event influences the price, but in the context of major product innovations it is of particular significance in its bearing on the decision of the innovating firm whether to take out its advantage in a price increase, or in an expansion of its share of the market. Assuming for simplicity that the product development is not one that involves an increase in cost, the gains in the former event consist in an enhanced excess of price over cost; in the latter event they consist, first, in a wider and surer foundation for the continuing business

[1] That is, the elasticity of the demand would govern the level of the price in these circumstances, if at and beyond the output where the d-curve intersects the no-entry ceiling $(c+m)$, marginal revenue as from the d-curve is greater than this marginal cost $(a.c)$, i.e.

$$mr = (c+m) \cdot \frac{\epsilon - 1}{\epsilon} > a.c, \text{ which reduces to the expression in the text,}$$

of the firm, and second, in the opportunity to invest more capital in this, the firm's own business, which would be, in general, the most profitable avenue of investment relative to the risk open to the firm.[1] If the industry demand is relatively elastic, then, the prospective gains under the latter heads are likely to exceed the former, and an expansion in the firm's share of the market will be the preferred course of action.

Of course, quite apart from the relative magnitudes of the prospective gains, one might refer to the desire for growth *per se*, as a partially independent factor weighting the balance in favour of a preference for expanding the share of the market. There is much weight in this argument.

Executives of large business concerns are prominent among those who share the belief that neither an economy, an industry, a business enterprise, nor even institutions of a different character (though not, one hopes, a university) is healthy unless it is becoming larger. For business executives the belief is strengthened by direct personal interest, since the growth of the business they control is likely to bring them more personal power, more prestige and a larger salary and other rewards. In general, so far as the policies of the big firm are designed to foster its growth, this obviously tends to discourage the worst of the alleged monopolistic vices, as e.g. restriction of output, suppression of new products and processes, and so on, and it also tends to bring the one expanding firm into healthy competition with others also desiring to grow.

In the event then that the innovating firm forces expansion in its share of the market, there is bound to be some downward pressure on the industry price in the resultant general upset to the established pattern of the market. And this downward pressure will tend to be greater and more prolonged where the second condition referred to above obtains.

This condition relates to the size pattern of the leading firms in the market, and to the source of the product innovation. It is not uncharacteristic of the modern oligopoly that there should be one firm with a market share of the order of 50 per cent. (or upwards), and other firms—say, two others—with market shares of the order of (say) 10 to 20 per cent. Now if it is the largest firm which appropriates

---

[1] This is reinforced by any tendency for capital to increase less than proportionately to output with the expansion in capacity, i.e. capital per unit declines (even if as is usual capital intensity, i.e. capital/labour ratio, increases).

the innovation, the possibility is to be noticed that the desire of such a firm for further growth in terms of a larger share of this market might be rather circumscribed. This is a very real consideration in the United States today in face of the present climate of antitrust opinion. It is said that firms in the United States become very wary about further growth when their share of the market verges on the 50 per cent. mark. (Indeed some years ago (1956) a committee of the United States Senate, in chiding the General Motors Corporation, proposed a recommendation that the corporation should limit its share of the market to its existing level.[1])

This consideration does not weigh so importantly in the United Kingdom. But it does serve to emphasize the present point, that the effect of product innovation on intra-industry competition tends to be greater if the innovation derives from one of the smaller of the competing oligopolists.[2] In this event both the 'carrot' of the prospective gains, and the 'stick' of the inferior position combine to motivate an aggressive attack on the established structure of the market. Now we have argued that this is likely to be successful because, quite apart from the institutional factor of the patent law, there is a necessary and often quite substantial lag between the initial innovation and its effective emulation by rival firms. During this interval the most effective weapon of retaliation is price, and where it is the larger firm which is under attack, resort to this weapon is the more probable and the magnitude of the downward pressure on price the greater. Moreover this pressure[3] would tend to persist beyond the interval during which the product development is being matched; because the enlarged share of the market

[1] Another committee of the Senate, however, took the corporation to task on the grounds that its profits (at about 34 per cent. on capital) were too large, and recommended that it should lower the prices of its products. The two recommendations presented the company with something of a dilemma. If it were to comply with the second and lower its prices, then since the smaller motor companies were earning only small profits (losses in at least one case) it would be bound to increase its share of the market!

[2] That this is a real possibility is evidenced by many practical instances. In the context of the large-scale modern oligopoly of course, even the smaller of the dominant firms (e.g. the Chrysler Corporation in the U.S. motor-car industry) are yet large and powerful concerns by any absolute standard. In general, it is a condition of effective competition in this sort of case that 'the "followers" should be able to keep near enough to the leaders to stay in the race' (Prof. J. M. Clark, *A.E.R.* Supplement, 1955, p. 453).

[3] I speak of 'pressure' intentionally in order to cover both actual price reduction, as well as the refusal to admit price rises which the general and progressive rise of costs in the full employment economy would indicate.

having been won, it is not easily reduced (save by further innovation elsewhere) and the pressure on price would tend to be maintained to this end. (In any event, prices having been once reduced it is more difficult to raise them again.) A circumstance which is often important in this connexion is the degree to which sellers operate in other markets. If the dominant firm under attack has large and profitable interests elsewhere, it can the better afford to initiate and maintain this sort of action.[1]

As the cumulative outcome of such a process of intra-industry competition then, one may expect a level of price over long periods below the potential maximum imposed by the no-entry ceiling, even in the circumstances of the large-firm modern oligopoly.

CONCLUSION

In concluding this Part, it is salutary to reflect on the variety of contributary circumstances which were called upon to yield the conclusions of the above analysis. Reference was made to at least six of primary importance: (1) the nature and magnitude of barriers to new entry into the market; (2) the character and frequency of developments in technique and produce design (both these factors are related, in general, to the nature of the product of the industry); (3) the number and size distribution of the competing sellers; (4) the rate of growth, or the potential elasticity, of the industry demand; (5) the objectives of individual firm policy—whether indeed profits are maximised, and if so, in what sense?—given the pressure of public opinion (or Government anti-monopoly action); and (6) the degree to which the sellers operate in other markets. There is a seventh factor which is often important, namely, the presence of a large buyer(s) in the market.

When one reflects on the variety of these conditions, and the enormous number of possible combinations that can arise with the variation of each one through all degrees, one comes back to the view that the probability is that every industry in practice is to some extent a special case. The scope for simple generalization, therefore, is limited. In my view the line of action which holds out the most promise of further progress is the detailed empirical study of particular industries (not particular firms, as such). The study of the British soap and detergents industry which follows is a contribution to this end.

[1] As the example of Unilever Ltd., described in Chapter 11, pp. 231-36 below.

PART II

THE BRITISH SOAP AND DETERGENTS INDUSTRY

CHAPTER 5

THE SOAP INDUSTRY

NATURE OF THE PRODUCT; DEMAND; PROCESS OF PRODUCTION

WE turn now to the study of the British soap and detergents industry. In its present form it is a good example of the so-called 'modern (national) oligopoly'; but the emergence of this form of industrial organization in the industry dates only from the decade of the nineteen-thirties. In order fully to understand and assess the structure and working of the industry since that time, it is necessary to go back much further than this. In this book we begin, in fact, with the nineteenth century (Chapter 6 following).

So far as the soap industry in this period was typical of consumer goods generally, the structure of the industry and the character of competition therein are of particular interest from the points of view of the opinion advanced in the preceding Part,[1] that the model of 'Perfect Competition' is not—and indeed never has been—structurally appropriate to the manufacturing sector of industry. This question apart, however, it is salutary to reflect on a number of significant facts which emerge from the study of this period. Thus the scale of production of the principal firms in the industry at this time was typically much larger than one (this writer at least) has been accustomed to think; and by the decade of the eighteen-eighties nearly all the well-known names (firms) in the industry were already established (Lever Bros. during that decade). Again, it was as early as these latter decades of the nineteenth century that large scale advertising emerged as the typical mode of selling in the industry. In the twenty years from 1886 to 1905, one firm's expenditure on advertising amounted to upwards of 12 per cent. of its total revenue from sales, and the name of the product was, and remains, a byword in the land.

In the subsequent chapters the course of the development of the industry from this date to the present day is traced and assessed. In turn we shall examine the formation of the massive Lever Combination (Chapter 7), the performance of the industry under this one dominant seller (Chapter 8), the emergence of national competitive

[1] Above, pp. 7, 25-31.

oligopoly in the nineteen-thirties (Chapter 9), and the exploitation of a major technological development—the so-called 'synthetic' detergents—in the post-World War II years (Chapters 10 and 11).

Before proceeding with the story, however, it is necessary to consider briefly the nature of soap, and the typical product-structure of the industry; the character of the demand for soap; and the process of production.

NATURE OF SOAP AND PRODUCTS OF THE INDUSTRY

'Soap' is the water-soluble organic, or paraffin-chain, salt of one, or more of the complex fatty (organic) acids.

Anyone who has studied school chemistry will be familiar with the reaction of an acid and a base (alkali) to form an inorganic salt, thus:

$$HCl \quad + \quad NaOH \quad \rightarrow \quad NaCl \quad + \quad H_2O$$

Hydrochloric acid	Caustic soda (Sodium hydroxide)	Common Salt (Sodium chloride)	Water

Similarly the organic acids react with caustic soda to form the organic salt which is soap, thus:[1]

$$R\text{-}COOH \quad + \quad Na\,OH \quad \xrightarrow{heat} \quad R\text{-}COONa \quad + \quad H_2O$$

Fatty acid	Caustic soda	Soap	Water

The fatty acids occur naturally in vegetable and animal oils and fats, e.g. palm, palm kernel, coconut oils; tallow; etc. The soap is manufactured (see below) by boiling oils or fats with caustic alkali, resulting in the formation of soap together with glycerine according to the equation:

$$C_3H_5(RCOO)_3 \quad + \quad 3NaOH \quad \xrightarrow{heat} \quad 3R\text{-}COONa + \quad C_3H_5\,(OH)_3$$

Fat	Caustic soda	Soap	Glycerine

The charge of oils and fats used in the process is termed the 'glyceride'. The process of boiling the fat with the alkali to form the soap is termed 'saponification'. The basic liquid soap run out from the soap kettle (see below) is referred to as 'neat' soap.

The principal finished soap products are as follows. *Household Hard Soap, in Bars and Tablets*. This, the staple product of the industry until the nineteen-twenties, may be a 'pure' soap or a 'built' (or 'filled') soap. Products of the latter class are mixtures of

---

[1] In this equation R stands for the 'hydrocarbon chain'—the 'organic'—component of the fat, or fatty acid. Thus in palmitic acid (from palm oil), R stands for '$C_{15}H_{13}$', and the corresponding 'soap' is sodium palmitate ($C_{15}H_{31}$-COONa); in stearic acid, R stands for '$C_{17}H_{35}$' and the corresponding soap is sodium stearate ($C_{17}H_{35}$-COONa).

soap ('dry', 66 per cent.), soda ash (6 per cent.), 'water glass' (2 per cent.), and the balance water.

Soap Powders. These are mixtures of soap (dry, 30-40 per cent.) and soda ash (30 per cent.) with traces of other ingredients, and the balance water.

In earlier times a hardened mass of the mixture was formed and then ground to a powder. From about 1925 this process was displaced by the development of the spray-drier. The liquid soap mixture is atomized by a rotating disc into minute hollow drops, which are cooled by a draught of fresh air, and dried as they fall through a large (tapered) cylindrical tower. The latter is erected externally to the factory, and may stand 40 to 60 feet in height.

Soap Flakes or Chips. These are fragments of pure soap (94 per cent. dry soap and the balance water) of a thickness of 0·0045 inch or less. Flakes are used for fine washing purposes.

Toilet Soap. Pure soap, no builders or fillers, with scents and colouring added.

Scouring and Abrasive Soaps. These consist of mixtures of soap (dry, about 10 per cent.) with fine sand, some soda ash and other builders.

Soft Soap. As the name implies this product is a slurry mass, which results from the saponification of oils and fats with the potassium rather than the sodium alkali (i.e. KOH).

The changing relative proportions in which these products have been produced by the industry over our period is discussed below (and see Table 18A, p. 238).

Glycerine is produced as an important by-product of the industry.

The basic raw materials of the soap industry are natural oils and fats. In Great Britain these are mainly imported.

As discussed in more detail elsewhere,[1] it takes overall about two-thirds of one ton of oils and fats to manufacture one ton of finished soap (household hard soap). The cost of this raw material is thus the principal component in the cost of production of soap— varying from the order of 50 to 80 per cent. as the market prices of oils and fats (which fluctuate widely) are low or high in relation to the more stable trend of wages and other manufacturing costs.

A secondary but indispensable raw material is caustic alkali (i.e. sodium hydroxide, NaOH). The conditions of the supply of this material are discussed in more detail in Chapter 7 below. With

[1] See Appendix 2 to Chapter 6 and the Appendix to Chapter 8.

the market prices of oils and fats 'normal', the magnitude of this component of the cost of production would not exceed 3-4 per cent.

Soapless Detergents. In recent years an entirely new variety of raw materials and a new range of finished washing products manufactured from them, have made their appearance. The nature of these, the so-called 'synthetic' or 'soapless' detergents, will be discussed in detail in due sequence below (Chapter 10 and Appendix 1 at the end of this Part).

The emergence of the soapless detergents has led to a new emphasis on the development of a wider range of washing products 'tailored' (i.e. specifically synthesized; hence the usage, 'synthetic') to a variety of particular purposes both in the household and industrial spheres; and further, they allow of recourse to a large and increasing variety of raw materials, principally derivatives of petroleum. The considerable importance of this is, that with these developments the likelihood of notable and frequent advances in product design and in the process of production (by virtue of new and cheaper raw materials) has been significantly enhanced. This, as discussed in the previous chapter, is a pre-condition of effective competition in the large-firm oligopoly.

THE DEMAND FOR SOAP PRODUCTS

Soap is a product in everyday household use, of low unit price, and habitually purchased. One should expect, therefore, the market demand for soap products to be relatively price-inelastic.

Mr. Richard Stone's well-known investigations of the demand for a variety of products includes soap, and would appear to confirm this expectation.[1] His estimate of the price elasticity of the market demand for soap based on data for the United Kingdom in the interwar period, is −0·381.

In the same calculation, the income-elasticity of demand is estimated at 0·317, thus also of only 'moderate sensitivity'. In this connexion, however, it is important to distinguish between short-term (cyclical) variations in incomes, and long-term changes in income per head (the 'standard of living'). An analysis of soap consumption in twenty-eight of the principal countries of the world has yielded the following results.[2]

[1] *J.R.S.S.*, 1945, pp. 321-3.
[2] Calculation by Lord Heyworth, Chairman of Unilever Ltd., presented in his speech to the shareholders of Unilever in June 1953 and published in *The Times*, 11 June, 1953.

No. of Countries, and total population	National Income per head	Average Consumption of Soap per Head per annum (*lb.*)
4 : 533 m.	Under $100	1
4 : 67 m.	$100—$200	5
5 : 142 m.	$200—$400	10
15 : 382 m.	Over $400	25

This considerable variation in consumption per head from 1 to 25 lb. over a range of income from $100 and under to $400 and over, suggests that the consumption of soap products in the longer run is closely dependent on the general level of real income, and tends to increase more than proportionately to the latter. And Table 10 (below, Chapter 9) indicates that since 1885 the periods of most rapid growth in the total consumption in Britain[1] have been periods of rising real income per head. (They have also been periods of intense selling pressure. But in other periods of such pressure, notably 1900-7, the rate of growth has been significantly less.)

In summary, therefore, the case might be put thus: in the short-term the market demand for soap is relatively inelastic both with respect to price and income; but in the longer term the price elasticity is somewhat greater,[2] and the income elasticity considerably greater.

THE PROCESS OF PRODUCTION

The process of production of soap is a comparatively simple one. It is traditionally a 'batch' process, and for the most part remains so today. (A complex plant for producing neat soap by a continuous process, which came into operation in this country in 1939, is noticed in Chapter 9, p. 192, n. 2.) The following brief outline will suffice for the purposes of this study.[3]

The basic component of the plant is the soap-boiling pan or *kettle*, a large iron vessel cylindrical in shape, and varying in diameter from 5-25 feet and in depth from 8-30 feet. It is fitted with an open steam coil for heating the contents, and outlet valves for running off the neat soap and the 'lye' (i.e. residual liquid after boiling, containing the glycerine).

The measured charge of oils and fats and caustic alkali are run into the

---

[1] The periods 1885-1900, 1929-39 (particularly the last quinquennium), and 1950-5.

[2] My conviction that this is so is based mainly on the experience of the post-depression years in the nineteen-thirties (Chapter 9 below).

[3] For further details see G. Martin, *The Modern Soap and Detergents Industry* (2 volumes; 3rd ed., London, 1950), vol. i, Sect. I.

kettle, and the whole vigorously boiled. Saponification ensues, after which the soap and lye are separated out by shovelling in common salt (in a solution of which soap is soluble, but the lye is not).

The boiling process may occupy a day, the mass then being left to separate out overnight. While the process is thus obviously of the 'batch' type, a continuous flow of neat soap for processing to finished soap products is achieved by installing a series of kettles.

The neat soap from the kettle is run off into a 'crutcher' (or mixing machine) where appropriate builders, colouring elements, and perfumes are added; thence[1] it is machine dried to an appropriate water content, and passed under pressure through a 'plodder' which extrudes the soap in a continuous bar. (The plodder is a machine rather similar to a home mincer, on a large scale. The soap is forced by means of a spiral screw through a cylinder tapering to a small 'mouth' at the end.) By a series of machines in line the soap is then cut into tablets of appropriate size, stamped with trade-mark, and wrapped.

In earlier times the soap from the mixer was run into rectangular frames, and when dried and solidified—this would take several days—the mass was slabbed and cut into bars. (This procedure is still in evidence in small, non-mechanized soaperies). These bars were the form in which the product was supplied to distributors, the retailer cutting off and himself wrapping the quantity desired by the housewife.

The important question in this connexion is the magnitude of the 'minimum optimum' scale of production. It is apparent from the preceding outline that the process of production is a comparatively simple one, and the basic plant and machines are more or less standard and in their broad design of long-standing. It is difficult to see in this much scope for economies of large scale. In a large factory the number of soap kettles is simply multiplied, the output of each one being relatively minute. Packing machinery is 'expensive' and complex; but the trend here has been towards the development of smaller machines of similar efficiency to large ones.

Discussion along these lines, however, is necessarily inconclusive. 'Engineering estimates' by authoritative persons in the trade are to be preferred. It has been stated to me, with reference to the period about 1950, that 'it would be uneconomic in the United Kingdom to run a soap factory under 100 tons per week, but after 500 tons there is no advantage in increasing the output' (because of certain difficulties not clearly specified).[2] Persons in the trade have emphasized that economy in the use of raw materials (prevention of waste,

[1] The following refers to the manufacture of ordinary hard soaps (household or toilet). In the case of powders, the mixture from the crutcher is run to the inlet valve of the spray-drying tower, previously referred to.

[2] On these points I am particularly indebted to Mr. L. G. Grimwade, then technical director of Lever Bros. (Port Sunlight) Ltd.

etc.) whatever the scale of production, is the dominant consideration in practice on the side of costs, and is likely to overshadow variations in other manufacturing costs with scale of plant. This qualifying comment suggests that the slope of the long-run cost curve between the limits of output referred to above is scarcely of practical importance.

Now this lower limit would indicate an annual output of the order of 5,000 tons. In 1951 the output of soap product per employee per annum was about 28 tons, so that an annual output of 5,000 tons would suggest a firm employing about 175 persons. It would appear that there were about 24 'establishments' of this or a larger size in the United Kingdom in 1951, accounting for nearly 80 per cent. of the total employment in the industry. (Nearly 50 per cent. of the total employment in the industry was in seven establishments employing 750 employees or over.)[1] It would appear therefore that plants were predominantly of the minimum optimum size at this date.

Some 110 'establishments' accounted for the remaining 20 per cent. of persons employed in the industry. The majority of these were very much smaller than the minimum optimum referred to. But as Lord Leverhulme pointed out to the Government Committee of Inquiry into the industry in 1920 (see further below), there is 'a certain economy in production and distribution [principally unaccounted overhead] based upon a very small scale of operations'.[2] In protected local or speciality 'pockets' of the market such firms flourish (more or less), but do not grow. Many would be manufacturers of toilet soaps. With this class of product the opportunities for varying scents and colours are unlimited; and most such firms do not manufacture neat soap at all, but purchase soap 'stock' from larger firms.

For previous years little information is available. (Employment data by size of firm were not collected in early Censuses of Production.) However, even as early as 1900 an output of 5,000 tons would have amounted to only about 1·5 per cent. of the total annual consumption of soap products in Britain at that time, and the minimum optimum scale would then have been considerably less. It is pretty clear from the discussion of the next chapter that most of the well established firms at that time would have been producing outputs larger than this; though then, as today, there was the large fringe of very small firms.

---

[1] Table 4, Report on the 'Soap, Candles, and Glycerine' Trade, Census of Production, 1951.
[2] *Report on the Soap Industry*, 1921 (Cmd. 1126), p. 6.

While the evidence is perhaps inconclusive, I think it is a reasonable presumption that the minimum optimum scale of production in this industry is—and has been—small relative to the size of the total market, and economies of scale thus unimportant. In concluding this discussion, however, it is necessary to emphasize that this refers to production only. Resort to large-scale advertising as the characteristic mode of sales promotion in the industry began early, as already noticed. In so far as this has involved selling to a national market, then because the sums that must be expended in this way for even minimum effectiveness are very large, it is probable that the selling optimum is substantially larger than the production optimum.

CHAPTER 6

THE SOAP INDUSTRY IN THE NINETEENTH CENTURY

THE objective of this chapter is to set the background of the modern soap industry, and to notice certain aspects of the structure of the industry in this period which have a bearing on the broad argument of Part I. It is not my purpose to write an adequate economic history of the industry.

The chapter falls into two parts. In the first (to page 143), the development and structure of the industry up to the eighteen-eighties is outlined. The year 1885 was notable for the entry of W. H. Lever into the industry, with results that were to be far-reaching indeed. Thus in the second part the manner of Lever's rise to leadership in the industry is examined.

THE SOAP INDUSTRY UNTIL ABOUT 1885

The origins of the industry are remote. But the modern soap industry may be dated from the beginning of the nineteenth century.[1] It was about this time that the classic researches of the French chemist Chevreul on the constitution of fats dispelled the ignorance as to the real composition of soap which had prevailed till that time. Chevreul showed that soap was not merely a mechanical mixture of fat and alkali, but resulted from a definite chemical reaction.

But it was not only ignorance of the real composition of soap, but the lack of an adequate source of alkali which restricted the development of soap-making. The only sources of alkali were the ashes of barilla (or seaweed) and limited natural deposits. This obstacle was overcome when Leblanc developed a process for the production of soda ash ('sodium carbonate'), and thence caustic alkali, from common salt. The first plant utilizing the Leblanc process in the

---

[1] See W. H. Simmons, *Soap: its Composition, Manufacture and Properties* (London, 1917), p. 2; and Charles Wilson, *History of Unilever*, two volumes, London, 1954, vol. i, p. 10. Mr. Wilson's book, hereafter referred to as 'Wilson, i (or ii)' is an excellent and authoritative study of the soap industry from the point of view of Lever Bros. Ltd., and in this chapter and the next I draw heavily upon it.

United Kingdom was established in 1814 at St. Helens, Lancashire, and thereafter this process was worked continuously in England.[1]

The discoveries of Chevreul and Leblanc thus established the scientific basis of the soap industry, and thereafter—despite the apparently retarding effect of a contentious excise tax on the product[2]—its economic development was rapid. In the early stages the industry relied primarily on home supplies of the principal raw material, tallow. Subsequently, however, with the rapid development of overseas transport, the expanding requirements of the industry were increasingly met by imported supplies. This was an important factor in determining the location of the industry, which tended to centre around ports—round Merseyside, Bristol, London, and Newcastle.[3]

With these developments in the supply of the principal raw materials and an expanding industrial population to purchase the product, the output of the industry consumed at home increased almost four-fold from the order of 24,000 tons in 1801 to 87,000 tons in 1851 (Table 2). Over this period the population increased by something like 80 per cent., so that the consumption of soap per head doubled (from about $3\frac{1}{2}$ lb. per head per annum in 1801 to 7 lb. per head in 1851).

[1] In the 1890's, the Leblanc process was superseded by the Solway process—a major innovation in this field.

[2] Soap had been subject to some form of excise tax almost continuously from 1631, when Charles I granted a monopoly of the trade to 'certain unpractised Gentlemen of Westminster' on condition that he should be paid £4 a ton on 5,000 tons a year. This patent was surrendered in 1637 by the 'Westminster gentlemen', who in the intervening years had 'vexed the whole kingdom with their white soap' which 'women and others in the street in open manner published, that . . . it spoyled and burnt the linnen, and fretted the hands of the washers'. (From *A Short and True Relation Concerning the Soap Business*, 1641, quoted in a special article 'Taxes on Washing' in *The Times*, 4 July 1953.) But the excise on soap was maintained. In our period the tax was as follows:

	Duty per ton £	Manufacturers' Price excluding duty £
1791	21	55
1801	21	53
1811	21	52
1821	28	40
1831	28	24
1841	14	24
1851	14	26

The excise duty on soap was finally repealed by Gladstone in the budget of 1853, when the loss to the revenue was £1,111,000. (Data from Mulhall, *Dictionary of Statistics*, 1890-1 edn., p. 542).

[3] Wilson, i, 10-11.

TABLE 2

Estimated Consumption of all Soap Products and Population:
Gt. Britain*—Nineteenth Century.

Year	Aggregate Consumption of all Soap Products† (Tons)	Estimated Population‡ (Millions)	Consumption of all Soap Products per Head (Lb.)
1801	24,107	15·0	3·6
1811	32,589	17·8	4·1
1821	41,964	20·9	4·5
1831	47,768	24·1	4·4
1841	75,893	26·7	6·4
1851	87,053	27·4	7·1
1861	104,000	29·0	8·0
1871	150,000	31·5	10·7
1881	218,000	34·9	14·0
1891	260,000	37·7	15·4
1900	320,000	41·1	17·4
1912	366,000	45·5	18·0

Notes:
* All British Isles (i.e. includes Eire).
† Data for 1801 to 1861, inclusive, from Mulhall, *Dictionary of Statistics* (1890-1 edn.), p. 542. Subsequent years from Wilson, i, p. 9 and *passim*.
‡ Official estimates, early years from Mulhall, op. cit.

No doubt many factors contributed to this increase in the consumption of soap per head. The progress of the 'industrial revolution' doubtless tended to render soap a necessity. Over the period the price of soap fell almost continuously—by 1851 to almost half the level prevailing in 1801. In part this was the fall in price typical of the early stages of the development of a new industry—or, as here, of an industry rejuvenated by major innovation (application of the Chevreul discoveries in the soap-making process, and of Leblanc's process in the manufacture of alkali). But after a precipitous rise in the first stages of the Napoleonic war (to 1801), the general price level was itself falling rapidly over the period.[1] Thus the influence of the price factor (and even the much-disputed tax itself) was probably not very significant, and the general rise in real income over the period the dominant factor.

[1] Thus:

	Index of Soap 'Price'	Siberling Index of General Prices
1791	100	100
1801	97·5	168
1811	96	160
1821	88·5	118
1831	68·5	96
1841	63	104
1851	52·5	87

(Soap 'price': total value of all soap products ex works (as recorded for excise purposes) plus the excise tax receipts, divided by the recorded quantity.)

The number of manufacturers of soap during this period was large. In 1801 there were 624 makers licenced for excise purposes, and as late as 1845 some 566. That many of these, however, were small and precariously established is clear from the record that 'during the next twelve months [1846] 393 failed or withdrew with varying losses'.[1]

By the middle of the century, however, the British soap industry was well established. It was reported that 'visitors to the Great Exhibition of 1851 . . . found a bewildering variety of soaps on show—honey soap, white curd soap, mottled soap, castillo and potash soap—shown by no less than 103 manufacturers'.[2] Certainly most of the well-known firms had been established by this time— Knight's, Cook's, Pears' in London; Christopher Thomas's at Bristol; Hudson's at Liverpool; Crosfields' at Warrington; Hodgson & Simpson's at Wakefield; Watson's at Leeds; Hedley's at Newcastle; Tennant's at Glasgow; and so on.[3] And it conveys some indication of the scale of production in the larger and well-established firm at the time, that 'In the 'fifties . . . [Knight's] was a sizeable business employing a hundred and fifty people and producing between two thousand and three thousand tons of soap a year'[4]—about 3-3·5 per cent. of the total national consumption of soap products.

The final repeal of the excise tax on soap by Gladstone in 1853 seems to have touched off another period of rapid growth in the demand for soap. With rising real wages,[5] the annual consumption per head again doubled from 1851 to 1881, reaching approximately 14 lb. per head in the latter year. Coupled with the increase in population, this meant a total home consumption of soap well in excess of 200,000 tons per annum, while some 20,000 to 25,000 tons was exported. And this output was produced by more than 100 firms of all sizes, and widely distributed throughout the country. It is clear that by the 'eighties of last century, soap-making was a large and firmly-established industry in Britain.

---

[1] From the *Case of the Soap Duties* (1846), quoted in the special article in *The Times*, previously referred to.
[2] R. Lucock Wilson, *Soap Through the Ages* (Lever Bros. and Unilever Ltd., 1952), p. 13.
[3] Wilson, i, 15.
[4] Idem.
[5] According to the index of G. H. Wood, real wages increased by 35 per cent. from 1850 to 1875.

It is of interest at this point to consider the question of how far the pattern of the industry at this time conformed to the Perfect Competition model of economic theory. For while the view advanced in earlier chapters—that the Perfect Competition model is structurally inappropriate to the circumstances of manufacturing industry —may be conceded in respect of present-day conditions, it is still sometimes suggested (or implied) that 'competition' in a form akin to that model was characteristic of the nineteenth century.[1] But in the case of the soap industry, at all events, this was not so. In this connexion a number of points should be noticed.

OLIGOPOLY IN THE NINETEENTH-CENTURY SOAP INDUSTRY

(i) There is no doubt that the industry was 'competitive' in the ordinary sense of the word (Chapter 1 above). It is true that as early as 1867 the Soap Makers' Association had been formed, and met regularly (twice yearly) thereafter. But the evidence suggests that the Association met with little success in any collective action to control the market, and in particular to determine prices by collective decision. The secretary of the Association at this time, one C. J. Cross, constantly repudiated any suggestion that it was any part of the Association's purposes to fix prices in that sense.[2] That, of course, will mean little to the cynical. It is quite certain, however, that the Association did attempt to *regulate* prices in the sense that it sought to bind members to observe their published price lists, and when conditions warranted it to take action to alter them at the same time.[3]

It has already been argued above that some tacit or overt collusion to this end is almost inevitable in the circumstances of manufacturing industry.

The difficulty, of course, is that the mere collective regulation of prices leads easily to the fixing of a price which is too high. Whether or not such a price can be maintained depends on the possibilities of new competition in such event. There can be few doubts on this point in the case of the British soap industry in the eighteen-eighties (see (ii) following).

In any event the Soap Makers' Association met with very

[1] For example, Mr. N. Kaldor speaks of 'the competitive markets typical of nineteenth-century capitalism—with individual industries consisting of hundreds of small or medium-sized businesses . . .' as being replaced by the modern oligopoly during the last forty years. 'The Economic Aspects of Advertising', *R.E.S.*, 1949-50, p. 15.
[2] Wilson, i, 60, 65.   [3] Idem.

indifferent success in its efforts to implement even a minimal measure of price regulation. Thus, according to Mr. Wilson:[1]

Some members . . . adopted the practice of 'booking forward', i.e. of offering long-term contracts which guaranteed the customer against the possibility of an increase in prices, and thus put themselves beyond the reach of the Association's agreed policy. Others were apparently in the habit of accepting, after an agreed rise in price, orders sent by return of post for delivery at the old rates. The temptation to undersell and try to get business at the expense of fellow members was almost irresistible. Dispute after dispute bore witness to the failure of the Association to agree even over such relatively straightforward issues as these.

Indeed, W. D. Knight, Chairman of the Association[2] in 1893, complained bitterly that 'the history of our Association is a history of exploded agreements'.

The importance of the regulation of price competition in the industry, however, in those intervals when 'good fellowship' in the trade did permit it (again see (ii) following), is indicated by several contemporary statements recorded by Mr. Wilson. Thus J. J. Crosfield wrote (1902) that 'good fellowship in the trade does undoubtedly add to the value in solid hard cash to us soap makers of our Association'. Similarly the chairman of the Northern Section of the Association thought 'good fellowship' was worth 'many thousands a year to its members', while W. D. Knight was more precise stating that it was 'worth 10 shillings a ton to the London makers'.[3] The manufacturers' price was about £20 per ton at the time, so this potential gain (or loss) would amount to about $2\frac{1}{2}$ per cent. of the sales price.[4]

But co-operation was more often broken down than not, so it would appear that notwithstanding the Soap Makers' Association the soap industry of the nineteenth century was competitive in a very real sense—but not, in the technical sense, 'perfect'.

(ii) Next as to the conditions of new entry. So far as the process of production is concerned, it is evident that new entry was both 'free' and relatively easy: there was ready access to the necessary raw materials, the process of production was simple, and the

---

[1] Wilson, i, 60-61.
[2] By this date reconstituted as the United Kingdom Soap Manufacturers' Association (U.K.S.M.A.).
[3] Wilson, i, 69-70.
[4] See also W. H. Lever's estimate of 'increased profit by combined selling' (at the time of the proposed amalgamation of 1906), below, p. 161. This he put at 'at least £1 per ton', or 4·15 per cent. of the then manufacturer's price of about £24 per ton.

capital necessary to set up the minimum plant relatively small. On the marketing side ('goodwill', or 'product differentiation' barrier to entry), the position is more complex. On the one hand, it appears that there was no new entrant of note in the soap industry after the decade of the 'fifties[1]—with the twofold and, in the light of later events, very important exceptions of W. H. Lever (begun 1885) and the Co-operative Wholesale Society.[2] On the other hand, there can be no doubt that the difficulty of new entry associated with the goodwill factor was at this time of a lesser order than is entry into the national (oligopoly) market of the present day.[3] Moreover, there was undoubtedly more scope for the small local firm, serving some corner of the market protected by the then high cost of inland carriage. In so far then as ready new entry into an industry is of the essence of a 'high' degree of competition, it may be conceded that in this sense the nineteenth-century industry was more 'competitive' than the present-day industry.

This readiness of entry was well exemplified in the mid-eighties. Mr. Wilson records that at a meeting of the Association the Chairman referred to 'the numerous small makers who were starting in business'. (One of them was W. H. Lever). He regarded this as 'a new trouble springing up', adding that while members 'would live to regret their introduction . . . he thought they should be got into the Association'.[4] This entry of the 'numerous small producers' in 1885-7 may possibly be interpreted in the following way.

On the one hand, the demand for soap (as we have seen) is not greatly sensitive to cyclical variations in general activity. On the other hand, the cost of the raw material forms a large part of the total cost of production (upwards of 60 per cent.); and the prices of oils and fats vary directly with the cycle and the amplitude of

---

[1] The firm of William Gossage and Sons of Widnes was established in 1855. By the 'eighties Gossages was the largest of the Northern soap makers, with an export trade of the order of 15,000 to 20,000 tons yearly.

[2] But in the one case, Lever (as argued in detail in the next section) exploited a major innovation in marketing method, which readily accounts for his success even although new entry were normally difficult. In the case of the Co-operative Wholesale Society (hereafter 'C.W.S.'): the embryonic beginnings of C.W.S. soap production date from 1874, when the Newcastle Committee purchased a small works at Durham ('having a capacity of 10 to 15 tons weekly'), P. Redfern, *The Story of the C.W.S.* (Manchester, 1913), pp. 78-79. In 1895 a new works at Irlam, near Manchester, began production. But it was not until the fortuitous boost to its sales due to the 'Soap trust' episode of 1906 (described in the next chapter), that the C.W.S. achieved a significant volume of production.

[3] Cf. Chapter 11, pp. 251-3 below.

[4] Wilson, i, 61.

fluctuation is considerable.[1] This being the case, it would seem that the most profitable times in the soap industry in the late nineteenth century (and the times of greatest harmony and good fellowship within the Soap Makers' Association!) were during the 'recovery' phase of the cycle, in Schumpeter's sense.[2] In the boom or 'prosperity' phase, the prices of raw materials were high, while competition in the product market in face of a relatively stable aggregate demand inhibited a corresponding advance in the price of soap. In consequence the soap manufacturers very often reported losses—at all events, 'difficult times'—towards the peak of the trade cycle.[3]

Now in these circumstances it may well have been true that to balance the low profits (sometimes losses) of the boom, the soap manufacturers would tend to be somewhat conservative in trimming

---

[1] Thus the price of tallow—still the principal raw material in the 'eighties—rose from £26 3s. per ton in the cyclical 'trough' year of 1885 (according to W. W. Rostow's dating, *British Economy in the Nineteenth Century*, Oxford, 1948, p. 33) to a peak of £34 6s. per ton in the 'boom' of 1888-9—an increase of 31 per cent. (Over the same period, the index of general prices fell by about 2 to 3 per cent.). The price fell again, irregularly, to £23 per ton in the 'trough' year 1894—a decrease of 33 per cent.—and fell even further, to £20 9s. per ton in 1896, when a drought in Australia entailed a heavy slaughter of livestock. (Over this period, 1889-96, the index of general prices fell by slightly more than 5 per cent.) By the turn of the century (Rostow cyclical 'peak', 1900), the price was up again to £32 per ton in 1901 and £32 16s. 8d. in 1902. And so on. (Data from Mulhall, *Dictionary of Statistics*.)

[2] J. A. Schumpeter, *Business Cycles* (New York, 1939), Vol. i, p. 149.

[3] Thus Mr. Wilson records that, in the several years before 1867 'soap makers profits had been falling . . . and the raw material situation was reported by one firm to be 'uniformly unfavourable' (i, 60). This period coincides with the prosperity phase of the cycle of 1862-8 (dating from Rostow 'trough' to 'trough'). It was this period, as already indicated, which saw the birth of the S.M.A.; the hope was that 'co-operation in the trade . . . would relieve their [the Soap Manufacturers'] difficulties'.

Again in 1889—a 'boom' year of the prosperity with cyclical peak in 1890—the Chairman of the Association referred to the 'deplorable conditions in the soap trade . . . now being carried on at a loss . . .' Raw material prices were at a peak at this time too (n. 1 above); but at the annual meeting of the Association (whose deliberations took on 'a greater appearance of seriousness, not to say acrimony') the cause of the trouble was sought in the product market, and in particular the 'absurd competition' stemming in the main from 'Messrs. Lever & Co.'

A similar tone marked the meeting of the Association in 1899, another boom year (Rostow peak 1900). Again the prices of raw materials were rising sharply, and we find the Chairman referring to 'the past years' losses'—the result of 'much unnecessary competition' (Wilson, i, 64).

In contrast the case was quite different in recovery, or even the depression phases of the cycle. Thus, conditions in 1885-6 (Rostow 'trough', 1886) are described as 'idyllic'. At the meeting of the Association, a member stated expansively that as a result of their meeting together 'our competition and rivalry becomes like a game at billiards or cricket. Animosity was driven out and we met on Change and elsewhere like a party of friends.'

Again there was prosperity in the trade during 1895-6 (Rostow cyclical 'trough', 1894). At the Annual dinner of the Association in 1895, the Chairman is quoted as remarking that 'the present was a time of profound peace in the trade'. And so on.

prices in the depression and recovery phases of the cycle. The period 1885-7 was just such a period of (relatively mild) depression and cyclical recovery. The appearance of 'numerous small makers' at this time is therefore readily explicable, and their competition no doubt served to moderate the price quotations of the established manufacturers.

(iii) Next, Perfect Competition postulates a large number of producers all small relative to the aggregate market; alternatively, it postulates quickly rising long-run marginal cost—which ensures the same result. It is apparent that in the soap industry of the eighteen-eighties this condition was by no means fulfilled.

Thus, in the first place, the condition implies a somewhat limited variation in the size of firms, with a tendency for the majority to approximate a definite and identifiable average, indeed an 'optimum', size. It is not possible to discern any such pattern in the soap industry of the 'eighties. Indeed the variation in the size of the firms was enormous—ranging 'from those [firms] producing a few tons a week and employing a handful of employees, to those making upwards of five hundred tons a week and employing several hundreds of work people'.[1] 'Five hundred tons a week' implies an annual output in excess of 25,000 tons—considerably more than 10 per cent. of the total national consumption of soap at this time. It is pretty evident that the size-distribution of the industry was of the typical reverse-J shape, i.e. a large number of very small firms and progressively fewer firms at larger scales of production, with an 'average' size (i.e. in the technical sense, not necessarily an identifiable 'typical' firm) of the order of 2,000 to 2,500 tons per annum, in terms of output.

This sort of size-distribution is typical of manufacturing industry, in present as in earlier times. It reflects a 'scale' (long-run cost) curve for the industry which at any given time is substantially horizontal over a very wide range of outputs. But it reflects also the difficulties which confront the firm seeking to expand its scale of operations along this curve, and primarily the difficulties of acquiring and extending goodwill. In the local or speciality market, it is relatively easy to acquire the necessary market connexion, and hence the large number of small firms.[2] But in the main body of the

---

[1] Wilson, i, 20.

[2] The speciality producer is more properly regarded as complementary to, rather than competitive with, the large manufacturers of more standardized products. Cf. P. W. S. Andrews, *Manufacturing Business*, p. 218.

market the scope is more restricted; and, in particular, the emergence of the large firm is usually associated with 'founder-ability' of a rare order, exploiting, initially, the momentum of an early start and/or other accidents of fortune, and subsequently maintaining and extending the position of the firm by sustained efficiency.

There is a second point to note in the present connexion. It is that quite apart from local or speciality 'pockets' of the market, a system of zones—conventional 'spheres of influence'—had emerged within the overall market, where for the most part 'preserves were respected and poaching kept to a minimum'.

Thus according to Mr. Wilson (i, 20):

A series of conventions, almost medieval in their parochialism, maintained a system of zones, so that Northern soap makers held the markets in the North of England, Norwich makers held the East Anglian market, while London makers held London and the South. In addition there were private treaties such as that by which Christr. Thomas's of Bristol obtained an undertaking from Gossage's of Widnes that they would not come south of a line drawn from Birmingham, north of Bristol, to the Severn in the West and to the Wash in the East.

And so on. There is no doubt that this sytem of conventional zones had its origins in the very real factor of the high costs of inland transport in earlier times. Soap in bulk is a heavy article selling at a relatively low price, so that the costs of carriage over any considerable distance were large. With the development of the railways these costs, of course, were greatly reduced: but the system of zones and conventional preserves continued, no doubt partly as the result of natural inertia, but also because to let it stand was a simple means of limiting unnecessary and costly competition and thus, on the whole, a comfortable and satisfactory arrangement of things.

This division of the overall market into a number of relatively distinct provincial sub-markets meant that the situation diverged even further from the conditions prescribed in the model of Perfect Competition than would appear at first sight. The large firm of the eighteen-eighties produced from 10,000 to 26,000 tons per annum, or from 5 to more than 10 per cent. of the total national production; taken as a proportion of the particular provincial sub-market served by such a firm, the percentage share of the market was very much higher (even allowing for the export component in the sales of these firms). If the oligopolistic character of competition in the soap industry was not sufficiently apparent from the discussion under

(i) above, it may now be deduced from the structure of the market—in terms of the number of firms supplying the great bulk of the trade in each of the relatively distinct divisions of the total market.

Mr. Wilson, an historian not trained in the definitional subtleties of economics, recognizes this. While on the one hand he refers to 'perfect competition'[1] on the other he speaks freely of Christr. Thomas's of Bristol as 'the leaders' of the 'West Country group of soap manufacturers';[2] of the fact that 'none of the other London makers . . . could really challenge the old-established supremacy of Knight's'[3]; of the toilet-soap market as being '. . . shared mainly by Pears', Gibbs' and the Vinolia company'[4] and so on. And indeed the leading (oligopolist) firms in each section of the market can be readily identified from Mr. Wilson's exposition: Crosfield's, Gossage's, Hazlehurst's (and in the soap powder sub-market, Hudson's) in the North-west; Watson's and Hodgson & Simpson's in the North-east; Knight's, Cook's, Harris's (and in the toilet soap market, Pears') in London and the South-east; and so on. The case is clearly one of oligopoly; *local* oligopoly, it is true, in contrast with the *national* oligopoly which was later to emerge; but still, oligopoly.

THE RISE OF W. H. LEVER TO LEADERSHIP

(i) Innovation in Marketing Method in the Soap Industry

Against this background it is now necessary to consider the emergence of William Hesketh Lever and his rapid rise to a position of dominance in the British soap industry.

Lever began the manufacture of soap in 1885 by acquiring a small factory at Warrington, and along with it the services of its works-manager, P. J. Winser, and soap-boiler, Edward Wainwright, both of whom, it appears, contributed largely to the technical perfecting of Lever's new 'oil' soap, 'Sunlight'—the product basis of the successful enterprise to follow and still a household word in many countries today.[5] The Warrington factory was producing only 'a

---

[1] i, 66   [2] Ibid, p. 14.
[3] Ibid, p. 18.   [4] Ibid, pp. 56-57.
[5] 'Sunlight' was a pure 'oil' soap, i.e. a soap manufactured largely from vegetable oils (palm kernel, copra, and cottonseed oil) rather than hard fats and not 'built' or 'filled' with additions of soda ash or 'water glass' (i.e. sodium silicate). Such a soap had been sold by Lever as manager of the Bolton and Wigan wholesale grocery business founded by his father, but it appears that its manufacture was not properly understood by the makers and it tended to go rancid and smell badly. To develop the potential of this soap appears to have been the primary cause of Lever's entry into soap manufacture (Wilson, i, 27-29)—along, no doubt, with an appreciation of the good profits in the industry in the mid-eighties (as noticed in the preceding section), and the prospective growth in the market with rising real income.

few tons a week'. But in 1886, the first full calendar year, production totalled nearly 3,000 tons—more than 50 tons per week. The expansion which followed was spectacular (see Table 3 and Fig. 9).

TABLE 3
Lever Bros. Ltd.: Sales of Soap, 1885-1907

Year	'Sunlight' (tons) (1)	Other Products: 'Lifebuoy' (1894) 'Monkey Brand' (1899) 'Lux' Flakes (1900) &c. (2)	Total Production (Sales) (3)	Total Sales as per cent. of Total U.K. Consumption (Selected Years) (4)	Sales of 'Sunlight' as per cent. of Household Hard Soap consumed at home (5)
1885	300	—	300		
1886	2,946	—	2,946	1·2	1·8
1887	9,669	—	9,669		
1888	14,183	—	14,183	5·7	8·2
1889	15,000*	—	15,000		
1890	18,100	—	18,100		
1891	22,500*	—	22,500	8·7	12·4
1895	38,788	1,000*	39,788	13·9	20·1
1896	36,000	1,500*	37,500		
1897	39,500*	2,500*	42,000		
1900	46,000	9,325	55,325	17·3	21·3
1901	45,000*	8,000*	53,000		
1902	48,000*	8,000*	56,000		
1905	55,000*	11,000*	66,000	18·9	23·1
1906	53,000*	10,000*	63,024		
1907	38-40,000*	10-12,000*	50,000	14·1	16·4

Source: Principally C. Wilson: *History of Unilever*, Vol. i.

* Estimated by logarithmic interpolation.

In 1889 production was removed to Port Sunlight on the Mersey; but in 1890 sales of 'Sunlight' were in excess of 18,000 tons. In the tenth year of operations, 1895,[1] they totalled 38,788 tons or the order of 20 per cent. of the aggregate national consumption of household hard soap;[2] and in 1900, 46,000 tons or approximately 21·3 per cent. of the national consumption. Thus did the former buyer of soap become, in a very short time, not merely the most formidable rival of the established manufacturers, but the recognized leader of the industry.

Now we have argued that new entry on any significant scale is

[1] A private company (with an authorized capital of £300,000) was formed in 1890, and the public company, Lever Brothers Ltd. (authorized capital, £1,500,000) was created in 1894.

[2] The total production of soap at Port Sunlight, which by this time included 'Lifebuoy' carbolic soap, amounted to the order of 14 per cent. of the total consumption of all soap products.

normally difficult. The question arises, therefore, in what manner is the phenomenal growth of Lever's enterprise to be reconciled with this doctrine? The answer can be put in a word, namely, innovation. The doctrine that new entry is difficult relates to settled (i.e.

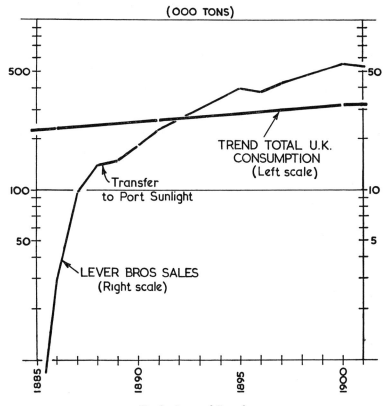

Fig. 9: Rates of Growth:
Total Consumption of Soap Products, and Production (Sales) of Lever Bros. Ltd.

static, approximately) conditions. But, as argued above (pp. 39, 118), in the event of major innovation the established pattern of the market may be decisively altered whether by an existing firm or a new entrant. There can be few better illustrations of this than Lever's entry and rise to dominance in the soap industry.

That Lever was an entrepreneur of the first class does not require argument. The question to consider is just in what the innovation he effected consisted. The answer is that it was primarily an innovation in marketing method.

It is true that the soap was itself new in some degree, as we have seen. Though soaps made predominantly from oils were not unknown at this time, they were to a greater or lesser degree 'filled' soaps. Lever's 'Sunlight' was a 'pure', i.e. unfilled, soap 'of excellent quality', which early on he dubbed 'Sunlight Self-Washer'—'because I claimed that it could wash of itself'.[1] There would be some truth in this claim because a pure oil soap would lather more freely, and would be less 'hard' in texture and more—though, with an appropriate fat content, not too—readily soluble in water. The manner in which 'Sunlight' and its imitators came subsequently to be referred to so readily in the trade as a distinct class of soap—the 'new' 'washer' soaps[2]—bears witness to the distinctive character of 'Sunlight'.

But Lever's striking success can scarcely be explained in terms alone, or even mainly, of this innovation in product; just because there *were* imitators and quickly. The leading firms among the established manufacturers, if—as will be noticed shortly—they were tardy in imitating his marketing methods, relatively quickly produced soaps of similar constitution to 'Sunlight'. Thus by 1888 Joseph Watson's, Christopher Thomas' and John Knight's were all marketing vegetable oil soaps in reply to Lever.[3] The difference in product, then, if it might well explain (in part) Lever's success in forcing an entry, scarcely accounts for the continued growth of his enterprise indicated above.

The explanation of this phenomenal growth is to be sought primarily in Lever's innovation in marketing method.

At the time of Lever's entry into the industry, soap was supplied for the most part in bulk[4] and unwrapped form. The grocer would cut off the length and weight the purchaser required from a long bar, wrapping it himself in a piece of paper, very much as quality cheese is sold today. If the soap bore any stamp or brand of the maker at all, it was not—from the final consumer's point of view—significantly branded: 'the housewife's choice of soap [was] based on the *kind* of soap—"Castile", "Windsor", mottled or curd, as supplied by her

---

[1] Wilson, i, 28.   [2] Or, simply, 'washers'. See Wilson, i, 67.

[3] Wilson, i, 62. Joseph Watson's of Leeds was apparently quickest to react in this way, perhaps as early as 1886.

[4] There were limited exceptions to this in the toilet soap field. E.g. Pear's famous transparent soap was from the first supplied in stamped tablet form.

customary retailer—rather than on the *make*'.[1] Within the trade soap-making reputations were built up on non-proprietary articles of the same general nature. Mr. Wilson quotes Christr. Thomas' comment—this well reflects the chagrin and indeed bewilderment of the established manufacturers in face of Lever's methods—'There is little or no difference in quality between different makes of Bar Soaps—there is a Thomas's Primrose, a Knight's Primrose, a Cook's Primrose—all the same soap. It is impossible therefore, by the nature of the case to . . . [attempt] through advertising to create a demand in favour of any one particular make.'[2] In a word, the situation was of the second broad class distinguished above,[3] that is, the case of consumer goods sold unbranded or under the brand of wholesaler or retailer.

Now the essence of Lever's innovation was to transform this situation into one approximating the third class of cases distinguished above. The innovation in marketing method had three aspects. First, the product, new in physical specification, was 'new' also in that it was produced in tablet form (one-lb. and subsequently 8-oz. tablets) as against the anonymous bulk of the customary bar soap; it was wrapped, at first in imitation parchment only, but later also in cartons; it was branded with the catch-name 'Sunlight' (Lever's registered trade-mark) on tablet, wrapper and carton; and it was advertised, not simply as soap but as 'Sunlight', in a manner unprecedented in extent and intensity and mainly directed to the final consumers in order to by-pass (so to speak) the acquired wholesaler-goodwill of the established firms.

Second, Lever was led to establish—if indeed he did not envisage at the outset—a national market for his product. In doing this he ignored and cut right across the accepted system of conventional zones and market preserves which divided the aggregate market, as discussed above. Lever began locally in the towns of Bolton and Wigan; 'When I got it [Sunlight] established there and making money' (his own words) 'I ventured forth to Liverpool and Manchester. Established there and making money I opened up in London, Scotland and elsewhere and covered the United Kingdom . . .'[4] Thus Lever's innovation consisted not merely in the branded speciality, but in the branded speciality recognized and selling at one price 'from Land's End to John o'Groats'.

---

[1] R. Lucock Wilson, *Soap Through the Ages*, p. 13.
[2] Wilson, i, 41.   [3] Chapter 2, p. 28n.   [4] Quoted by Wilson, i, 32-33.

Third, it seems clear that Lever realized it was in the working-class households throughout the land that the greatest opportunities for expanding sales of soap resided. As Mr. Wilson interprets his thought (i, 38):

The working classes alone had numbers sufficient to realize his ideal of making large-scale enterprise depend on a low rate of profit and a huge turnover; and rising wages had brought soap within their means. Here was a vast potential market yet only partially exploited.

While no opening in the whole market that it was practicable to tap was overlooked, it is apparent that, at least initially, this is where Lever concentrated his main effort—as the pivotal slogan of the early campaigns, 'Why does a Woman look old sooner than a Man?', obviously directed to the factory housewife, bears witness.

These, then, were the essential contours of Lever's innovation in marketing method. With these factors exploited with the resource and energy of an entrepreneur of Lever's stature, his rapid appropriation of so large a share of the market is easily explained.

Thus, if his principal rivals were quick to retaliate with new soaps of a similar constitution to 'Sunlight', they were slow to appreciate the significance of the heavily-advertised manufacturer-branded product. Reference has been made to the bewilderment and concern apparent in the statement of Christr. Thomas of Bristol, quoted above. From the vantage point of the present, this is difficult to appreciate because the idea would seem to be such a simple one; but at that time and regarded through the blinkers of established modes of thinking about marketing methods in the soap industry, it was not. Lever's way of doing things was just not customary, and was at best a risky experiment. His methods were regarded with indifference or contempt by some, and with alarm by others; but is clear from Mr. Wilson's narrative (i, 40 ff.) that as late as 1889, and while some of the Northern makers—the first to feel the pinch —were in fact beginning to retaliate by wrapping their own soaps in imitation of Lever,[1] many in the S.M.A. were still speaking of his competition and his methods as 'absurd', and were hesitant about copying them.[2] Meanwhile Lever was exploiting the growing

[1] In particular, Joseph Watson's of Leeds. Wilson, i, 62.

[2] Among the larger firms it would appear that Knight's of London were the most tardy to follow Lever. This was because they feared that 'aggressive advertising' was 'contrary to their established custom and liable to offend the very customers they wished to attract'. These were defined as 'high-class family grocers and substantial professional men . . . and ladies scheduled in the Ladies Court Book' (Wilson, i, 16). But in the early 'nineties, they like the others felt compelled to follow suit (p. 63).

momentum of his early start to the full. The 'superior' qualities and actual practical benefits of the new product were pressed home by every available means—by the newspaper advertisement, the billboard poster on the railway station and road-side, and (from as early as 1887) the offer of prizes in exchange for wrappers and cartons. With the price maintained comparable to rival unbranded products, it was entirely rational of the consumer to purchase the advertised product. And the manner of her response is sufficiently indicated by the fact that in the period before the counter-competition of the established firms became in any great degree effective, it would appear that the practical limit to sales was not the (rapidly expanding) demand for the product, but the physical capacity of the plant to produce in sufficient quantity (i, 32).

Lever's expenditure on advertising was 'prodigious . . . by contemporary standards'. Mr. Wilson records that in all, his advertising costs during the twenty years 1886-1905 amounted to some £2,000,000 (i, 43). In ratio of sales, this may be roughly estimated (see Appendix I to this chapter) at about 12-13 per cent. of the ex-factory value of sales of 'Sunlight', on which product it was mainly concentrated—a ratio higher than for the 'soapless detergents' in recent years.[1] The very great effectiveness of this advertising, particularly in the first five to ten years, is only too apparent and cannot be denied. This, of course, does not conflict with the strictures concerning the efficacy of (competitive) advertising, discussed above (pp. 33-34). In a context of major innovation, advertising can be very effective (in the present instance, large-scale advertising, as a new mode of final-consumer selling, was itself innovation). Very often—and particularly in the event of innovation in product design—large-scale advertising is essential to exploit the advantage so conferred, and to this extent such advertising may be a necessary condition of a significant alteration in market shares; it is not, however, a sufficient condition.

Next Lever proceeded (as already noted) by gradually extending his operations, area by area, to achieve a national, indeed, an international, market for 'Sunlight'. This is in itself a factor in explaining the somewhat tardy reactions of some of the established soap manufacturers; London or the West Country were sufficiently remote from Lever's home territory in the North-west not to feel the full impact of his expansion for some time. But the fact of a

[1] Below, Chapter 11, p. 249.

national market for 'Sunlight' is also important in explaining the actual order of magnitude of Lever's ultimate share of the aggregate production of soap—upwards of 20 per cent. of the total national production of household hard soap (Column 5 of Table 3 above).

Mr. Wilson records (i, 62) that the very idea of a soap supplying a national market 'came as a shock to the older makers'; certainly most of their number were slow to seek to do likewise. In this, therefore, they were necessarily at a disadvantage in competing volume-wise with Lever. To appropriate a 20-25 per cent. share of any of the conventional sub-markets of the kingdom would have been, perhaps, the maximum result attainable; but this in itself would not have amounted to much more than the order of 4-5 per cent. of the aggregate (national) market.[1] To realize a rate of production of the order he wished, then, Lever extended his sales throughout the nation, appropriating (as it were) a 20 per cent. share, more or less, in each of the conventional market areas. In such terms the magnitude of his achievement, while still evoking admiration, may at least be understood.

Finally a contributory factor in Lever's success was the growth in the total demand for soap over the period in view. From an average of 220,000 to 230,000 tons in the first quinquennium of the 'eighties, the annual aggregate consumption of all soap products in the United Kingdom increased to 320,000 tons at the turn of the century.[2] It is apparent that this increase was at once a condition, and an effect, of Lever's success.

The increase, in absolute terms, was almost twice the total of Lever's sales which stood at 55,000 tons in 1900. While there was a decisive change in (relative) shares of the market in Lever's favour, therefore, this was achieved without any decrease—indeed, along with some increase—in the absolute volume of sales of all other soap manufacturers taken together. The magnitude of Lever's sales would almost certainly have been less had it been necessary for him to

---

[1] This envisages five major sub-divisions of the total market (say, the North-west, North-east, West Country, London and South-east, in England and Wales, and Scotland as the fifth): all assumed approximately equal for the sake of argument.

[2] The available evidence suggests that after a period of rapid growth in the decades of the 'sixties and 'seventies (see Table 2) the consumption per head was barely stationary—and hence the rate of growth of the aggregate consumption much slower —in the first quinquennium of the 'eighties. The growth from the mid-eighties to 1900, therefore, while slower than in the earlier decades, represents a recovery in the rate of advance.

wrest his market entirely, or in some greater degree than was in fact the case, from those of the established manufacturers.

This, however, is scarcely to subtract from the measure of his achievement. The increase in the total consumption was due in approximately equal proportions to the increase in population over the period (of the order of 15 per cent.) and to the increase in consumption of soap per head (from the order of 14 lb. per annum to 17½ lb. per annum or approximately 25 per cent.); and the main element in the latter was undoubtedly the increased consumption of soap among the working classes. Lever, as suggested above, foresaw the potential of this market and by his aggressive selling to the 'factory housewife' actively fostered it. To this extent, therefore, the increase in the aggregate consumption was not merely a condition of Lever's success, but also (partially) its effect.

Lever suffered the first reverse in the upward trend of 'Sunlight' sales in 1896. The upward trend was soon renewed, however; but from that time onwards, the rate of growth in Lever's total sales did not greatly exceed that of the aggregate consumption of the market as a whole (see column 5 of Table 3 and Fig. 9). In terms of the analysis of Chapter 2 (above pp. 32-37) this tendency to a comparative stability in the relative division of the market is what we should expect: because by this time the impetus of Lever's innovation had slackened; and even the most conservative of the established firms (e.g. Knight's of London, as noted above) were imitating or otherwise adapting his methods to suit their own markets, so that a rough balance of competitive strength had re-emerged. There was, in a word, an approach to industry equilibrium.

(ii) Unstable Equilibrium, 1896-1905

It was, however, an 'equilibrium' full of life and movement, as is evident from Mr. Wilson's account. As sales of 'Sunlight' fell in 1896, Lever set new advertising schemes afoot to retrieve the position (i, 52), and loud complaints of 'ruinous' and 'unnecessary' competition were soon heard in the Association (p. 64). So intense, indeed was the competition and such the expenditure on advertising, that Lever himself in 1898 decided that not only would he stop advertising prizes, but that he would commence (in his own words) 'a policy of discouragement of that system of business'. The argument was that such schemes had outrun their usefulness 'because in spite of heavy outlay on prize schemes in that year [1897] the increase in sales was not more than a normal one' (i, 52).

But this view of the situation was faulty, because with the impetus of his innovation well-nigh run out, and in the absence of agreement all round to restrain advertising, even a 'normal' increase could be achieved only by heavy advertising. Thus in the event, Lever did not succeed in his purpose. His competitors, now fully awake to the significance of the methods they had earlier resisted, immediately pushed 'most energetically schemes for giving prizes for wrappers as we [Lever Bros.] withdrew from that method of advertising'. Subsequently, in face of an actual decline in sales in 1901, Lever conceived the idea of a new wrapper scheme with not 'cutlery and fancy articles of doubtful value' as prizes, but rather Lever Bros.' own soaps, since no other soap manufacturer could offer these (Wilson, i, 54). With this, sales of 'Sunlight' resumed their upward trend, but not significantly faster than the growth of the total market, which itself had now levelled off to a rate not much in excess of the growth of population.[1]

In assessing this stage of the development of the soap industry, two points must be made. First, the development at this time stopped considerably short of the emergence of national oligopoly in the soap industry; though the latter outcome might confidently have been predicted during the early years of the Lever revolution, and did ultimately emerge in the nineteen-thirties (Chapter 9 below). This is readily explained in terms of the number and 'staying power' —within their respective traditional territories—of the already large and well-established firms in the industry at the time of Lever's entry thereto. While somewhat slow in imitating his methods fully, these firms were yet able to 'hold the line' (so to speak) during the initial period (assisted by the growth in the total demand), and subsequently matched Lever's advertising and selling methods with equally aggressive advertising of their own.

Thus (second) the character of the situation which emerged is pretty clear. Not all the 'frenzied competition' of the period to 1906, with its 'increasingly pretentious and extravagant advertising',[2]

---

[1] The Wood index of 'Real Wages allowing for Unemployment' following the rapid rise from the mid-'eighties to 1900, fell some 10 per cent. between 1900 and 1910. If the exploitation of the mass market represented by the working-class households of the nation was the main factor in the increase in the consumption per head to 1900, the subsequent fall in real wages (and a Modigliani factor) no doubt explains the almost stationary consumption per head in the first decade of the twentieth century.

[2] Mr. Wilson's phrases, i, 55.

issued in any significant and lasting change in the relative positions of the leading firms: albeit there were considerable fluctuations of fortune with the varying successes of particular advertising campaigns, as evidenced by the variations in Lever Bros.' sales just noticed in the penultimate paragraph. The situation was thus akin to that referred to in Chapter 3 (p. 101 above), and one would expect to observe, therefore, some significant excess of productive capacity in the industry at this time. The evidence of the Census of Production of 1907 would seem to bear this out. The year 1907 was a cyclical 'peak' year according to W. W. Rostow's dating previously referred to, but the Census Report on the 'Soap, Candles, and Glycerine' trade for that year states:

Firms accounting for 64 per cent. of total soap production (4,756,000 cwt. of 7,440,000 cwt.) stated that their maximum annual capacity was 8,180,000 cwt.; thus their output was 58 per cent. of their maximum capacity.

In assessing this, the special factors affecting sales in 1907 to be discussed in the next chapter must be taken into account; but the existence of a considerable measure of excess capacity in the industry at this time is beyond doubt. As suggested above in the analysis referred to, this under-utilization of capacity involving a greater incidence per unit of output of fixed 'establishment' charges, is likely to have had some influence on prices because of the tendency of entrepreneurs in this sort of situation to 'take full cost literally'. There was in addition the pressure on prices from the build-up of excess expenditure on advertising. In the event, until the end of 1906,[1] it would appear that the effect was rather that prices were upheld at the levels previously prevailing when otherwise the decline of raw material prices which occurred would have led to some reduction in the price of soap, while at the same time net profits were reduced as revenue was appropriated to finance increasing advertising expenditures. (This crucial question of the relation of prices to costs is examined at length in Appendix 2 to this chapter.) The situation was scarcely a stable one, and the manner in which in the event it was resolved is discussed in the next chapter. But to many it would appear that the last state was worse than the first.

---

[1] The retail price of 'Sunlight' (lb. tablet) which had remained unchanged at 3d. since its first appearance, was increased to 3½d. in October 1906. (Of course, there had previously been movements up and down in the wholesale price.)

APPENDIX 1

LEVER'S EXPENDITURE ON ADVERTISING IN RELATION TO TURNOVER

The sales of 'Sunlight' soap in the twenty years 1886-1905 have been estimated as in column 1 of the following table:

Year	Sales of Sunlight	Value ex-factory @ £23 8s. ton (000 £'s)
1886	2·9	69
1887	9·7	231
1888	14·2	338
1889	15·0	356
1890	18·1	430
1891	22·5	535
1892	26·5	630
1893	30·0	713
1894	34·0	808
1895	38·8	923
1896	36·0	856
1897	39·5	940
1898	42·0	1,000
1899	44·5	1,060
1900	46·0	1,096
1901	45·0	1,070
1902	48·0	1,142
1903	51·0	1,214
1904	54·0	1,285
1905	55·0	1,310

Total Sales: 672,700 tons
Total Value: £16,006,000

The 'value ex-factory' has been estimated at an average of £23 8s. per ton. This figure has been arrived at on the basis of data relating to whole-sale and retail trading margins for this type of product, as given in the *Report of the Committee of Inquiry into the Soap Industry*, 1921 (Cmd. 1126) and elsewhere. These sources would indicate an inclusive traders' margin of the order of 15 per cent. of the retail price. (This may seem rather low for the period. The effect of a larger figure would be to enlarge even further the estimated ratio of advertising to sales revenue.) Subtracting this from the constant retail price of 'Sunlight' over the period in view, namely, 3d. per lb. or £28 per ton, we arrive at the figure of £23 8s. per ton—as a rough estimate of the manufacturer's price over the period on the average, though of course it varied above and below this from time to time. (This may be compared with the round figure of £24 per ton mentioned by Lever himself as quoted by Wilson, i, 117.)

Now Lever's total expenditure on advertising during these twenty years amounted to the order of £2,000,000. This represents some 12·5 per cent. of the total estimated revenue from sales of £16,006,000.

APPENDIX 2

TREND OF SOAP PRICES IN RELATION TO TREND OF COSTS, 1901-13

1. Some indication is required of the trend of soap prices in relation to the trend of costs.

At least until pre-World War II, it was a rough rule of thumb in the soap trade that 'the' cost of production per ton of soap (including 'normal' profit) could be estimated approximately as:

> 2/3 realized cost per ton of oils and fats
> *Plus* 'manufacturing cost' (q.v.)
> *Less* value of glycerine recovered per ton of raw
> material.

This rule is also suggested by the calculations of the Government Committee of Inquiry into the Soap Industry, 1920-1: see *Report on the Soap Industry*, 1921, Cmd. 1126, pp. 10-11.

'Manufacturing cost' in this rule of thumb refers to the following: wages, coal, chemicals, packing materials, freight, also selling, distribution, and establishment charges.

The sum of these costs per ton of best quality household soap was supplied to the Committee for a number of years by 'a representative manufacturer' (*Report*, p. 10). Over the period shown I have found (as one might expect) that the variation in these data is closely correlated with the G. H. Wood index of money wages, as tabulated and extended by W. T. Layton and G. Crowther, *Introduction to the Study of Prices* (London, 1938), Appendix E, pp. 271-5.

2. A rough calculation of the trend of costs per ton of best quality household soap for the period 1901-13 has thus been essayed in Table 4 as follows:

In column 1 the G. H. Wood index of money wages is entered. For 1913 (the earliest year for which a figure was supplied to the Committee of Inquiry) the composite item 'manufacturing cost' was stated to be £6 11s. per ton. On the basis of the index, this is estimated for each year 1901-13 inclusive as in column 2.

In columns 3, 4, and 5 the mean (annual) prices of the three principal oils and fats used in the manufacture of good-quality household soaps are entered. (These data have been kindly supplied by Unilever Ltd.) The Committee of Inquiry found that by taking 2/3 of a simple average of

TABLE 4

Trend of Costs—Prices, 1901-13

	G. H. Wood Index, Money Wages 1	'Manufacturing Cost' Component £ per ton 2	Palm Oil £ per ton 3	Tallow £ per ton 4	Copra £ per ton 5	Sum (3+4+5) £ 6	⅓ col. 6 × ⅔ £ 7	Estimated 'Cost', £ per ton, Soap (2+7) 8	Index of Cost 24·7=100 9	Index of Price 3d.=100 10
1901	179	6·22	26	32	17	75	16·67	22·89	92·7	100
1902	176	6·11	28	32·83	17	77·83	17·30	23·41	94·7	100
1903	174	6·04	29	27·5	15·5	72	16·00	22·04	89·2	100
1904	173	6·01	26·5	27·5	19	73	16·22	22·23	90·0	100
1905	174	6·04	28·5	27·5	18	74	16·44	22·48	91·0	100
1906	176	6·11	33	27·5	19	79·5	17·67	23·78	96·2	100
1907	182	6·32	31	34·25	23·5	88·75	19·72	26·04	105·4	116·7
1908	181	6·28	28·5	31·25	16·75	76·5	17·00	23·28	94·3	116·7
1909	179	6·22	31	31·25	21	83·25	18·50	24·72	100	116·7
1910	179·5	6·24	37	35	25·75	97·75	21·72	27·96	113·0	100
1911	179	6·22	34·5	31·25	25·88	91·63	20·36	26·58	107·4	100
1912	184	6·40	34	33·5	24·95	92·45	20·54	26·94	108·9	100
1913	188·5	6·55	36	35	30·75	101·75	22·61	29·16	117·9	116·7

the market prices of the principal oils and fats, an estimate of the oils and fats component of the cost of production of soap was arrived at which corresponded almost identically with figures for this cost component supplied by the 'representative manufacturer' previously referred to. (*Report*, p. 10, and see the Table, p. 11). In column 7 of the accompanying table, therefore, the sum (in col. 6) of the values in cols. 3, 4, and 5 is divided by 3 (for the simple average) and 2/3 of the resultant entered in the column.

For the purpose of our index of costs, the sum of columns 2 and 7 is then taken (column 8). In absolute terms, and apart from the further qualifications noticed below, this overstates the cost of production in that the value of glycerine recovered should be subtracted. This refinement is not attempted here first, because no adequate data relating to glycerine prices over the period, nor to the 'typical' composition of output as between crude and refined glycerine by soapmakers, are available. (Even in the Census year 1907, as stated in the *Report* for this trade, the position is not clear because of double counting between the crude and refined outputs.) Second, however, data supplied by the Soapmakers' Federation to the Committee put the credit on account of glycerine recovered as £1 15*s.* per ton for the year 1918. At this time the price of glycerine had no doubt been elevated by the pressure of war demands for explosives: in pre-war years this credit is unlikely to have exceeded (say) £1 per ton. It is clear that in absolute terms this element is small relative to the total cost of production, so that for the purpose of an index over time variations in this small element can be ignored without sensible error.

If, however, it is reasonable to assume that the credit on account of glycerine recovered was in fact of the order of £1 per ton in the pre-war period, this provides some check on the validity of the above rule of thumb. Thus Mr. Wilson refers to the air of gloom and misery at the Soap Makers' Association dinner in 1909 ('all present agreed that they were suffering', i, 117), and a passage quoted from a letter written by W. H. Lever about this time mentions the round figure of £24 per ton as the manufacturer's net price of soap. Now the estimates of cost in col. 8 of the table herewith for 1908 and 1909 (£23·28 and £24·72 respectively) less £1 in each case, give £22·28 and £23·72 for the cost of production per ton in these two years. These estimates would appear to be not wide of the mark. If the manufacturers' net price was in fact £24 in 1909, this would indicate a pretty tight relation of price to cost in that year; while in the preceding year (when the retail price of 'Sunlight', at least, was nearly 17 per cent. higher and probably therefore wholesale prices generally also) the estimate for the cost of production is lower and profits were therefore probably 'good'. Thus the estimates suggest a 'tight' position in 1909, and a decline in fortunes from the previous year: this would adequately account for the general gloom at the dinner of 1909, which in this way provides some limited confirmation of the general validity of the estimates.

Because of the apparent close relation of price to cost in 1909, I have taken this year as the base year for the indexes in cols. 9 and 10, i.e. for the cost series £24·7 = 100, and for the price series 3*d.* = 100. (The price data here used are the retail price of Lever Bros.' 'Sunlight' per 'lb.' bar, kindly supplied by Unilever Ltd.) These indexes are graphed in the accompanying Fig. 10. It is to be emphasized that the positions of the two graphs relative to each other depends entirely on the choice of bases.

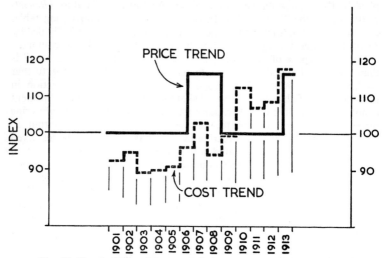

Fig. 10. Trend of Soap Prices in Relation to Trend of Costs: 1901-13

3. The calculation suggests that costs were indeed low in the period of 'frenzied competition', 1903-5/6, as suggested in the last paragraph of the text of the preceding chapter. By the same token, however, one might conclude from the graph at first glance that soap was sold at less than cost in the years 1910-12/13. This, however, does not follow. First, as already stated, the position of the graphs relative to each other depends on the choice of bases, and this is in the last analysis arbitrary. (However, for the reasons advanced above I believe myself that the choice of 1909 is reasonable.) Second, as publicized by the *Daily Mail* press campaign referred to in the next chapter, the 'one lb.' bar of soap was reduced to 15 oz. with the rise in the prices of oils and fats in the latter months of 1906, and this expedient could doubtless have been resorted to again. Third, the extent of the rise in the prices of oils and fats during and after 1906 (resulting from the increased demands of the margarine industry, referred to in the next chapter) varied—see the much greater relative rise in copra in the table. The possibilities of substitution in favour of the relatively cheaper oils and fats are not taken into account in the above calculation. For these reasons, despite the trends shown in the graph, soap was doubtless produced at some profit in this period. It is significant, however, that Mr. Wilson's account of Lever Bros. during the period 1906-14 (Part II of the Volume) is entitled 'The Difficult Years'; that dividends on the Preference capital in 1909 were able to be met only from the profits of the Associated Companies overseas (Wilson, i, 110); and more such in similar vein.

CHAPTER 7

THE LEVER COMBINATION MOVEMENT, 1906-21

THE dominant factor in the development of the British soap industry from about 1908 to the early 'twenties was the rapid growth in the extent of Lever's control within the industry. By purchase outright (or of majority share-holdings), he acquired one British soap business after another. The dimensions of this combination movement are indicated by the following. In 1905 the total sales of all soap products by Lever Bros. in the United Kingdom was 66,500 tons, or approximately 19·2 per cent. of the aggregate national consumption of all soap products. In 1914 the total sales in the United Kingdom of the Lever 'group'—i.e. companies wholly owned or controlled by Lever Bros. Ltd.—was of the order of 236,000 tons or 61 per cent. of the aggregate national consumption; and by the early 'twenties this proportion was nearer 70 per cent. (representing annual sales of the order of 260,000 tons in 1920-1), while the group's exports amounted to some 90 per cent. of the total export trade in soap.

With this, the competitive structure of the British soap industry had been transformed.

The causes of this development and the extent to which it was implicit (so to speak) in the developing situation of 1905-6 will now be examined.

THE ABORTIVE AMALGAMATION OF 1906

According to Mr. Wilson (i, 75) 'nothing is more probable' than that Lever had considered the possibility of combination in the soap trade as early as 1903, and primarily as a means by which selling costs (and particularly advertising expenditures) could be reduced to offset the high prices of raw material prevailing at the turn of the century. Subsequently prices fell, but as we have seen advertising became the more intense and lavish with resultant pressure on profits.

It is probable that an important determining factor in the desire for combination was a belief that the (long-run) industry demand for soap at this time was rather elastic—at least for a rise in price.

Certainly since the turn of the century, the aggregate consumption of soap products had ceased to expand at the (relatively) rapid rate of preceding decades (refer Table 2 above). And notwithstanding all the 'extravagant' advertising of the period, the consumption of soap products per head continued barely stationary; no doubt the fall in real wages after 1900[1] was the proximate cause of this. From all accounts of the period, it was becoming increasingly necessary for the housewife to prune her budget, and soap —still at the margin of necessities—was the sort of item likely to be among the first to be cut, and particularly in face of an increase in price.

In these circumstances, the situation described at the end of the preceding chapter was brought to a head by a rise in the prices of oils and fats in July 1906 unprecedented in its suddenness and magnitude (prices advanced by $33\frac{1}{3}$ per cent. to 50 per cent. and over). This rise was the beginning of a permanent readjustment of prices in the oils and fats market, the new factor in the situation being the rapid expansion in the margarine industry. (This provides an excellent example of the textbook 'external pecuniary diseconomy', shifting the cost curves of all firms in the soap and margarine industries bodily upwards.) The potential elasticity of the demand for soap, then, meant that this increase in raw material costs could not readily be passed on in the form of higher prices.

With this Lever revived his ideas on combination, and from July 1906 plans for an amalgamation of twenty of the leading soap firms—including Joseph Watson's, Gossage's, Crosfields', Christr. Thomas', Cook's and others—developed rapidly, with Lever and Joseph Watson (of Leeds) the principal architects. The amalgamation '. . . was to be achieved by a "working arragment" between soap makers based on an exchange of shares. Firms coming into such an arrangement would cease "frenzied advertising" but would in general retain control over the running of their own businesses.'[2] This summary of the objectives of the combine makes it quite clear where the economies, which were to offset the increased costs of raw materials without an advance in the price of soap, were to be sought, namely, in an all-round reduction of the costs of selling. It is worth noting that even Mr. Percy Redfern, contemporary historian

[1] The Wood index of Real Wages, previously referred to, declined 12 points (nearly 7 per cent.) from 1900 to 1905. The 1900 peak level was not recovered until the immediate post World War I years.
[2] Wilson, i, 76.

of the C.W.S., conceded the 'innocence' of the soap makers' motives 'in this case'.[1]

Mr. Wilson records Lever's private estimates of the economies which could be made as follows (i, 79):

		£
(1)	Advertising, at least	200,000
(2)	Increased profit by combined selling, at least £1 per ton	250,000
(3)	Benefits of combined buying of soda ash, sundry supplies, cardboxes, etc.	100,000
(4)	Benefits of combined buying of raw material, oils, tallow, etc.—not capable of estimation but certainly large	—
(5)	Economies in agents, travellers, travelling expenses, branch offices, management of salesmen and selling expenses generally, at least	100,000
(6)	Economies in manufacture, by centring certain soaps at certain works, and mutual helpfulness in reducing costs of manufacture, obtained by comparing methods of working; say 5s. per ton at least	50,000
	Actual Economies	£700,000

It is apparent at a glance that economies in selling dominate the picture. The meaning of item (2) is not immediately obvious, but doubtless the reference is to revenue lost by the competitive shading of wholesale prices. If that interpretation is correct, then it represents a 'cost' of competitive selling to the manufacturers, no less than items (1) and (5). These three items together amount to £550,000 of the total estimate of £700,000.

We may estimate the order of magnitude of these anticipated economies as follows. The wholesale price of household soap at this time was about £24 per ton. At this figure the manufacturers' total receipts for 225,000 tons[2] would be £5,400,000. The anticipated economies, in excess of £700,000 per annum, therefore, would amount to more than 13 per cent. of total revenue. The cost of

[1] P. Redfern, *The Story of the C.W.S., 1863-1913* (Manchester, 1913), p. 242.

[2] The expected combined weekly output was estimated by Lever at 4,500 tons—above 225,000 tons per annum.

oils and fats would be 70 per cent. of the latter (Table 4). Thus the proposed economies would enable an increase of nearly 20 per cent. (i.e. 13/70) in the cost of these raw materials to be absorbed without an increase in the price of soap (other costs, and the level of profits, remaining the same) in accordance with the professed objective of the amalgamation.

In the event, however, the scheme proved abortive. It is not necessary to dwell here on the famous campaign of 1906 in the press, principally the *Daily Mail*.[1] Ostensibly to protect the interests of the public but doubtless motivated in large measure by chagrin at the prospective loss of advertising revenue (Lever and Watson were actively engaged in reducing or cancelling advertising contracts throughout September), the *Daily Mail* launched a vitriolic attack on the 'soap trust'—as it chose to call the proposed combine—which was mainly directed under a thin disguise at Lever himself and his business. Other newspapers and publications joined in the attack. In November when the effect of the newspapers' attacks on the sales of the associated firms became very evident, all idea of the combine was finally abandoned.[2]

The final outcome was a court action for libel, brought by Lever against Lord Northcliffe, proprietor of the *Daily Mail*. In this Lever was successful, and the final damages awarded him— £91,000 from all the publications concerned—were 'enormous by contemporary standards'.

This, however, must have been small compensation for the difficulties of the next few years. From the beginning of the press attack there was a notable fall in the sales of Lever Bros.' products, principally 'Sunlight'. In November of 1906 sales were 60 per cent. below those for the same month in 1905; for the full year 1907, production at Port Sunlight was down to 46,000 tons—a reduction of 27 per cent. from the peak of 63,000 tons in 1905; by 1910 it had recovered to 53,000 tons but the 60,000 tons mark was not again exceeded until 1917.[3] The effects on other firms of the proposed combination, however, were uneven; Watson's also suffered

---

[1] See Wilson, i, 79-88, and Redfern, op. cit., pp. 242-3.

[2] At a meeting of 23 November. Mr. Redfern records that *Punch* duly printed a satirical epitaph:

> Stranger, please drop a tear upon the dust
> Of one that did spontaneously bust;
> Had I lived on, they would have killed me dead,
> So I committed suicide instead.

[3] Data from Wilson, i, 82.

a severe loss of sales, but Crossfield's and Gossage's scarcely at all.

It is thus not clear that this outcome was due only to the press attack, as is perhaps too readily assumed by Messrs. Wilson and Redfern. For in the event Lever did raise the price of 'Sunlight'—to $3\frac{1}{2}d$. at the end of October 1906—and this price was maintained until January 1909.[1] There is no evidence as to whether the other soap manufacturers followed suit. But some of them, at all events, might well not have done so, because 'good fellowship' in the soap trade was pretty clearly at its lowest ebb in the period following the failure of the amalgamation. This then would go far to explain the notable falling off in Lever Bros.' sales.

GROWTH OF C.W.S. SOAP PRODUCTION

Of even greater significance is the fact that the sales of C.W.S. products received an impetus from the press attacks on the so-called 'soap trust', which carried it to the first rank as a competitor in the soap industry.

We have already noted above the beginnings of C.W.S. soap production, and the establishment of the factory at Irlam in 1895. During the following ten years, the production of soap products at Irlam increased from an average of 72 tons to 265 tons per week,[2] the latter representing an annual rate of production of the order of 14,000 tons. With the press attacks on the 'private' soap makers in 1906, 'a demand for C.W.S. soaps arose hitherto unheard of. . . . The Irlam works ran every available machine night and day, and then could hardly meet it. The maximum weekly output jumped to 660 tons . . .'[3] representing an annual rate of production of the order of 34,000 tons. (This provides a striking illustration of the flexibility of the short-run limits of 'capacity' of a given plant; see above, pp. 63-64.) The C.W.S. proceeded to build two new factories, one at Silvertown, London, and the other at Dunston, near Newcastle-on-Tyne. Thus by 1909-10, the soap manufacturing capacity of the C.W.S. was in excess of 40,000 tons annually.

[1] See Appendix 2 to the preceding chapter. (Precise data as to the retail price of 'Sunlight' has been kindly supplied to the writer by Unilever Ltd.)

[2] Redfern, op. cit., p. 241.

[3] Redfern, op. cit., p. 243. The *Grocer* for March 1907 reported: 'This diversion of the soap-trade from ordinary channels will be regretted by all interested in the success of private enterprise; . . . the soap manufacturers concerned will find it difficult to recover the trade they have lost and which the C.W.S. has gained.' The substantial truth of this prognosis is borne out by the figures already given above for the sales of Lever Bros.' products (and see following).

TABLE 5

Co-operative Wholesale Society:
Sales of all Soap Products
(Tons)

Year	Volume of Sales
1905	14,000
1908-10	26,000
1920	43,186
1923	39,812
1926	43,031
1929	53,000
1935	49,791
1938	55,880
1939	58,835
1951*	29,145
1954*	31,000
1955*	31,500

Source: Data kindly supplied by the Society.
* Includes soapless detergents (powder and liquid) as follows: 1951—n.a.; 1954—5,900; 1955—4,500 tons.

It was not for nearly a decade, however, that the C.W.S. achieved an actual volume of sales commensurate with this capacity. As Mr. Redfern puts it, after Lever Bros. and the other firms of the abortive combination had been '. . . restored to respect [by the successful Court action] and congratulated by a press and public that previously had joined in the hunt, . . . [these] firms naturally put forth unusual efforts to regain the lost trade'.[1] Thus after the artificial heights of 1906-7, sales of C.W.S. own-manufactured soap products, in the face of a resurgence of coupon schemes and other inducements to buy, steadied at a level of the order of 26,000 tons annually (Table 5)—which nevertheless represented nearly a doubling of sales as compared with 1905.

But according to the C.W.S. Committee, the total sales of soap products through co-operative stores amounted to the order of 42,000 tons in 1909. From this date, then, the Committee of the C.W.S. resolved to attack the share of the co-operative trade supplied by the private soap makers, and amounting to some 16,000 tons of soap products. With the failure of a court action brought by Lever Bros. in 1910, seeking to enforce co-operative stores to sell Lever products,[2] large numbers of these stores discontinued selling the products of the private makers.

With this the competition of the C.W.S., backed up as it was by appeals to working-class ideology, became formidable indeed. Each

[1] Redfern, op. cit., p. 245.   [2] For details, see Redfern, op. cit., pp. 245-51.

of Lever's national brands was matched by a comparable C.W.S. product—'C.W.S. Flakes' to match 'Lux', C.W.S. 'Parrot Brand' scouring soap to match Lever's 'Monkey Brand', and so on; and wherever possible inquiries for the Lever, or other private, products were diverted to the comparable C.W.S. product. By the early 1920's, C.W.S. sales in England were in excess of 40,000 tons annually, or fully two-thirds of the production of Lever products at Port Sunlight—a further increase of more than 50 per cent. on the level of C.W.S. sales in 1909-10.

Moreover, like Lever's, the C.W.S. was actively engaged in the search for raw material in Africa. And as early as 1897 a permanent C.W.S. representative had been placed in Sydney (Australia), where 'as a sequel to the direct purchasing so begun, a small factory for receiving, refining and exporting coconut oil and tallow was purchased at the end of April 1901; Fiji subsequently being explored by the C.W.S. Sydney representative in the quest of copra . . . [indeed] no vegetable oil-producing country was, in 1913, escaping the survey of the Society'.[1]

Here, then, was a formidable competitor whom Lever could never hope to buy out.

THE LEVER COMBINATION MOVEMENT, 1907-1921

The voluntary amalgamation of 1906 had failed; but the problems of excessive competition in the sale of soap, the increased prices for oils and fats, and the long-run elasticity in the demand for soap, remained. In these circumstances (and for another reason shortly to be examined) some measure of combination in the soap industry seems to have been inevitable. And combination there was. But its ultimate limits—that it was carried so far—can surely be explained only in terms of the particular factor, namely, the generous business horizons and commercial genius of Lever himself.

From 1906 on, Lever began to acquire existing British soap businesses at an ever-increasing rate. The first acquisitions in 1906 were, as Mr. Wilson puts it, 'more or less involuntary'. These were Hodgson & Simpson's of Wakefield and the Vinolia Company (toilet soap). Lever had purchased these companies as part of the plan for the 1906 amalgamation, and was left with them on his hands when the negotiations broke down. However, they were put to good use: the first as a means of breaking into the market for ordinary

---

[1] Redfern, op. cit., p. 244.

bar soaps (particularly the export trade, largely the province of Crosfield's and Gossage's) and the second for entering the toilet soap market (i, 78, 119-20). Next, in 1908, the Hudson soap powder business was acquired. (As early as 1900 Lever had sought to introduce a soap powder, a powdered version of 'Lifebuoy'. It had been energetically pushed for some years, but had never been successful. Mr. Wilson writes (i, 57) '. . . Lever never knew why. Probably the answer was that housewives had bought Hudson's for seventy years and meant to go on buying it, no matter what Lever Brothers did.' This is a very good example of the difficulty of entering an established market without major innovation.)

In 1910, Lever Bros. acquired Barrington's of Dublin and Tyson's of Liverpool, and also the larger firms of Cook's, in London, and Christr. Thomas's in Bristol. In 1911 Hazlehurst's was added to the list; and in 1912-13 Lever acquired a 'substantial holding' in two of his largest rivals—Joseph Watson's of Leeds and John Knight's of London. Thus at the outbreak of World War I Lever's through wholly-owned or associated companies controlled (as previously stated) some 60 per cent. of the total production of soap for the home market.

During the war the process continued. In 1917 the remaining shares in Joseph Watson's were acquired, and also a half-interest in 'Crossage's' (as the combined business of Gossage's and Crosfield's, both of which firms had been acquired by Brunner Mond & Co. in 1911, had come to be known). In October 1919 the remaining interest in Crossage's was purchased, and Knight's in April 1920. Other firms, including the old-established soap and candle firm of Price's of London were also added in this year.

At this point no soap manufacturer of any consequence, with the important exception, of course, of the C.W.S., remained outside the combination.

The causes of the development thus briefly summarized, apart from Lever's own imperial designs, were three.

First, the objective of the abortive 1906 amalgamation, namely, to restrain excessive competition and by thus reducing selling costs to absorb the increased cost of oils and fats without a significant advance in the price of soap, still stood. Indeed personal animosities had been sharpened by the unequal incidence of the losses

incurred at that time, and competition in the industry was, if anything, more virulent than ever.

Second, sales of Lever Bros.' products, and particularly 'Sunlight',
the foundation of the business, had shrunk significantly, as we have
seen; and the lost ground seemed virtually impossible to recover.
The loss was particularly severe in London. To take over other
existing businesses and their 'goodwill' or sales connexions with
them (and in cases of inefficiency transferring part, or all, of the
production to the idle capacity of Port Sunlight) was the only way
to recover the lost ground.

These two objectives—to limit competition and to restore lost
sales—were undoubtedly uppermost in the acquisition of the
business of Cook's, Knight's, Christr. Thomas's and Watson's.
Knight's first, and Cook's, a close second, were Lever's leading
rivals in the London market; while Watson's had been, all along,
the chief imitator of Lever's own selling methods, and therefore a
leading force in the 'build-up' of selling expenditures in the markets
of north-east England, where that firm had long ruled. The acquisition of Christr. Thomas's of Bristol, on the other hand, served
primarily to give Lever access to the widespread West Country
connexions of that firm.[1]

In the third place, however, there was another cause which may
well have led to a measure of combination in the soap industry
even in the absence of excessive competition and the rise in prices
in the oils and fats market. This was the growing control of Brunner
Mond & Co., the large chemical firm, over the supply of soda ash
for the manufacture of alkali, the secondary but indispensable raw
material in the manufacture of soap.[2]

Brunner Mond presented a twofold threat to the Lever business.
First, as the dominant single seller in the alkali market, it was in a
position to dictate terms to the divided soap manufacturers. The latter
were obliged to enter into exclusive-purchase contracts running for

---

[1] Wilson, i, 118.

[2] The firm of Brunner Mond was founded in 1881, to exploit the new Solway
(ammonia-soda) process for the manufacture of soda ash—a major innovation in
technique designed to replace the Leblanc process referred to above (p. 133). Such
was the superiority of the Solway process that Brunner Mond rapidly appropriated
a dominant share of the trade in soda ash, and maintained this position thereafter.
(In 1925 Brunner Mond merged with the United Alkali Company—formed by an
amalgamation in 1890 of fifty-one of the Leblanc firms—to form Imperial Chemical
Industries Ltd.) This account is based on (1) *Centenary of the Alkali Industry*, 1924
(issued by the United Alkali Co.); (2) P. Fitzgerald, *Industrial Combination in England*,
London, 1927, pp. 79-81.

a period of years. And the contracts included other terms—for example, the 1907 contract with Lever strictly bound the latter not to go into caustic manufacture (earlier, in 1904, at the renewal of the contract Lever had been obliged to sell to Brunner's a caustic plant he had installed), but there was nothing to prevent Brunner Mond from taking up soap manufacture.[1]

This then was the second danger: that Brunner Mond, which was allied to Crosfield's of Warrington, one of Lever's principal competitors, should itself enter the soap business (either in association with Crosfield or independently) as 'the most powerful of all competitors'.

On both these counts there was an incentive to an entrepreneur of Lever's stature to build up a position of strength in the soap industry, comparable to Brunner Mond's in the alkali industry. In this light the development of the Lever combine takes on an air of inevitability, quite apart from the other determining factors in the situation. When, subsequently, the struggle for position with Brunner Mond extended from the market for alkali to that for oils and fats themselves,[2] Lever in acting for his own interest was, in effect, acting to protect the interests of the soap industry as a whole. In these circumstances it is reasonable to assume that the lesser soap makers of England were not at all unwilling to enter the Lever 'family', and this no doubt greatly facilitated the formation of the combination.

STRUCTURE OF THE BRITISH SOAP INDUSTRY, 1920-1

By 1920 (as previously stated) the Lever combination embraced all the leading soap manufacturers of the kingdom apart, of course, from the C.W.S. The resulting structure of the British soap industry about 1920-1 may be described as follows:

(i) The aggregate annual production of all soap products in the United Kingdom at this date was of the order of 450,000 tons. Of this total, the traditional household bar soap made up some 70 per cent.; thus it was still, as it had long been, the staple product of the

[1] Wilson, i, 126.

[2] This latter threat related to the new 'hydrogenation' process, by which certain oils quite useless in their natural state for soap or margarine manufacture, could be 'hardened' by causing them to combine with hydrogen (hence, hydrogenation) and thus converted into useful fatty raw materials. The soap firm Crosfield's had acquired an alleged master patent for the process; so that when in 1911 Brunner Mond in the course of the conflict with Lever purchased the capital of Crosfield's (also Gossage's), Brunner's not only became thereby direct competitors in soap itself, but bid fair to monopolize the supply of hardened fats. Lever in the end successfully met this challenge, but litigation on this and related issues did not end till 1919. (Wilson, i, 127-34, 245-6.)

industry. (Subsequently, the relative importance of household bar soap in the total output of the industry was to decline appreciably, to be replaced by the relatively more expensive soap powders.)

Of this total production, about 16 per cent.—or an annual rate of more than 70,000 tons—was exported. These exports consisted predominantly of household bar soap. (Retained imports were small, amounting to about $2\frac{1}{2}$ per cent. of the aggregate U.K. consumption.)

(ii) This output was produced by 220 'firms' in the United Kingdom, counting all businesses with a distinct legal identity as separate firms.[1] Most of these were specialist soap (and candle) manufacturers. Many were very small indeed: some produced for limited local markets; others were speciality producers of textile (industrial) soaps. Some were manufacturers of toilet preparations, who also produced a toilet soap using 'neat' soap stock purchased from other soap manufacturers. The scope for variations in the scenting and colouring of toilet soaps is endless, and there have always been a great variety of them to suit the whims of taste of relatively small numbers of consumers.

Now of these 220 soap makers, ninety were members of the United Kingdom Soap Manufacturers' Association (U.K.S.M.A.).

The aggregate output of these ninety firms amounted to about 80 per cent. of the total British production.[2]

(iii) Of these ninety members of the Association, thirty-seven were members (owned wholly or in part) of the Lever group. The combined output of these firms (including, of course, Lever Bros. Ltd., itself) amounted to about 90 per cent. of the aggregate output of members of the Association, or about 70-75 per cent. of the total British production.[2]

In the export trade, member firms of the Lever group were predominant, contributing about 90 per cent. of the total exports of soap products. Gossage's alone supplied perhaps 50 per cent. of the total trade, and Crosfield's 16 per cent. It would be quite wrong, however, to suggest that there was any unified control, or even unanimity of policy, in the 'Lever' export business; as Mr. Wilson has recorded it, 'the traditional rivalry between the three biggest exporters

---

[1] See *Report of the Soap Industry*, 1921 (Cmd. 1126), p. 6. (This Report was prepared by a sub-Committee of the Standing Committee on Trusts established under the Profiteering Acts, 1919 and 1920. The Chairman of this particular sub-committee was Sir William Beveridge.)

[2] Ibid.

in the family—Lever's, Crosfield's, and Gossage's—died hard'.[1]

It follows then that the share of the Lever group in the aggregate consumption of all soap products at home—a total of about 390,000 tons annually including imports—was about 67 per cent., representing a volume of sales of the order of 260,000 tons per annum.[2]

In each of the five main product-divisions of the market, namely household bar soap, soap powders and flakes, toilet soaps, scouring soaps, and soft soaps, the output of member-firms of the Lever group predominated. (In the soap powder market, the dominant position of the group was due to the early purchase by Lever of the Hudson soap powder business, referred to above.)

(iv) Apart from the Lever group and the other members of the U.K.S.M.A., there were 130 independent firms outside the Association producing 20 per cent. of the total British output—about 90,000 tons annually at this time. Most of these 'firms' were very small indeed. The one large firm among them (of course) was the C.W.S., whose output in 1921 was about 42,000 tons or 10·8 per cent. of the aggregate annual consumption of soap products at home.

(v) Finally, it is to be noted that it was one of the declared objects of the U.K.S.M.A. as at this time 'to maintain the minimum net prices and conditions at and upon which . . . soaps are offered and sold' in the home market.[3] Minimum prices, both manufacturers' and retail, were fixed by three Committees of the Association (each of seven members)—for hard soap, toilet soap, and soft soap,

---

[1] Wilson, ii, 303. Quite apart from the export division, very little was done until the nineteen-thirties to rationalize the production and selling organizations of the component firms of the Combination. Indeed the competition of the various firms continued, within its framework, very much as it had always been. The Government Committee of Inquiry expressed itself as follows:

We think we are justified in recording our impression, gathered from the testimony of competent witnesses, that, although the acquired companies have the benefit of the advice of Lever Bros.' experts and of their laboratory, they nevertheless, generally speaking, have continued their individual organizations and have effected little or no economy in any of the items which go to make up the cost of the manufacture of soap. The same works are generally continued under the same management, the existing titles and goodwill are maintained, necessitating separate travellers, advertising, and distribution. . . . (*Report*, Cmd. 1126, p. 13).

The statement of the Committee may be compared with Lever's own statement at the annual meeting of Lever Bros. on 10 April 1924, that not only did each of the Associated Companies have its own board of directors, but 'all are in the closest competition with one another'. 'That', he added, 'was the only way the string of the bow was kept tight.' This sort of statement, one might venture to remark, is not untypical of the 'founder mentality' of great entrepreneurs, who are frequently little prepared for the exploitation of the economy of the businesses they create.

[2] i.e. 72 per cent. (between 70-75—see penultimate paragraph) of 450,000 tons (total production), less 90 per cent. of the total export of about 70,000 tons.

[3] *Report*, Cmd. 1126, pp. 4-5.

respectively. The minimum prices were binding on all members of the Association with these reservations: (*a*) proprietary brands or 'specialities' were not included; (*b*) no decision of a Committee was binding unless adopted *unanimously* by the members present when the resolution was passed.

It was argued before the 1921 Committee of Inquiry that this requirement of unanimity prevented the Lever group dominating the Association, and 'safeguarded the interests of the independent and small manufacturers'. Certainly if there had been some large firms among the fifty in the Association which were not members of the Lever group, this requirement would have given plenty of scope for wranglings along the pattern of the old Soap Makers' Association. In fact, however, the mean output (per firm) of these fifty firms was less than 1,000 tons per annum so that should any one of them consistently resist the wishes of the Lever group it could no doubt easily be bought, or driven, out of the trade. If willy-nilly one or a number should hang on, then the Lever group—outside the Association—could set its own prices for the 90 per cent. of the output of the Association it controlled, while meeting the lower prices of the dissentients only in the latter's own (relatively minute) markets. One can only agree, therefore, with the Committee's conclusion (p. 6) that

We find it difficult to believe . . . that an independent [i.e. non-Lever but within the Association] manufacturer could, for any considerable period, prevent the definite and considered wishes of the Lever combine from being put into effect.

More significant, perhaps, was the fact that the U.K.S.M.A.'s formal price fixing did not cover proprietary brands or specialities. This no doubt did give some opportunity to individualists within the Lever group (including Lever himself) to 'paddle their own canoes' upon occasion.

In fine, however, it seems clear that the formal price-fixing machinery of the U.K.S.M.A. was merely a substitute for the lack of such an organization within the as yet but loosely-federated Lever concern itself. It was therefore only the logical conclusion of this when Lever Bros. withdrew from the Association altogether in 1927. Clearly, the Lever group—so long as it was possible to discipline its own members—could fix its own price; but at what level in the not-so-long long run depended, as always, on the competition of the C.W.S. and such other competitors as should arise, or threaten to arise, from time to time.

CHAPTER 8

THE SOAP INDUSTRY WITH ONE DOMINANT SELLER

BY the beginning of the decade of the 'twenties the British soap industry had been transformed from the fiercely competitive industry of the early nineteen-hundreds into an industry dominated by a massive, albeit loosely-federated, combination of the leading firms. The question immediately arises as to whether, and to what extent, the dominant position of the Lever group was, or could be, exploited to fix prices in excess of a 'reasonable' level.

This is ultimately a question of the degree to which entry into the industry remained free and relatively easy. This was, more or less, the case.[1] And thus, while it is certain that at least in the abnormal conditions of the immediate post-World War I years,[2] the Lever group did succeed in exploiting its market control to maintain the price of soap too high; yet notwithstanding that control, it remained subject to real and formidable competition, as events in the inter-war period amply show.

In this chapter the course of the development until 1929 will be reviewed, and in the next the period of the 'thirties.

NEW COMPETITION—1921-5

It is important for a proper understanding of events in this period to realize that the businesses acquired by Lever Bros. Ltd. during World War I and the immediate post-war years were not confined to soap firms. Some of the most spectacular acquisitions were in the sphere of raw materials.[3] These included the Southern Whaling and

---

[1] The situation was thus akin to that noticed in Chapter 3, pp. 101-2, above, and that analysis is indeed suggestive in respect of the events of this period.

[2] With the cessation of hostilities in November 1918 there was an upsurge in business activity, with expectations everywhere sanguine as wartime controls were rapidly removed and normal business conditions restored after the restrictions and frustra-tions of the war years. The boom reached its high-point in the summer of 1920, after which there was a rapid collapse and the post-war depression of 1921-2. There followed the rather slow recovery and indifferent prosperity of the 'twenties.

[3] The objectives of Lever's raw material ventures were two. First, the demand for oils and fats—a derived demand from end products (soap, margarine, etc.) in rela-tively steady demand—was inelastic. It would appear that the purpose of Lever's early ventures (plantations in the Solomons and the Congo) was so to add to the marginal supply in the market as to ensure that prices would 'rule reasonably and in

Sealing Co. (based in South Georgia) to secure an annual supply of about 4,000 to 5,000 tons of whale oil for margarine manufacture;[1] the Barton & Waterhouse (of Hull) oil-milling business; and the mammoth Niger Company trading in West Africa.

The objective of the second of these purchases was to enter the oil-milling business.[2] This industry was a development of the long-established business of crushing oil seed for the manufacture of cattle cake. On the Continent the character of the milling industry had always been different; there seeds were crushed to obtain oils for the manufacture of margarine. During the war, however, supplies of West African oil seeds for crushing were diverted from Germany to England, while the demand in England for oils for margarine manufacture grew rapidly. As a result, the crushing of seeds for oil ('oil-milling') expanded greatly in England during the war. At the end of the war the largest firm in the industry was the British Oil and Cake Mills Ltd. (B.O.C.M.), a group formed by the amalgamation of a number of the leading oil-milling firms. There were other firms, including J. Bibby & Sons Ltd., of Liverpool, and the Olympia Oil & Cake Mill of Joseph Watson at Selby, Yorkshire. It was when Lever was outbid for the latter by Jurgens, the margarine manufacturers, that he acquired the smaller Barton & Waterhouse mill at Hull.

Here, then, was a group of well-established and able firms, handling a great variety of oil-bearing seeds, skilled in the trade in oils and fats, and already competitors of Lever Bros. in the manufacture of cattle cake—a subsidiary Lever product since 1896. Thus 'adjacent' to the soap industry both horizontally and vertically, these firms were potential competitors in a very real sense. And in 1921 this potential competition became actual.

The reason is not far to seek. There can be no reasonable doubt that following the reverse of the post-war boom in mid-1920 the

his favour'. (Wilson, i, 184). Apparently Lever had always been suspicious of 'combines' and 'rings' among the oils and fats dealers—i, 159. But these fears were largely groundless. Thus another sub-Committee of the Committee on Trusts inquired into this trade in 1919-20, and concluded that 'the possibility of a corner in any particular oil or seed by any one group has been carefully considered, and we are of the opinion that this would be impracticable. . . . There is no sign of any monopoly in the trade.' *Oils Fats and Margarine Trades* (Cmd. 982, 1920. p. 5). Second, there was the object of ultimate complete vertical integration—to secure a supply from wholly-owned sources sufficient to meet all the requirements of the Company. In the event Lever did not succeed in attaining either objective.

[1] Lever Bros. entered the margarine business with 'Planter' brand margarine early in the war. Wilson, i, Ch. XVI.
[2] This paragraph is based on Wilson, i, 245, 278-9.

Lever group exploited its quasi-monopolistic control over the manufacture and sale of soap to maintain prices too high in relation to
costs.

The evidence of the Government Committee of Inquiry, previously
referred to, is conclusive. On the basis of data supplied by the
manufacturers themselves, the Committee found that the 'cost' of
best-quality household soap in December 1920, with the retail price
of the product at 11*d*. per lb., was £22 19*s*. per ton (or about 2·45*d*.
per lb.) less than when the price was first raised to 11*d*. in August
1919.[1] Alternatively the Committee showed that, calculating the
cost of production on the basis proposed in a memorandum of
1918 by the Soap Makers' Federation,[2] the cost per ton in December
1920 was £5 7*s*. 4*d*. per ton less than the Federation's cost figure
submitted to justify a price of 9*d*. On either basis, the Committee
concluded (p. 12), the price of soap in December 1920 ought to
have been 'not more than 8½*d*. or 9*d*. per lb. instead of 11*d*.' If
this view is correct, then the price for some four or five months had
been maintained at a level 22-29 per cent. in excess of a reasonable
cost of production.

Was this gratuitous profit-taking merely, or were there more
definitive reasons for this high price policy? There appear to have
been two factors bearing on the case, the second of which was
indeed compelling.

First, there was the incidence of the wartime Excess Profits Tax,
still in force. In his evidence to the Committee of Inquiry, Lord
Leverhulme[3] himself argued as follows. After the decontrol of oils
and fats, prices rose steeply[4] and profits increased because of the

[1] *Report*, Cmd. 1126, p. 11 and Appendix C(1).

[2] A temporary body founded during the war at the request of the Government to
allocate raw materials released by the Ministry of Food for soap making.

[3] Lever was raised to the peerage in June 1917.

[4] Oils and fats were decontrolled in March 1919. The prices of certain oils and fats
(as recorded in the Committee's *Report*, p. 11) in June 1914 ('pre-war normal') and
on 14 August 1919 (the date when the retail price of best household soap was first
raised to 11*d*.) were as follows (£'s per ton):

	Australian Tallow	Lagos Palm Oil	Palm Kernel Oil
June 1914	36	28·5	39
14 August 1919	105	90	103

The highest and lowest points of the market up till November 1920 were as follows:

	Australian Tallow	Lagos Palm Oil	Palm Kernel Oil
February 1920	108	98	115
19 July 1920	68	53	65

policy of basing the price of soap on replacement costs. This policy, however, had been abandoned when prices began to fall, because, Leverhulme claimed, Excess Profits Duty had absorbed profits which would otherwise have been available to meet raw material losses.[1] The argument amounts to this, that the profits of the boom were mainly the effect of stock appreciation; that in the absence of the Excess Profits Duty they would have been largely absorbed in maintaining the existing scale of operations; and that again in the absence of the Duty, they would merely have offset the corresponding losses when prices fell. Whatever the merits of the argument, it did mean that the Excess Profits Duty was being passed on to the then current consumers of soap, and that the Lever combine did have the power to set prices 'to suit themselves'—at least, for a season.

In the second place, however, it would appear to be beyond doubt that soap profits at this time were being used to offset severe losses elsewhere in the Company's operations, and to relieve the very great financial strain of over-sanguine expansion in the immediate post-war years.[2] Only in terms of this pressure, I believe, can the failure to reduce the prices of Lever soaps in the latter part of 1920 be explained. Thus it may be that Leverhulme was speaking with his tongue in his cheek when he argued emphatically to the Committee of Inquiry that new competition—home production or imports—would soon frustrate any attempt to charge excessive prices; but I do not think so. He can only have been too well aware of the strength of his competitors overseas, particularly Procter & Gamble and Colgate-Palmolive in the United States. And it would surely be an insult to his rare business insight to suggest that he could be unaware of the potential threat of new competition at home from the oil millers, the margarine manufacturers, and other kindred trades, particularly in view of his own incursions into those fields. Only the dire necessity to maintain soap profits in view of

[1] *Report*, Cmd. 1126, p. 12.
[2] Cf. Wilson, i, 262-3, 279. The West African Niger Company, for example, was purchased precipitately early in 1920 only for a price of £8·5m to be paid in cash (not in Lever Bros.' preference shares like most of the other acquisitions) by 1 July. Meanwhile, the boom collapsed, and the Niger Company was involved in heavy losses on its large stocks of oils and fats. To add to the difficulty, the Company's overdraft of £2m—discovered (apparently) only after the purchase!—had also to be repaid. Again, with the cessation of rationing at the end of the war, and butter again plentiful, losses were incurred on Lever Bros.' wartime margarine product, 'Planter'. On top of all, money had to be found to meet the dividends of the large volume of preference capital issued in acquiring the group companies.

the financial straits of the company, so it seems to me, could have induced Leverhulme to take the calculated risk of maintaining the price of soap at this time at a level clearly in excess of the cost of production.

Both Leverhulme's assertion that in the event that the price was excessive new competition would emerge, and the Committee's contention that the price *was* excessive, were speedily verified when in 1921 new competition in fact materialized.

Early in that year two of the largest of the oil-milling firms, namely the British Oils and Cake Mills (B.O.C.M.) group, and J. Bibby & Sons of Liverpool, began the manufacture of soap.

The competition of the B.O.C.M. was apparently the more effective, at least initially. It set up a new company, the British Soap Company, and produced a soap called 'New Pin' 'very much on the lines of "Sunlight" itself'.[1] The new product was intensively advertised throughout the country, with a lavish gift scheme (in return for soap coupons) on the old familiar pattern.

The sales of 'New Pin' amounted to but 3,000 to 4,000 tons in 1922; in 1923 they leapt to over 21,000 tons. The retail price of 'Sunlight', which had been reduced from the 11*d*. of 1920 to 10*d*. in January and to 8½*d*. per lb. in April 1921, was further reduced to 7*d*. in January 1922 and to 6½*d*. in October of that year. That this reduction in the price by nearly 25 per cent. in the first ten months of 1922 was precipitated by the growing competition of 'New Pin' and Bibby soap cannot be doubted; though a reduction of this, or an even greater, order seems to have been indicated by trends in the level of costs—see Fig. 12 (below, p. 185) and Table 9 (appendix to this chapter). The sales of 'New Pin' continued to grow and amounted to 34,000 in 1922. One can gauge the effectiveness of the competition of 'New Pin' from this, that in the same year the sales of 'Sunlight,' against which brand it was principally directed, could not have exceeded 40,000 to 45,000 tons; and the volume of 'New Pin' sales amounted to nearly 13 per cent. of the total United Kingdom consumption of all grades of household bar soap.

Three comments on this development need to be made here. First, in a limited way this transfer of the active competitive leadership in the British soap industry from the Lever colossus (or rather, from

[1] Wilson, i, 279. (Data as to the sales of 'New Pin' in the following account, from this reference.)

any one of its constituent firms, most of which, as we have seen, still retained their separate legal identities and competed relatively freely with one another) to the ebullient British Soap Company of the B.O.C.M., provides an illustration of that 'passing to and fro' of the industrial leadership which, as argued above, is of the essence of competition in practice. In this case, however, the new 'leader' firm was also an entirely new firm.

Second, it is again necessary to refer to the position argued above, that in the absence of major innovation, to force an entry—and to appropriate a significant share of the market—is normally very difficult. For in the case of 'New Pin' there was no innovation: the product was, as already stated, very similar to 'Sunlight' itself, and the methods of selling were those characteristic of the industry. Yet by 1925 it had appropriated some 13 per cent. of the market for household hard soap, and a much larger share of the market for strictly comparable products. This seeming conflict is, however, easily resolved.

In the proposition that entry is difficult, 'normally' implies not only that conditions are settled (more or less), but that the price is in a proper relation to the cost of efficient production; and further it is presumed that all the competitors in the field seek actively to maintain the overall balance of competitive persuasion brought to bear on the consumer.[1]

Now in the present instance, it is indeed true that conditions were settled (no innovation, and known methods of production more or less fully exploited). But, as we have seen, the prices of Lever soaps were initially too high, and the Government Committee of Inquiry had publicized this circumstance. And in the second place, the selling methods—and particularly the lavish prize schemes—of the manufacturers of 'New Pin' were not fully matched by the Lever companies. To put an end to prize schemes, which had become in the early days such an intolerable burden on the industry, had been a primary objective of Leverhulme's policy since 1906; he was determined to prevent so far as possible their reappearance now. To this end, there were in the latter months of 1924 long negotiations between Lever Bros. and the British Soap Company; but they proved abortive.[2] The 'New Pin' prize schemes continued, and were countered only tardily and with half-measures from the Lever companies.

[1] Cf. Chapter 2, pp. 37, 33-35, above.   [2] Wilson, i, 280.

The third comment is this. The setting up of additional capacity on such a scale by this, and the other, new firms, and largely consequent upon the early (short-run) exploitation of its market control by the Lever combination, undoubtedly contributed to the excess of productive capacity which would seem to have become more or less chronic in the industry.[1] By 1924 recovery from the slump of 1921-2 was well advanced, but the Report on the 'Soap, Candles, and Glycerine Trade', of the third Census of Production (1924) gives the following figures:

Year	Proportion of actual output to Maximum Capacity*
1907	58%
1912	64%
1924	63%

* Firms furnishing information

That the basic plant in the trade—the array of soap kettles for boiling the neat soap—is very long-lived was, of course, a particular contributary factor.

The new competition of the oil-milling firms in the market for household hard soap was not the only challenge to the Lever group in this period. In the toilet soap sector of the market new competition from abroad was soon making itself felt.

Lever's with the early acquisition of the Vinolia Company (1906) and subsequently also the business of A. & F. Pears and D. & W. Gibbs, were no less dominant in the market for toilet soaps than in the market for household soaps. Early in 1923, however, this position was challenged by the Palmolive Company of the United States of America with their green toilet soap 'Palmolive'.[2] This, it would appear, was the first incursion by the dominant American soap makers into the British market. So seriously was this new competition regarded, that by 1924 Lever Bros. had developed a green soap of their own, 'Olva', as similar to Palmolive in appearance as possible. This is a good example of the efforts of a competitor to 'match' the product variant and selling line of a rival.[3]

---

[1] Cf. pp. 101-2, above.   [2] Wilson, i, 280.

[3] Cf. above, p. 37. Mr. Wilson writes that the Palmolive Company 'made great, play [in their advertising] with the name and the ingredients [Palm and Olive Oil] and in 1923 Leverhulme was writing angrily of 'the pretentious claim of the Palmolive people to a monopoly of the words Palm and Olive Oil'. In their turn, the Palmolive

The gains of the imported toilet soaps, and Palmolive chiefly among them, are evidenced by the following data of imports and exports of toilet soap in this period.

TABLE 6

Toilet Soap: Exports and Imports,
Great Britain, 1920-4

Year	Exports	Imports
	(cwt.)	
1920	147,800	9,700
1921	33,800	19,200
1922	56,900	41,600
1923	60,100	71,900
1924	67,000	65,000

Source: Annual Statements of the Trade of the United Kingdom.

The period covers a peak cyclical year (1920), followed by recession and slump, and recovery in 1923 and 1924. Despite this imports increased notably through 1923, and declined in 1924, by which date a more proper relation of price to cost would appear to have been restored and Lever's with 'Olva' were vigorously countering this new competition.

From the Census Report of 1924 we have also the data in Table 7.

TABLE 7

Exports, Imports, and Home Consumption of Soap,
Great Britain, 1924

Product	Exports	(Tons) Imports	Home Consumption	% Share of home market supplied by British Producers
Household Soap	67,100	6,800	264,350	97·4
Toilet Soap	3,350	3,250	24,650	86·8
All Soap, exc. Toilet Soap	73,350	10,100	385,250	97·4

Source: Census of Production, 1924.

Thus in the case of household soap (and other soaps apart from toilet) where new competition developed at home, the traditional dominance of home producers was maintained, with exports exceeding imports some tenfold and the latter accounting for only 2·6 per cent. of the national consumption. With toilet soaps imports in this year were nearly equal to exports and accounted

'people' complained that the marketing of 'Olva', so similar to their own product was 'not entirely ethical' (i, 281). The late Mr. L. P. James, founder and proprietor of the British Hydrological Corporation, who was employed in the sales dept. of Lever Bros. at this time, has entertained the writer with many anecdotes concerning the rivalry in the field of the two companies' salesmen during this period.

for 13·2 per cent. of the national consumption. The only other year for which comparable data are available is the early pre-war Census year 1907. In that year exports of toilet soaps were nearly three times as large as imports with the latter accounting for 7 per cent. of the national consumption; while in the case of household soap, exports exceeded imports fivefold, with imports 4·5 per cent. of the national consumption. (It is perhaps worth emphasizing that the efficacy of overseas competition cannot be gauged adequately from data of the relative magnitude of imports in a single year. Like the extent of actual competition at home, the actual magnitude of imports may be low; this would give no indication of what the value ɔf imports *might* be if the price were excessive.)

Throughout this period of intense competition and counter-competition, the C.W.S., with the resources of the whole movement severely strained by the general collapse of prices in 1920-1, barely maintained its volume of sales. In 1920 the sales of C.W.S. soap products totalled 43,186 tons; in 1923 the total had fallen to 39,812 tons (above, Table 5). In 1924-5 to counter the advertising of the 'private' soap firms (particularly 'New Pin'), the C.W.S. itself embarked on prize-scheme advertising. A total of £10,000 in prizes was offered for the correct or nearest estimate of C.W.S. soap sales, the entries to be accompanied by numbers of coupons derived from the purchase of C.W.S. soaps.[1] According to Mr. Redfern, 'the scheme justified itself', but was not repeated in this form. Subsequently towels were offered in exchange for C.W.S. soap wrappers—the Committee now recognized that 'the days of unwrapped bars were past'—and this proved 'a more popular form of sales-stimulation'. At all events, with sales in 1926 at 43,031 tons, the 1920 situation had been restored.

It should be noticed, too, that it was during this period—in 1922 —that the C.W.S. first began to sell its soap products at fixed retail prices, nationally advertised.[2] Thus by the early 'twenties the Society had emerged as a national competitor of the private soap manufacturers in the fullest sense.

The position in 1924 and early 1925 is indicated by the second row of Table 8 on p. 183. The table sets out the volume of sales, and the percentage shares of the aggregate consumption of all

[1] P. Redfern, *The New History of the C.W.S.* (Manchester, 1938), pp. 364-5.
[2] Ibid., p. 282.

soap products of the three largest firms in certain years. The drift of the data for the interwar period as a whole is brought out in the associated Fig. 11.

Thus in 1924-5 the total sales of the Lever group had scarcely advanced, indeed had fallen a little, from the levels of 1920-1; a new competitor in the British Soap Company, and others (as Bibby's of Liverpool) less successful initially but ultimately to prove more tenacious, had emerged; the toilet soap market had been invaded by the powerful Palmolive Company of America; and the C.W.S., after a setback in 1922-3, had returned to the fray with a national sales policy similar to and scarcely less aggressive than the private soap makers' own. Moreover the relation of prices to the cost of production does not seem to have been too disparate by this time (see Fig. 12). Thus despite the dominant market position of the Lever group, it remained subject to real and effective competition.

C.W.S. COMPETITION—1925-9

But where one colossus controls so large a proportion of the supply of a commodity as did the Lever combine in soap, if there is not monopoly in the sense that the appearance of new competition can be actually prevented, yet the charge is frequently made (on the grounds that every man has his price) that such a firm has a virtual monopoly in that, with its great resources, if new competition does become effective it can always be 'bought out'. There is much substance in this view; but on the other hand, it does not take adequate account of the great variety of ways in which a challenge to the power of the established position may arise.

It is true that in the case of the British Soap Company, this is precisely what took place. The amalgamation of Lever Bros. and the B.O.C.M. was effected on 27 May 1925, when the former acquired all the ordinary share capital of B.O.C.M. in exchange for Lever Bros.' preference shares.[1] Immediately the 'New Pin' prize schemes were ended, and the threatened build-up of prize-scheme advertising was thus restrained. (The British Soap Company was then allowed to die, sales of 'New Pin' falling from the 34,000 tons of 1925 to 6,000 tons in 1928.)[2]

But the C.W.S. and other competitors, mostly small but lively, remained, and the monopolistic position of the combine was to this extent circumscribed. The C.W.S., ideologically opposed to the

[1] Wilson, i, 280. (Lord Leverhulme died about this time.)   [2] Ibid, p. 302.

private ownership of large aggregations of capital, was one competitor Lever Bros. could not buy out; and, taking a long view, the existence of the C.W.S. as a competitor in the soap trade cannot be regarded as fortuitous.

Thus it can fairly be argued that the Co-operative movement in England (and elsewhere) came into being just because of the threat, real or imagined, to the consumer interest from the ever-increasing scale of modern industry. It was basically with the object of opposing the large, and hence strong, seller with a large, and also strong, buyer, that the Wholesale Co-operative Society was formed—'to combine the purchases of the retail co-operative stores, and thus to enable them to obtain goods as pure and as cheap as those who have the largest capital'.[1] The development of the large multiple and chain stores, of course, may be attributed to similar causes, and the effects are much the same;[2] indeed their relatively late emergence in Great Britain as compared with the United States of America was no doubt due in large measure to the very development of the C.W.S. in Britain early on.[3] But this well illustrates the variety of forms the challenge to the strong position of the established seller may take.

At all events, from 1925 onwards the competition of the C.W.S. made itself increasingly felt. It is possible that with the demise of the British Soap Company, the level of soap prices as fixed by the U.K.S.M.A. (that is, virtually, by Lever Bros.) continued firm somewhat above reasonable levels: see again Fig. 12 below. Certainly spokesmen for the C.W.S. would have it that way. Thus a delegate speaking for the Liverpool Society at the C.W.S. Financial General Meeting in April 1926 maintained that 'C.W.S. soap at that date was still £9 a ton cheaper [about 15 per cent. of the then current Association retail price of best quality hard soap] and 10 per cent. better in quality than that of certain other makers'.[4] Allowance must be made for the occasion, of course, and certainly the case requires careful assessment. In particular the structure of demand was changing significantly, as soap powders and flakes were increasingly substituted for hard soap in household use, and a variety

---

[1] From a letter of 23 January 1861 by one William E. Bond (quoted Redfern, *New History*, p. 18) which strikingly anticipated the actual C.W.S. which was born in 1863.

[2] Cf. P. W. S. Andrews, 'Competition in Retail Trade', *O.E.P.*, 1950.

[3] Cf. J. K. Galbraith, *American Capitalism* (London, 1952) p. 132.

[4] Redfern, *New History*, p. 363.

TABLE 8

British Soap Industry:
Volume of Sales (in 000 tons) and Market Shares (a) of the Principal Firms, Selected Years

Year	Lever Bros. & Associated Companies (later Unilever) Sales	%	British Soap Company (B.O.C.M.) Sales	%	Co-operative Wholesale Society Ltd. Sales	%	Thomas Hedley Ltd. Sales	%	Aggregate U.K. Consumption	Combined Share of the 'Big Three' %
c. 1921	260	67·0	(b)		42	10·8	(b)		390	77·8
1924-25	255	61·5	31	7·5	42	10·2	(b)		413	71·7 (79·2(c))
1929	260	60·0	(b)		53	12·2	(5)	(1·2)	434	72·2
1935	258	53·5	—		50	10·4	40	8·3	480	72·2
1938	263	51·5	—		56	11·0	70	13·7(d)	510	76·2
1954(e)	297	50·5	—		34	6·0	207	35·0	590(e)	91·5

Notes: (a) That is, volume of sales as percentage of the Aggregate Consumption shown in the last column but one.
(b) Negligible.
(c) Including British Soap Company.
(d) Sales of approximately 67,500 tons represented 15 per cent. share of 'Household' consumption, which totalled approx. 450,000 tons in 1938.
(e) Data in this row relate to U.K. 'Household' consumption (market). See n. 1, p. 240 below.

of other factors contributed to a lessened demand for the latter; thus a smaller production, more frequent and varied deliveries, and so on all possibly contributed to a relatively high price for household hard soap within the structure of soap prices.

At all events the C.W.S. rapidly expanded its sales of soap after 1925. From 1925 to 1929 the national consumption of all soap products in Great Britain rose by only 5 per cent., but sales of C.W.S. soaps increased by 25 per cent. (Table 5 above). A new factory adjacent to the original works at Irlam, 'with a roof garden

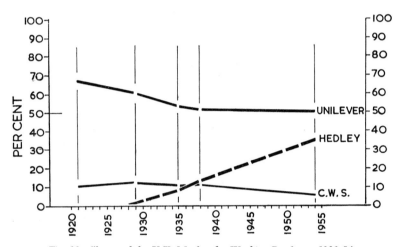

Fig. 11: Shares of the U.K. Market for Washing Products: 1921-54.
N.B. During the period, 1939-40 to 1949-50, these graphs have only notional significance, owing to the dislocation of production during the war years and the post-war shortage of oils and fats.

above it and a sports ground beside it', was opened on 27 July 1926; and in 1929 extensions were made to the factory at Silvertown, London (and again in 1935). At all the works, Irlam, Dunston, and Silvertown, 'much new machinery' was installed during this period, and amenities for the employees increased.[1]

Thus 'monopoly' in the soap trade was not to be permitted a quiet life. The effect on the Lever concern was to spur on, at long last, moves to effect a measure of rationalization within the Group. The need for it was underlined by the fact that with forty-nine soap-manufacturing companies in the Group, there were no less than

[1] Redfern, *New History*, p. 365.

forty-eight separate sales organizations![1] But this would take time. Meanwhile, when one remembers the heavy commitments of Lever Bros. to pay preference dividends (the legacy of the high prices paid, in Lever Bros.' preference shares, for many of the associated companies), it is scarcely possible to doubt that the failure of the Company up to this time to appropriate in any significant measure the economies of combination which were undoubtedly available, meant that soap prices were higher than they might otherwise, or should have, been—as suggested by Fig. 12.

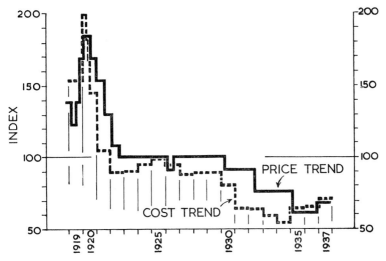

Fig. 12: Trend of Soap Prices in Relation to Trend of Costs: 1919-37
(Source: see Appendix to this chapter.)

At any rate, the combined share of the Lever companies in the total United Kingdom consumption of all soap products had declined to 60 per cent. by 1929 (see the third row of Table 8). In absolute terms, the volume of sales was still about the same as in 1920-1, and it was considerably less than the combined sales of the Lever companies and the British Soap Company in 1924-5. The C.W.S. on the other hand, with sales at 53,000 tons in 1929 (above,

[1] Wilson, ii, 345. See also the comment by the Government Committee of Inquiry recorded in the previous chapter. At this time also Lever Bros. withdrew from the U.K.S.M.A. (Wilson, i, 304), which body thereafter, if it had not already, ceased to be a factor of importance in the soap industry, and will not be referred to again in this book. It became the meeting place of the smaller makers, where they could freely voice their endless complaints at the severity of the competition of the 'big three' (post 1930).

Table 5) had increased its share of the national consumption from about 10 per cent. in the middle of the decade to upwards of 12 per cent. Such then was the position in 1929, the eve of the purchase of Thomas Hedley Ltd. of Newcastle by Procter & Gamble, the leading soap manufacturers of the U.S.A. With this a decisively new chapter in the development of the British soap industry was begun, the full story of which will occupy our attention to the end of this book.[1]

APPENDIX (Chapter 8)

TREND OF PRICES IN RELATION TO TREND OF COSTS, 1919-37

(as in Fig. 12 above)

1. The calculation set out in the accompanying table is similar to that for the period 1901-13 described in Appendix 2 to Chapter 6 above.

2. The figure of £23 for the 'manufacturing cost' component of 1920 is that accepted by the Government Committee of Inquiry, *Report*, Cmd. 1126, p. 10.

Reference was made in Appendix 2, Chapter 6, to the possibilities of substituting the relatively cheaper for the more expensive oils and fats. Over this period tallow was consistently higher in price than palm oil. In the calculation, therefore, palm oil is weighted 2 to tallow 1: in col. 3 of the table, the price of palm oil is multiplied by 2, and the sum of cols. 3 and 4 is taken in col. 5. (Supplies of copra were limited during the period, and this is omitted.) This sum is first divided by 3 (to give the weighted average price per ton of oils and fats) and then multiplied by $\frac{2}{3}$ to give the oils and fats component of the cost in col. 6 (corresponds to col. 7 of Table 4 in Appendix 2, Chapter 6).

3. The position in the year 1925 has been taken as a base for the index series in cols. 8 and 9. This choice has been governed by the consideration that the competition of the British Soap Company probably approached its peak in the latter part of 1924, and the retail prices then prevailing were maintained during 1925, and even reduced for a short period in 1926. This suggests the probability that the relation of price to cost during 1925 was a reasonable one. It is necessary to emphasize again, however that the choice of base is ultimately arbitrary, and so also therefore is the position of each graph as a whole relative to the other.

4. It would appear from the graph that prices were rather below cost for a brief period in 1920, and in the late 1930's. Apart from the question of the choice of base, it should be noted: (*a*) with respect to the former

---

[1] In this same year there was arranged the amalgamation of Lever Bros. Limited and the great group of companies of Dutch origin known as the 'Margarine Unie'. The new business in Britain was called, initially, 'Unilever Limited'. For short it will be referred to hereafter as Unilever.

TABLE 9

Trend of Costs—Prices, 1919-38

Year	Wood Index, Money Wages 1	'Manufacturing Cost' Component £ per ton 2	2× Palm Oil £ per ton 3	Tallow £ per ton 4	Sum, cols. 3 and 4 5	$\frac{1}{3}\times\frac{2}{3}$ (col. 5) £ per ton 6	Estimated 'Cost' £ per ton, Soap (=2+6) 7	Index of Cost (43·4=100) 8	Index of Price‡ 6½d.=100 9
1919	403	16·9	138·5	86·53	225·03	50·01	66·91	154	138·6 123 138·6 169
1920 (i)†	550	23		*		63·33	86·33	199	185
(ii)	550	23				56·00	79·00	181·6	185 169
(iii), (iv)	550	23				39·33	62·33	145·5	169
1921	517	21·7	68·0	40·45	108·45	24·10	45·80	105·4	154 131
1922	398	16·7	65	36·95	101·95	22·65	39·35	90·6	131 108 100
1923	364	15·2	70·5	38·33	108·83	24·19	39·39	90·7	100
1924	369	15·45	77	42·22	119·22	26·49	41·94	96·5	100
1925	371·5	15·53	80	45·4	125·4	27·87	43·40	100	100
1926	371	15·5	75	41·88	116·88	25·97	41·47	95·6	100 92·3 100
1927	372	15·55	66	36·55	102·55	22·79	38·34	88·7	100
1928	368	15·4	69	38·59	107·59	23·91	39·31	90	100
1929	367	15·35	68	39·05	107·05	23·79	39·14	90	100
1930	363	15·2	56·5	33·5	90	20·00	35·20	81·1	100 92·3
1931	358	15	37	22	59	13·11	28·11	64·7	92·3
1932	352	14·72	34·5	25·5	60	13·33	28·05	64·6	92·3 76·9
1933	347	14·5	30	20	50	11·11	25·61	59	76·9
1934	347	14·5	22·5	17·75	40·25	8·95	23·45	54·1	76·9
1935	351	14·7	33	25·5	58·5	13·00	27·70	63·8	61·5
1936	360	15·05	35	25	60	13·33	28·38	65·4	61·5
1937	371	15·5	44	25·5	69·5	15·45	30·95	71·3	69·2

* For each period estimate of cost of oils and fats direct (in col. 6) from *Report*, Cmd. 1126, p. 11.

† (i)≡First quarter, etc.

‡ Successive figures in a particular row indicate price changes within the year. The precise dates of these changes are set out in par. 6 of the accompanying Appendix.

period, that at the very high prices of oils and fats then prevailing, actual purchases of raw material were small; and (*b*) with respect to the later period, that the calculation presumes that overhead costs were at the level of the early nineteen-twenties, but in fact these had been significantly pruned by the latter 'thirties (see Chapter 9 following, pp. 198-9).

5. One final observation. Mr. Wilson (i, 284) quotes P. Fitzgerald (*Industrial Combination in England*, London 1927) as stating that the price of 6*d*. for 'Sunlight' in 1926 was 'below what the Committee of 1921 would have considered reasonable'. The price of 6*d*., however, was maintained only for a period of three months (April to July) in 1926, and Fig. 12 suggests that the reference to this brief interval is rather misleading.

6. The actual dates of the price changes ('Sunlight' soap, retail price per lb. bar) indicated in column 9 of the table were as follows:

1919:	Initial	— 9*d*.	1922:	23 Jan.	—7*d*.
	21 March	— 8*d*.		3 Oct.	—6½*d*.
	23 May	— 9*d*.	1926:	22 April	—6*d*.
	14 August	—11*d*.		12 July	—6½*d*.
1920:	27 Jan.	—1*s*. 0*d*.	1930:	29 April	—6*d*.
	27 April	—11*d*.	1932:	30 May	—5*d*.
1921:	Jan.	—10*d*.	1935:	14 Jan.	—4*d*.
	9 April	—8½*d*.	1936:	21 Dec.	—4½*d*.

CHAPTER 9

THE THIRTIES: NATIONAL OLIGOPOLY IN THE SOAP INDUSTRY

IF first the British Soap Company and thereafter the C.W.S. proved not ineffective competitors of the Lever Group in the 'twenties, in the nineteen-thirties an even more formidable competitor emerged in the firm of Thomas Hedley and Company of Newcastle-upon-Tyne. In the first quinquennium of the decade, Hedley's attained to the full stature of a national competitor in the industry, and by 1938 Unilever, Hedley's, and the C.W.S. supplied between them upwards of 75 per cent. of the home trade in all soap products. With this the structure of the British soap industry had been transformed from the local oligopoly of earlier times, through the quasi-monopoly of the 'twenties, to a situation of national oligopoly. In tracing the development of the industry from this time to the present day, our problem in the main is to assess the working and effectiveness of competition under this latter form of industrial organization, in the particular case of the British soap industry.

We begin with an outline of the origins and development of Thomas Hedley Ltd. An analysis of the pattern of competition in the 'thirties follows which takes up the balance of this chapter. The important development of the 'soapless detergents' in the post-World War II years is taken up in detail in the next two chapters.

THOMAS HEDLEY AND CO., LTD., NEWCASTLE-UPON-TYNE

The business of Thomas Hedley Ltd. dates back to a partnership begun in 1837. It was formed into a Company about 1890, with a trade principally in good quality household soap and mainly confined to Newcastle and the surrounding area. In the 'twenties the firm was one of the more important of the many small independent members in the industry, with an output of the order of 100 tons weekly.

Towards the end of that decade, however, the business was in need of considerable re-organization and capital expenditure if it were to survive as an independent. A direct approach was made to

Procter & Gamble Ltd., largest of the American soap makers, and in 1930 that Company purchased almost the whole of the share capital of Hedley's.[1]

With this the firm was rejuvenated, and Unilever's most formidable competitor in the soap industry had emerged.

It was perhaps not entirely fortuitous that the American company entered the British soap market about this time. Thus as early as 1888 W. H. Lever had visited New York to arrange for an American export agency to distribute 'Sunlight';[2] and by 1900 two factories—one at Boston and the other at Philadelphia—had been acquired.[3] In the period before World War I, it appears that little progress was made (particularly with 'Sunlight', which was eventually abandoned in the U.S. market). But with the prosperity of the war period, Lever Bros., Boston, succeeded in expanding its turnover some fifteenfold by 1920.[4] And this expansion continued unabated in the nineteen-twenties. By 1929 the volume of sales was of the order of 91,000 tons, as compared with 21,105 tons in 1920[5]—the former figure representing some 8·1 per cent. of the aggregate American production of 1,122,800 tons in 1929.[6]

It is thus evident that by the late 'twenties the rapid expansion of the Lever company's share of the U.S. market constituted a major threat to the leading American soap manufacturers. With the issue so joined, it was almost inevitable that the latter should look to the prospects in Lever Bros.' home territory, Great Britain. As noticed

---

[1] The following brief account of the American company is based on *Into a Second Century with Procter & Gamble* (privately printed in Cincinnati, U.S.A., 1944, and kindly supplied to the writer by Thomas Hedley Ltd.): the firm was founded in 1837 (the same year as Hedley's) when a partnership was begun at Cincinnati between James Gamble, who had been manufacturing soap since 1819, and William Procter, a candlemaker. The weekly production of soap by the two partners was about 6 tons. The heroic period in the firm's growth appears to have been in the years following the development of its 'Ivory' brand soap—a white, pure soap, originally developed as a floating soap. The product was heavily advertised—the firm took its first full-page advertisement as early as 1882—and within a few years some 200,000 cakes per day were being produced. In 1885 a large new factory, Ivorydale, at Cincinnati was opened; and the business was organized as a company in 1890. In 1904 a second factory was built in Kansas City; and in 1907 'Port Ivory' at Staten Island, New York—Port Sunlight the inspiration?—began production.

By 1937—the Company's centenary—there was in the Procter & Gamble group sixteen soap factories in all, including the Canadian business at Hamilton, Ontario (begun 1915) and the English factories of Thomas Hedley's and sixteen oil mills (mainly for the production of cottonseed oil). The principal factories in the United States were those of Cincinnati, Staten Island (Port Ivory), Baltimore, St. Louis, Long Beach, Dallas, and Kansas City. In all Procter & Gamble's share of the aggregate United States market exceeded 50 per cent.

[2] Wilson, i, 90.   [3] Ibid., i, 104.   [4] Ibid., i, 285-6.   [5] Ibid., ii, 354.
[6] Census of Production in the United States (U.S. Dept. of Commerce).

in the previous chapter, the Colgate-Palmolive Company seized the favourable opportunity of 1922-3 to enter the British market for toilet soaps. With the acquisition of Hedley's of Newcastle in 1930, Proctor & Gamble followed this lead. In this way then, the entry of U.S. capital and business enterprise into the British soap industry may be interpreted (at least in part) as the normal outcome of the free working of competitive forces, projected on to the wider canvas of the international market for the product. Few indigenous 'monopolies' are free (national tariff policy permitting) from the threat of such competition.

From being a predominantly local firm prior to 1930 (though with the beginnings of a wider distribution of its main brand, 'Fairy' household soap), Thomas Hedley's aspired during the decade of the 'thirties to the full stature of a national competitor in the British soap trade.

One by one each of the principal Lever products was matched with a corresponding Hedley product:—'Fairy' soap in household bar soap; 'Oxydol' soap powder to match 'Persil' and 'Rinso'; 'Sylvan' flakes to match 'Lux' flakes; 'Mirro' scourer powder, in the circular carton, to match 'Vim'. (Hedley's did not produce a toilet soap. In the toilet soap market, as we have seen, Lever's were already being strongly challenged by Colgate-Palmolive and into this battle of giants Hedley's no doubt judged it prudent not to intrude. Nor did Hedley's enter the trade in soft soap. The manufacture of soft soap had never been very profitable for the large firm, because of the extreme simplicity of the process of production and the resultant ease with which small firms could supply the market.)

Each of the Hedley products was heavily advertised on a national basis, and in the result a dramatic expansion in sales was achieved. The sales of Thomas Hedley's in 1930 could not have far exceeded the order of 5,500 tons annually. By the end of 1932 the volume of sales had about doubled, and by 1935 were of the order of 40,000 tons annually.

By this date the original factory at Newcastle had been re-organized, and a large new spray-drying tower for the production of soap powder had been added. In 1933 (begun 1932) a second factory at Trafford Park, Manchester, was opened; at the time this was probably the most modern in design in the world. This factory was enlarged in 1935-6, and has been several times expanded since then. It remains the biggest factory in the Hedley group.[1]

As the growth of sales continued (about 70,000 tons in 1938, or nearly 15 per cent. of the aggregate U.K. household consumption of soap products: see Table 8 above), a third factory was begun at West Thurrock, Essex, and opened in 1940. This plant was noteworthy in that a new, highly complex continuous process of manufacture was substituted for the ordinary batch process using the traditional soap kettle.[2]

Thus by the end of the decade the small Newcastle business of pre-1930 had been transformed.

THE PATTERN OF COMPETITION IN THE 1930'S

A number of factors contributed to this rapid growth of the Hedley business. Again it is necessary to refer to the proposition argued in Chapter 2, namely that in settled conditions (and in particular, in the absence of major innovation) the established pattern of shares of the market tends to remain more or less constant. What then were the circumstances which enabled the rapid growth of sales in the present instance?

(i) In the first place, there was the relatively rapid growth in the total national consumption of all soap products during this period (see Table 10). From 1907 to 1924 the aggregate consumption increased from 353,000 tons to 412,000 tons, an increase of only 17 per cent. in as many years and then mainly the result of a renewed growth in the consumption per head with the high incomes of the war period. This slow (average) rate of growth continued throughout the 'twenties; indeed, the Chairman of Unilever spoke of the soap trade as having reached 'a fixed state'.[3] He was, however, quite wrong. In the 'thirties the aggregate consumption expanded more rapidly than in any period since the nineteenth century—from 434,000 tons in 1929 to about 530,000 tons in 1938-9, an increase

---

[1] *Scope*, 1948, p. 58.

[2] The essentials of the new process were: continuous fat-splitting into fatty acids and glycerine (at high pressure and temperature), followed by continuous distillation, and continuous neutralization with caustic soda. The whole process is highly instrumented. The soap is made from raw fats to finished product in a matter of hours instead of days, and it is claimed that it permits of greater flexibility in the output flow, more accurate control, increased glycerine recovery, and smaller space requirements over the whole process of production. (For further details, see G. W. McBride in *Chemical Engineering*, vol. liv, No. 4 (1947), pp. 94-97 and 133-7.)

[3] Wilson, i, 299; ii, 341.

of over 22 per cent. in the decade. Moreover these figures of total tonnage do not tell the whole story, for there was a considerable shift during the period to consumption of the relatively more expensive soap powders, of which more below.

TABLE 10

Rates of Growth in Aggregate Consumption, All Soap Products:
Selected Periods

Period	Significance of period	Rate of growth per annum %
1885-1900	Rise of W. H. Lever to dominance	1·85
1900-7	Period of 'frenzied' competition	1·42
1907-24	Development of Lever combine (includes World War I years)	0·95
1924-9	One dominant seller in the industry	1·05
1929-39	National oligopolistic competition with emergence of Hedley Ltd.	2·02*
1939-49-50	War and post-war shortages	1·24
1950-5	Exploitation of soapless detergents	2·5

* Assuming aggregate consumption of 530,000 tons in 1939, based on projection from 1937 Census of Production data.

The apparent causes of this increase in the aggregate consumption were the customary ones, namely, a notable increase in real incomes after 1933, and a very considerable reduction in the price of soap made possible in part by the fall in the prices of oils and fats.[1] The aggressive new competition of the Hedley Company itself undoubtedly contributed in some measure to this increase in the overall consumption. And under the pressure of this competition the price of soap was brought down to a level, it would appear, in close relation to that indicated by the trend of costs—in contrast to the position in the 'twenties. (See Fig. 12, previous chapter.)

If, however, the increase in the aggregate consumption was in part the effect of the aggressive new competition of the Hedley

[1] After 1932 the reduction went far beyond the fall of retail prices generally, thus:

Retail Price Indexes (1929 = 100)

	All soap products	General price index		All soap products	General price index
1929	100·0	100·0	1934	80·9	86·0
1930	95·7	96·2	1935	75·1	87·2
1931	93·6	89·9	1936	75·6	89·6
1932	87·1	87·8	1937	79·3	93·9
1933	81·3	85·4	1938	80·4	95·1

Source: R. Stone, 'The Analysis of Market Demand', *J.R.S.S.*, 1945.

company, it was also on the other hand a significant factor in making possible the rapid growth in the company's sales. It meant that by 1938 the Hedley position in the market had been attained without any absolute decline in the sales of either the Unilever group or the C.W.S.; though under pressure of the heavy competition between Hedley's, Unilever, and the C.W.S. the 'small men' in the industry, i.e. producers other than the three mentioned, had lost some ground. It is virtually certain that without the net increase in the aggregate consumption to cushion the impact, the resistance to Hedley's by Unilever, the C.W.S., and even the smaller independent firms would have been more aggressive and stubborn, and the ultimate success of Hedley's considerably less.

(ii) Moreover, second, within this growth of the aggregate market there was (as already referred to) an acceleration during this period of the basic long-term trend in the structure of demand for soap products, namely, the increasing preference for soap powders and flakes as against the traditional household hard soaps. This trend is brought out in Table 18A (below, p. 238). Thus, in 1907 nearly 70 per cent. of the total national consumption was of household hard soap. In 1924 the proportion was still 64 per cent.; but by 1937 it had fallen to 45 per cent. Soap powders and flakes, on the other hand, which comprised only 11·3 per cent. of the total consumption in 1907, had increased to 35 per cent. by 1937.

The significant point for our present purposes is the acceleration in this trend in the latter 'twenties and throughout the 'thirties. (This was in part the result of an innovation in the manufacture of soap powders, namely, the development of the 'spray-drying' technique about 1925.[1] Previously soap powders had been of the ground type; the modern spray-dried powder, on the other hand, is a granulated powder, consisting of hollow globular particles with a wall thickness of about 0·05 mm. As compared with the old, the modern powder is freer-flowing, more readily soluble, and comparatively free from dust. With this development of the product, the powder became the preferred washing aid, but because relatively more expensive than ordinary bar soap its increasing usage was dependent on rising levels of real income.)

Hedley's, then, entering the market in 1930 (with 'Oxydol' soap powder), were just in a position to share in this expansion, and to

---

[1] J. W. McCutcheon, 'Soap Progress since 1900', *Soap and Sanitary Chemicals*, 1951, p. 20.

grow as this sector of the market grew very largely of its own momentum. There is some evidence, too, to suggest that in their advertising relatively greater weight was given to the soap powder product (and 'Sylvan' flakes).[1] With its narrow range of products and unified control—as compared with the decentralized Unilever organization—the Hedley Company was in a strategic position thus to assess, and to promote, the natural course of the overall development.

(iii) This brings us to our third point in explaining the rapid growth of the Hedley company: the conflict between Hedley's and Unilever in this period, despite the dominance of the latter in terms of sheer size, was nevertheless to some extent an unequal one with the odds in favour of Hedley's.

Thus backed by the resources, knowhow and some personnel of Procter & Gamble, Hedley's were at no insuperable disadvantage in these respects. In others, the advantage was positively in Hedley's favour. As late as 1930, very little headway had been made in rationalizing the many separate selling and production units within the Lever group. The problem, indeed, was beset with many difficulties, and the fact was that there was no person in the concern with the authority to shape and impose a programme of rational reform.[2] So, one Unilever brand continued to compete with other Unilever brands of the same class of product, as well as with 'outside' brands. Hedley's, on the other hand, concentrated their effort from the beginning on but one brand in each product-sector of the market. All their products were thus complementary to one another, and there was no intra-product dissipation of the sales effort as inevitably occurred with the variety of products marketed by the component firms of Unilever, each charged with the obligation of standing on its own feet. In this way, Hedley's were in a better strategic position to appropriate the lion's share of the increase in the aggregate consumption which its own efforts were partially instrumental in bringing about.

This bears on a second point which should be noticed in this connexion. It was argued above[3] that the costs of national advertising are large in absolute amount, and to a considerable extent independent of the sales volume of the particular firm—being determined

---

[1] For a long period prior to the war, 'Sylvan' flakes retailed at a significant price differential, weight for weight, below the 'Lux' packet.

[2] Wilson, ii, 344-5.   [3] p. 29 and Appendix, Chapter 2.

by such factors as the density and accessibility of the population, the necessities for repetition given the nature of the product (its 'period' of consumption, etc.), and so on: so that the firm which would advertise nationally, if it is to survive at all, must attain a very large volume of sales to 'spread' these costs adequately. Now a perusal of Table 8 (above, p. 183) would suggest, at first sight, that Lever's—with a sales volume of the order of 260,000 tons— should possess a decisive advantage on this score over Hedley's with a sales volume in the later 'thirties of the order of but 60,000 to 70,000 tons.

But to argue thus is again to overlook the composition of the Unilever sales. In the first place, there was the greater variety of brands to be advertised on a national or semi-national basis, in contrast to Hedley's narrow range of products. It is true that only one of the Lever firms—Port Sunlight—had an indisputably national market for all its proprietary products ('Sunlight' soap, 'Rinso' powder, 'Lux' flakes, 'Lux' toilet soap, and 'Vim' scourer). But at least four others—Crosfield's, Watson's, Gossage's, and Knight's— had wide regional markets and some grip on the national market for certain products, (e.g. Crosfield's 'Persil' soap powder, manufactured under licence from a Continental firm).[1]

The rest of the Unilever firms in the main served local markets, in unbranded or not-heavily-advertised local brands of soap. In the second place, therefore, it is necessary to allow for this output in judging the relative incidence of advertising costs as between Hedley's and Unilever. (Subsequently, of course, the variety of brands of the Unilever group was reduced, as the rationalization programme went ahead.)

(iv) A final factor enabling the rapid expansion in the Hedley business was the possibility of appropriating sales from the 'small men'.

Thus in 1929 Lever's and the C.W.S.'s share of the aggregate consumption was 72·2 per cent. But by 1938 the 'big three' had appropriated 76·2 per cent. of the market. (See col. 10 of Table 8.)

A similar tendency had been observable in the early 'twenties, with 'New Pin' competition. After Lever Bros.' amalgamation with the B.O.C.M., however, the small independents had more than restored the position in the latter 'twenties.

When conditions had been restored to something approaching

[1] Wilson, ii, 344.

normal after World War II, this tendency towards concentration of the production in the hands of the 'big three'—or rather, 'big two'—was to become even more pronounced.

Yet when all this has been said it appears that the growth of the Hedley business was slackening in the latter years of the decade. Indeed, as one person in the trade put it to the writer, 'the company had [by the outbreak of World War II] just about reached the limits of expansion possible in the conditions of that time'. In a word, conditions in the soap industry—the design and specification of its principal products, and the basic processes of manufacture— were 'settled'; so that as the intensive rationalization programme within the Unilever concern restored its competitive power, the emergent shares of the market were hardening into a continuing pattern.

With this the possibilities of the Hedley Company's further growth were severely circumscribed. And so it would have continued—one can safely assert—if conditions had remained static. In fact, after the war, Hedley's apprehended and in due course exploited with the utmost vigour a major innovation in the industry, and thereby succeeded in doubling their share of the total trade in washing products. This story is unravelled in the two following chapters.

NATIONAL OLIGOPOLY IN THE SOAP INDUSTRY

The position in the years immediately preceding the outbreak of World War II, then, is indicated by the fifth row of Table 8 above.

Hedley's with its rapid expansion had by 1938 appropriated some 13·7 per cent. of the aggregate United Kingdom market for all soap products—or about 15 per cent. of the market for household products.

The share of Lever's in the aggregate consumption, in contrast, had receded from the 65 per cent. of 1920-1, to a little over 50 per cent. in 1938; though in absolute terms the volume of sales had been more or less maintained.

Meanwhile the C.W.S., after its gains during the period 1925-9, lost ground somewhat to remain in 1938 in much the same relative position in the market—with about 11 per cent. of the national consumption of soap products—as in 1920-1. This, however, involved an increase of fully one-third in its actual volume of sales as compared with the earlier period.

The combined sales of these three firms in the United Kingdom in 1938 totalled nearly 400,000 tons, or (as previously stated) some 76·2 per cent. of the aggregate consumption. And within that total, there had by that date been a significant increase in the share of the national or semi-national brands, as the sales effort in the Unilever group was increasingly concentrated on a more restricted range of its more popular brands. With this the situation in the British soap trade was, in the full sense, national oligopoly.

On the whole, it would appear that the emergence of national competitive oligopoly in the soap industry in this period served the consumer well.

With the transfer of the active competitive leadship to Hedley's, the Unilever concern—the so-called 'monopolist' in the soap trade —had indeed been contained. Further there can be no doubt that the aggressive new competition of the period led to a speeding up in the Unilever programme of rationalization and increased efficiency. One cannot escape the conclusion that soap prices were high in relation to (theoretical) costs in the latter nineteen-twenties (Fig. 12, p. 185), not because prices were held up gratuitously to yield excessive profits, but because realized costs including only 'reasonable' profits were too high: in a word, the protection which the quasi-monopolistic position of the Unilever group afforded, enabled it to maintain an organization of production and sale which was outdated, top-heavy, and inefficient. Some of the details of the economies achieved in the 'thirties by the concentration of production and selling, as set out by Mr. Wilson, amply bear this out. Thus (ii, 347)

. . . In one year, 1932, in the West of England the travelling staff was cut from 220 to 154, and the number of 'packs' from 852 to 294. And all this without any loss to total sales in the area.

Later the Gossage plant at Widnes, three factories in the London area, the two Hudson soap powder factories, the 'New Pin' factory at Hull, the ancient Thomas's works at Exeter, and others were entirely closed down. And 'those factories that survived had to undergo vigorous internal reorganization'. Efficiency less than it might be, and costs accordingly too high, is perhaps the principal objection to 'monopoly' (above, p. 95); it would seem that such a charge was indeed justified in the present instance.

Some indication of the overall increase in efficiency in the trade as a whole is provided by the change in output (all soap products by weight) per employee between 1924 and 1937, as shown in Table 11.

TABLE 11

Production per Employee, 1924 and 1937

Year	Total Production all Soap Products (including Exports) (tons)	No. of Employees*	Production per Employee (tons)
1924	473,250	30,064	15·7
1937	523,100	22,920	22·8

* Includes 'Operatives' and 'Administrative, Technical and Clerical Employees'.
Source: Census of Production, 1924 and 1937. (The results of the latter were published with the results of the 1948 Census.)

No doubt there is some lack of strict comparability in the data, but the trend is clear enough. Moreover it is to be borne in mind that the output in 1937 consisted of a much larger proportion of the relatively more expensive, because of more complex processing, soap powder products.

Finally with the resumption of strong competition and the increase in efficiency (the two thus not independent), and with a notable expansion in output made possible ultimately by rising real income, the price of soap, it would appear, was brought down in closer relation to the trend of theoretical costs than had previously obtained. Doubtless profits continued 'good', and particularly so in view of the increased turnover. But on the whole the consumer interest would seem to have been well served.

CHAPTER 10

THE SOAP INDUSTRY IN THE POST-WAR PERIOD

I. SOAPLESS DETERGENTS

In the nineteen-thirties the situation in the British soap industry had become, in the full sense, national oligopoly. Within that oligopoly the Unilever concern, despite the transfer of the active competitive leadership in the industry to Hedley's, remained at the outbreak of World War II as the 'number 1' in the soap trade. With the restrictions and dislocations of the war years, the competitive struggle abated. But in the post-war years Hedley's challenge to Unilever's dominant position was renewed with more vigour than ever.

The history of the industry in these post-war years is dominated by the development of soapless detergents—or as sometimes referred to, the 'synthetic' detergents.[1] At the outset, therefore, it is necessary to indicate briefly just what is meant by a 'soapless detergent'. The main thread of the narrative of the preceding chapters is not resumed until the next chapter.

NATURE AND PROPERTIES OF SOAPLESS DETERGENTS

A detergent may be defined briefly as any agent which facilitates the washing process. Soap, defined above as the sodium ('hard') or potassium ('soft') salt of one or more of the complex fatty acids, is such an agent. Research indicates that soap is an effective detergent (*a*) because it is 'surface-active', which means that it acts to reduce the tensions, one, between the washing water and the article washed, thus facilitating the thorough 'wetting' of the article, and two, between the 'dirt' and the article washed, thus facilitating the removal of the dirt; (*b*) because it assists in dispersing and holding the dirt in the washing water, and in preventing the dirt being redeposited

---

[1] The significance of the 'synthetic' is that the products in question have been scientifically synthesized as substitutes for the common soap. But soap itself does not occur naturally; it, no less than the (so-called) 'synthetic', has to be synthesized by man. This usage, accordingly, has been resisted in this study.

on the article washed—again, in part, because of its surface activity, this time in reducing surface tensions as between the dirt and the water; and (c) because of its foaming or lathering power—lather is possibly important in initially holding the loosened dirt before it is suspended in the water.[1]

A soapless detergent, then, may be defined thus: an organic compound other than the water-soluble salts of the organic acids, which is surface-active, facilitates the washing process in the ways indicated, and in particular does not contain the 'carboxyl group' of the fatty acids.[2] (The technical chemical term is unavoidable: the significance of this point will be explained below.)

A great variety of such components have been developed; the more important commercially will be discussed in due sequence in what follows. That so great a variety of detergent compounds have been developed has resulted, in part, from the possibility of 'tailoring them to measure', i.e. of synthesizing a special compound for the particular purpose in view. This is an important general advantage of the soapless detergents as against soaps, particularly in the industrial field.[3]

Apart from this the soapless detergents exhibit two fundamental advantages, and one disadvantage, vis-à-vis soap.

To take the disadvantage first. Whereas soap as such is an efficient detergent for most purposes, the principal soapless detergent compounds, i.e. the organic base materials as such, are not. On their own they are certainly surface-active, but they are not effective washers. Precisely why not, is as yet imperfectly understood; but it

[1] Whether or not lathering assists the washing process is debated in the technical literature. However, because of the identification of cleansing power with lathering power in the popular mind, it is almost essential that any household detergent should possess lathering power. Products which do not lather (e.g. 'Stergene'), while in fact very efficient, are regarded with some suspicion. On the other hand, such a detergent is of positive advantage in certain industrial processes.

[2] As already noted above (Chapter 5), the general formula for a fatty acid R-COOH. R represents the paraffin chain; $-$COOH is known as the 'carboxyl acid group'. Its molecular character is better indicated thus:

$$-C\overset{\displaystyle O}{\underset{\displaystyle OH}{\diagup}}$$

[3] But this is true also in the field of household soapless detergents. Thus one detergent compound which is lacking in the power to maintain dirt in suspension, but is powerfully surface-active, may be a very effective dish-washer, because the opportunities for dirt redepositing on a dish are relatively small; whereas for laundering fabrics, where the opportunities for redeposition are large, a different type of detergent, less surface-active but with superior suspending power, is more effective.

would seem to have to do with their ability, or rather lack of it, to prevent the redeposition of the dirt on the article before its removal with the dirty washing water.[1] Soap, on the other hand, is effective in this.

By experiment, however, and then only fairly late in the piece, it was discovered that the synthetic base plus certain inorganic compounds (though not soda ash, hitherto the most common 'builder' in washing products) formed a very efficient detergent indeed, perhaps even more efficient than the corresponding soap product. Such products are now referred to as 'blended' soapless detergents.

The considerable significance of this point for the post-war development of the soap and detergents industry will be indicated below.

Next as to the two advantages of the soapless detergents.

The first is that they do not form the familiar 'scum' or 'curd' in hard water as do soaps; in other words, the soapless detergents are stable in hard water. This is because they do not contain the 'carboxyl group' of the fatty acid, present in soap. It is this group which promotes combination with the 'hard' traces in water to form the 'lime soaps' making up the scum.[2] These lime soaps, being wax-like solids, also promote the adhesion of dirt to fabrics, which is the reason for the greyish colour imparted to white goods with continual washing with soap in hard water.

The soapless detergents' property of stability in hard water thus means both that the washing is cleaner, and that a given quantity of a suitably blended detergent will do more washing in hard water than the same quantity of otherwise equally efficient soap product —and the harder the water, the greater this advantage of the soapless product. The soap product, that is, will first neutralize the 'hard' traces in the water by the formation of lime soaps, before any effective washing at all is done.

The extent of this wastage of soap has been estimated by one witness before the post-war Water Softening Committee of Inquiry,[3]

---

[1] On this see the article in *Industrial and Engineering Chemistry*, 1950, pp. 856 ff.

[2] The lime-soaps are mixtures of calcium and magnesium oleates, palmitates, and stearates, formed by combination of the soap with the calcium bicarbonate and magnesium bicarbonate traces in the hard water.

[3] This was a Sub-committee of the Central Advisory Water Committee appointed about 1946 to inquire into the desirability of softening British water supplies, etc. The Committee's Report, *Water Softening*, was published by H.M.S.O. in 1949. The present reference is to §§ 41-45, pp. 14-17, of the Report.

to be at least 30 to 40 per cent. of the consumption of soap by
users in water of 200 p.p.m. of hardness, i.e. 6 to 8 lb. of soap for
an annual per capita consumption of 20 lb. of soap per annum.
(The Committee itself was of the opinion that the wastage was
higher even than the latter figure.) On these figures, in water of this
hardness, 1 lb. of otherwise equally efficient synthetic detergent
would do the work of between 1·43 and 1·67 lb. of soap, the
correct figure being nearer the latter. The Committee also stated
that 'It may be assumed without significant error that the soap
wasted is proportional to the hardness'. We may deduce, therefore, the relations illustrated in the accompanying graph (Fig. 13)
indicating the upper and lower limits on the foregoing data of the
relative efficiency of soap and soapless detergents in hard water.[1]

It should be noted that elsewhere the Committee gives the data
shown in Table 12, relating to the hardness of British water supplies
in relation to the population using the water. These data indicate

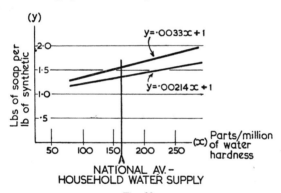

Fig. 13.
Relative Efficiency of Soap and Soapless Detergents in Hard Water.

that the average degree of hardness of the British water supply,
taking the country as a whole, is 163·4 p.p.m.[2] Referring to Fig. 13,

[1] Let x stand for the degree of hardness of the water in p.p.m. of hardness. We have
that C, the per capita consumption, is equal to $14 + (6/200) x$, for the lower figure of
soap wastage, and to $12 + (8/200) x$, for the higher figure. But the lbs of soap per lb.
of synthetic (call this y) is equal to $C/14$ in the first case, and $C/12$ in the second.
Hence the two relationships are:

$$y = (6/200 \cdot 14) \, x + 1$$
$$= \cdot 00214 \, x + 1$$
$$\text{and } y = (8/200 \cdot 12) \, x + 1$$
$$= \cdot 00333 \, x + 1$$

[2] This average has been calculated assuming that the average of the 'Over 300'
class is 350. Some of the water supplied in this class exceeds 660 p.p.m.

TABLE 12

Percentage of Population of England and Wales Supplied with Water of Different Degrees of Hardness

Hardness (p.p.m.)	Described as:	% of Population
0—50	Soft	20·5
50—100	Moderately soft	14·1
100—150	Slightly hard	11·9
150—200	Moderately hard	8·5
200—300	Hard	39·7
Over 300	Very hard	5·3

Source: Report, *Water Softening* (H.M.S.O., 1949), § 17, p. 8.

this would suggest that on the average the relative efficiency of soap and soapless detergents in use is about 1·5 : 1; or, to put it another way, that on the average 1 lb. of soapless detergent products displaces in use about 1·5 lb. of soap products.[1]

This conclusion has been utilized in calculating the 'soap equivalents' in Table 18A of the next chapter (p. 238)—see the entries in the Table for 1951 and 1954. It will be emphasized below that in the form in which the soapless detergent powders were in fact marketed during 1950-5, the ratio of 1·5 : 1 by weight expresses an equivalence *not only of 'washing power' but also of volume and of value*, i.e. 1·5 lb. soap powder has been of approximately the same volume as 1 lb. of detergent powder (less dense than the soap powder), and also of the same value.

In what follows, constant reference will be made to this superior technical efficiency of the soapless detergents, weight for weight, in hard water.

The second advantage of the soapless detergents *vis-à-vis* soap is the variety of raw materials which may be used in the manufacture of the soapless detergents. The principal raw materials utilized are

---

[1] It can be argued, in the extreme, that such comparisons are entirely meaningless. If, for example, one were to take a bucket of hard water and introduce a very small quantity of soap, then this could be wholly used up in neutralizing the hard elements in the water, leaving none at all for washing. In the same bucket, the same quantity (by weight) of synthetic would enable *some* washing; so that the ratio of 'washing power' by synthetic to that by soap would be infinity. Merely by increasing the quantity of soap and synthetic introduced, or again, varying the quantity of water, the ratio could be varied at will.

But this is to look at the matter from the wrong angle. In fact, what is envisaged is an 'average' housewife obliged to carry out a 'normal' weekly wash, in her 'customary' tub-full of water. The question is then one of the quantity of soap product which will do the job as compared with the quantity of synthetic, expressed as a ratio of lb. of soap per lb. of synthetic. This problem is quite meaningful, though any calculation is necessarily imprecise because of the difficulty of fixing upon the appropriate 'averages' involved. However, the degree of refinement to which one major soap company at least carries its research in these matters has to be seen to be believed.

petroleum or coal-tar fractions, rather than natural oils and fats—
the soapmakers' traditional raw materials. (However, a high-class
soapless detergent can be, and has been, manufactured from natural
fats.)[1] Thus the petroleum and organic chemical industries have
become important suppliers of raw material to the soap and detergents manufacturers, and indeed they have competed directly with the
latter in certain markets and have become potential competitors
in others. Thus with the development of the soapless detergents, a
major technological change, the competitive 'field' of the established
soap manufacturers has been very significantly extended.

With this preliminary survey, we may now return to our main
theme. The discussion is divided into two parts.

In the first, which takes up the balance of this chapter, the broad
contours of the development of soapless detergents manufacture in
Great Britain are traced, with particular reference to the varieties
of organic detergent base material which have been utilized to date.

In its early stages, this development took place for the most part
outside the major soap companies. But from 1948-9 the history of
the further progress of the soapless detergents merges with the
general development of the soap industry as we have followed it,
hitherto, in the preceding chapters. Thus the second part of the
following narrative (Chapter 11) will be concerned with events in
this wider setting since 1949-50.

THE DEVELOPMENT OF SOAPLESS DETERGENT MANUFACTURE
IN THE UNITED KINGDOM

The commercial development of the soapless detergent in Britain
was largely a wartime and post-war phenomenon. But like any major
technical development, it had its antecedents—in the 1930's and
even earlier; and we must first notice these briefly.

Thus, as far back as the latter decades of the nineteenth century,
the disadvantages of soap as a general surface-active agent in certain
industrial processes had led to the development of the first of the
(so-called) sulphonated oils, namely, 'Turkey Red Oil', which takes
its name from its principal application in the dyeing of fabrics with
Turkey Red. The sulphonated oils may be regarded as the fore-
runners of the 'alkyl sulphates'—the class of detergent which,

---

[1] The *primary* alkyl sulphate' type of detergent base (see Appendix 1 to this Part),
which is a fine detergent comparable to an 'alkyl aryl sulphonate' (see below).

until 1949-50, formed the basis of the British soapless detergents industry.

Apart from the sulphonated oils, the development of synthetic surface-active agents (and detergents in particular) was not taken beyond the laboratory stage within the British organic chemicals industry during the inter-war years. Throughout the period the supply of natural fats remained plentiful; so that, at least so far as the chemical industry itself was concerned, there was not a sufficient stimulus for the practical development of expensive substitutes for the traditional soap.

The case of the major soap companies was different. Both Unilever and Thomas Hedley had introduced soapless detergent products in the latter 1930's, more or less experimentally. Both firms had been influenced by the early development of soapless detergents outside the United Kingdom—in particular in Germany and the United States of America.

The stimulus to development in Germany had been the chronic shortage of natural fats, as a result of the pressure on the balance of payments of reparations payments, and then rearmament. The German I. G. Farben chemicals group was the leader in this field, and in 1933[1] Unilever negotiated an agreement with I. G. Farben whereby the latter should supply basic materials for a soapless powder to be marketed by Unilever. By 1938 Unilever was competing with Henkels, the German chemical manufacturers, for the trade in soapless washing powders in Germany; but this development was cut short by the war. In the United Kingdom, Joseph Watson's of Leeds introduced a soapless shampoo ('Eve') in 1935, and an experimental soapless powder ('Leda') for washing fine fabrics a year later.

In the United States the stimulus to the development of soapless detergents in the 1930's was the great urban populations in areas of hard water. By 1935 the recorded production of soapless detergents was already in excess of 20,000 tons per annum[2]—a sizeable figure, though small in relation to the present development of the market in that country. Procter & Gamble played a leading role in this development; and it was doubtless on the basis of the experience of the parent firm that Hedley's in Great Britain developed the

---

[1] Wilson, ii, 352.
[2] 'Survey of Recent Literature on Soaps Versus Synthetic Detergents', U.S. Dept. of Commerce, 1950, Table 1, p. 2.

fine-washing soapless powder 'Dreft', which was introduced experimentally in 1938.

These experiments in the marketing of household soapless detergents in this country were cut short by the outbreak of war; and they were not to be resumed by the major soap companies for nearly a decade. But they presaged much larger developments, if and when the circumstances of their production and sale should become propitious.

Such a situation arose with the increasing shortage of oils and fats in the United Kingdom during and after World War II.

In the immediate pre-war years, some 95-97 per cent. of the U.K. consumption of (visible) oils and fats including butter, amounting to 1,380,000 tons, was imported. With the increasing difficulties of transportation and the shipping losses of the war, edible fats of all kinds were severely rationed, and in February 1942 so also was soap. Nor did the problem come to an end with the cessation of hostilities. In 1946 the production of soap products in the U.K. was at the rate of only 300,000 tons per annum, compared with the 1937 production of 523,000 tons. And in July of that year the soap ration was cut still further, to reduce the rate of production to the order of 260,000 tons per annum.

It was not till the end of 1949 and 1950 that the world supply position in oils and fats eased. In 1947 world production was still some 10 per cent. below the pre-war average of 20·7 million tons, while the world population was estimated to have increased by nearly 9 per cent. In 1948, while world production approached more nearly the pre-war level, world exports were only about 60 per cent. of the pre-war level mainly owing to the drop in exports from India, China, and the (then) Netherlands East Indies. Even by 1950 world production was running at only 6 per cent. above pre-war levels (with world exports approximately 92 per cent. of pre-war). But while thus the overall supply of oils and fats in relation to the increase in world population (14 per cent.) and aggregate food requirements remained short (indeed, continued so until 1954), it appears that for soap products in the U.K. the shortage of oils and fats ceased to be a factor at this time. The *Annual Report* of Unilever Ltd. for 1950 (p. 9) speaks of '. . . the tendency for supplies of raw materials to be more plentiful, which had developed during 1949'. And on 10 September 1950, after a period of some months during which it was reported that the soap ration had not been fully taken up, soap rationing was finally abandoned.[1]

The development of the soapless detergents in the United Kingdom thus falls naturally into two phases. The first is the period from the outbreak of World War II to 1949-50. In this period the oils and fats shortage was the decisive factor. The first phase was thus the use of soapless detergents—or, more accurately, 'soap substitutes', worthy and otherwise—in place of soaps to meet the unsatisfied margin of demand for the latter in their more essential uses, first in the industrial field (principally the laundry, catering, and textile trades), and then in the field of household washing products.

But the development of soapless detergents was ultimately to be favoured by more permanent factors than the shortage of oils and fats, as already presaged above, and this is evidenced by the continued rapid growth of production and sales in the period after 1949-50. This, the second phase of the development, was a period of substantially free competition between the soap and synthetic products on a comparative price/performance basis, and it began even before the rationing of soap was formally abandoned in 1950. And at least in the case of Thomas Hedley Ltd., it merges into what may be distinguished as a third phase of the development, namely, the conscious and aggressive effort to replace soap on a permanent basis.

(i) *The Development to 1949-50*

Two products dominated the early history of the soapless detergents industry in the United Kingdom, namely, 'Teepol', manufactured by Technical Products Ltd. (later Shell Chemicals Manufacturing Ltd.), the petro-chemical subsidiary of the Shell Petroleum Company;[2] and 'Lissapol', manufactured by Imperial

---

[1] It was appreciated, too, that the consumption of oils and fats for soap-making normally absorbed only some 13-15 per cent. of the total consumption of oils and fats; with the increase in production of the soapless detergents, it was unlikely in any event that the consumption of soap should increase by more than 10 per cent. and that would affect the aggregate consumption of oils and fats by about 1·5 per cent. However, the then Ministry of Food retained its control over the prices and supplies of oils and fats until 1954.

[2] 'Teepol' may be classified as a secondary alkyl sulphate. (See the notes to Table 13 in Appendix 1 to this Part.) The basic raw material is 'slack-wax', a waxy solid at normal temperatures obtained as a by-product from the refinery in the production of lubricating oil. This material is vapourized and fed into a specialized cracking plant, a sizeable and complex installation. The 'olefine' (unsaturated hydrocarbon) material thus obtained is reacted with sulphuric acid, neutralized with caustic soda, and further refined to produce 'Teepol'.

TABLE 13

Production and Use of Soapless Detergents (Finished Products and Base Materials): United Kingdom, 1942-55
(000 tons)

Column groupings: columns 2–6 fall under *Aggregate Consumption in U.K.* (columns 2–4 under *Household*). Columns 8–12 fall under *Output Consumed in U.K. by Type of Organic Detergent Base Material (20-25 per cent. active material)* (columns 8–9 under *Anionics*).

Year	Total Prodn.	Powder (All grades)	Liquid	Total, Household	Industrial	U.K. Consumption	Export	Primary and Secondary Alkyl Sulphates (e.g. 'Teepol')	Alkyl Aryl Sulphonates (e.g. 'Santomerse')	Cationics (e.g. 'Deciquam')	Non-ionic (e.g. 'Lissapol')	U.K. Consumption	Year
	1	2	3	4	5	6	7	8	9	10	11	12	
1942	6	*	*	*	*	6	—	5	—		1	6	1942
1943	10	*	*	*	*	10	—	8	—		2	10	1943
1944	19	*	*	*	*	19	—	16	—		3	19	1944
1945	31	*	*	*	*	31	—	26	—		5	31	1945
1946	37	5	23	28	9	37	—	30	—		7	37	1946
1947	52	9	33	42	10	52	—	42	—		10	52	1947
1948	62	15	35	50	11	61	1	46	..		15	61	1948
1949	74	30	30	60	13	73	1	55	..		18	73	1949
1950	77	35	22	57	14	71	6	36	21	..	14	71	1950
1951	98	49	18	67	19	86	12	27	44	..	15	86	1951
1952	135	84	14	98	26	124	11	33	76	..	15	124	1952
1953	185	127	11	138	28	166	19	29	124	..	13	166	1953
1954	223	150	8	158	34	192	31	28	149	1	14	192	1954
1955	253	156	6	162	38	200	53	30	155	1	14	200	1955

(Sources and notes to this table: see Appendix 1)

* Not estimated separately   .. Negligible

Chemical Industries.[1] The latter was first introduced on a commercial scale in 1940 at the Billingham division of I.C.I.; the production of 'Teepol' was begun in 1942 at Stanlow, Cheshire.

The production of these products was expanded rapidly up to 1945. In that year the output of 'Teepol' has been estimated at some 20-25,000 tons (21 per cent. active), and that of 'Lissapol' at 5,000 tons (see Table 13). Taken together, therefore, these products accounted for the bulk of the estimated total production of 31,000 tons in 1945. Apart from these there was a variety of products of the 'primary alkyl sulphate' class, but all produced on a small scale, e.g. 'Estraline' (manufactured by the Stockport Chemical Company), 'Gardinol', 'Lorol', etc.

Of this total output for 1945, about 75 per cent. was utilized for industrial purposes (including some export), and only 25 per cent. as a base for the preparation of household washing products. These proportions were to change rapidly after 1946.

There were a number of reasons for the dominance of sales to industrial consumers in this early period. First, the manufacture of washing preparations for the retail market was the recognized province of the soap companies. The outbreak of the war had put an end to their early experiments in the marketing of soapless detergents, and subsequently the general conditions of the war emergency precluded the full-scale effort required, at least so far as the major soap companies were concerned. Moreover, neither 'Teepol' nor 'Lissapol' was suitable as a base for the large-scale manufacture of domestic washing products, particularly powders— though Unilever, subsequently, did go ahead with a 'Teepol'-based powder ('Wisk'). 'Lissapol' was not suitable for a powder at all; the difficulty in its case was that it did not foam (lather), which presented a complex selling problem in a market where cleansing power has always been virtually identified with lathering power.

Second, so far as the producing companies (I.C.I. and Shell) were concerned, a custom based on direct sales to laundries, catering establishments, and firms in the textile trades was to be preferred to production for the retail market, since neither company possessed

---

[1] 'Lissapol' belongs to the non-ionic class of detergent materials. In these early years it was manufactured from a hydrocarbon fraction (an 'alkyl amide') derived principally from coal tar. This material was condensed with ethylene oxide (ethylene is a gas obtained in large quantities in the 'cracking' of petroleum), and further refined to produce 'Lissapol'.

either the distributing organization or the experience necessary for selling to the latter market. In any event, I.C.I. had a close and long-standing association with the textile trades via its sales of dye-stuffs and other chemical products.

In the conditions of general shortage, then, I.C.I. with 'Lissapol' progressively acquired a considerable custom in these trades, in which it served a variety of purposes. In addition, it was utilized in dishwashing machines and other industrial processes for which its property of foamless surface activity made it ideally suitable.

The principal market outlet for 'Teepol', on the other hand, consisted in sales to laundries and catering establishments, with a more limited outlet in the textile industries.

In the household sector of the market, there was during the latter war and the immediate post-war years, a 'mushroom' growth of small firms producing packaged non-soap washing products. These firms were licenced by the Ministry of Food, as manufacturers of 'worthy soap substitutes', and in 1946 there were over 500 of them. (Up to the end of 1949 more than 2,000 such licences had been issued.)

These products varied widely in quality, but even the best were inferior by present-day standards. In the conditions of acute shortage of soap, however, they found a ready market, and the limit to production and sales was imposed only by the restricted supplies of the detergent base material. Thus from a volume (as marketed) of the order of 48,000 tons in 1946, the sales of household 'soap substitute' products increased to 85,000 tons in 1948 and 91,000 tons in 1949. (In terms comparable to the data in Table 13 for recent years, i.e. washing material containing at least 20 per cent. by weight of the active detergent base, these outputs would read 28,000 tons, 50,000 tons, and 60,000 tons respectively for the years referred to).[1]

In 1946 some 23,000 tons—or upwards of 80 per cent. of the production expressed in the latter terms—consisted of liquid detergent products. But the outstanding, though not unexpected feature of the post-war development, was the increase in the manufacture of powder products, the form in which the consumer undoubtedly prefers her general-purpose washing aids. Sales of such products increased from a negligible volume in 1945-6 to

[1] See P. A. R. Puplett, *Synthetic Detergents* (London, 1957), pp. 27-29.

the order of 50,000 tons (as marketed) in 1948, and to 61,000 tons in 1949.[1]

For the most part these products were of poor quality. They consisted in the main of mixtures of 'Teepol' with soda ash, to form on drying a lumpy powder. There were also, however, some better-class products based on the 'primary alkyl sulphates'.

The most significant event of these years was the re-entry of the major soap companies into the field in 1948. In July of that year Thomas Hedley's revived 'Dreft'. This was a mild detergent powder specifically designed (and advertised) as a product for fine washing only, and competitive with soap flakes of the 'Lux' or 'Sylvan' variety rather than with powders such as 'Persil' or 'Oxydol'. Some months later Unilever brought out 'Wisk', advertised as an all-purpose detergent. At this date 'Wisk' was a heavily-built 'Teepol'-based powder, suited mainly to the heavy family wash and rather severe in its effect on the skin.

But notwithstanding this entry of the major soap companies into the field, business continued easy throughout 1948 and most of 1949 for the 500-odd independent producers remaining in the field. In comparison with the years before the war there was still plenty of leeway to be made up in consumption of washing aids. Thus the aggregate household consumption of hard soap and soap powders and flakes amounted to some 356,200 tons in 1937; while in 1948 the available supplies of these products for household purposes amounted to but 273,400 tons—a decrease of 23 per cent. over a period when the population had increased by nearly 6 per cent. In these conditions of continued soap shortage, the demand for the soapless detergents continued strong, notwithstanding a retail price ratio of synthetics to soap in excess of 2 : 1 at this time.

Subsequently the intensive competition of the major soap companies, based on a vastly increased scale of production, was to reduce this ratio—the normal fall in (relative) price with the competing-down phase in the development of a new industrial process. But it is worth noticing that in the prevailing conditions of small-scale production, a price ratio in the region of 2 : 1 was not greatly

[1] With this the sale of liquid detergents as a proportion of the total production had declined to about 50 per cent., and this trend has continued. Today, liquid detergents, used mainly for dishwashing, account for only about 4-5 per cent. of the total household consumption of detergent products (cf. Table 13). 'Stergene' (introduced 1947 by Domestos Ltd., and principally 'Lissapol') accounts for about 60 per cent. of this market. The other main product in this field is Unilever's 'Quix' (principally 'Teepol').

out of line with the relative costs of production of the synthetic and soap products at this time. Apart from difficulties in the process of manufacture not yet overcome, the ratio of the prices of the active synthetic-detergent base material and neat soap stock was itself of the order of 2 : 1. Thus the average trade price of soap stock in 1948 was £98 2s. per ton;[1] and this would be of approximately 70 per cent. dry soap content. The trade price of 'Teepol' (20 to 25 per cent. active) at this time was in the range £60 to £70 per ton. The price per ton of active material comparable to that of soap stock, therefore, would be £185 to £215.

With the striking expansion in the sales of powder products in 1948 through 1949, Hedley's 'Dreft' and Unilever's 'Wisk' were brought into large-scale production. Then towards the end of that year Colgate-Palmolive, which company hitherto (as we have seen) had confined its attentions in the United Kingdom to the toilet soap market, brought out 'Fab', then manufactured and packaged in this country for Palmolive by Marchon Products Ltd. of White-haven; at the beginning of 1950 the C.W.S. began to market their own powder 'Cascade': and in the spring of 1950 Hedley's intro-duced their all-purpose detergent 'Tide'. With the appearance of these products the major soap companies were in the market in earnest. Competition in the 'soap' trade was to become even more intense than ever before.

(ii) *1949-50 to date*

With the introduction of 'Tide' by Hedley's in 1950 a new type of organic detergent base, namely the alkyl-aryl sulphonate, was rapidly to displace any other as the active detergent material in household powder products. Before we proceed with the main story, in the next chapter, a word must be said concerning this new type of detergent material.[2]

While this type of active detergent material was not utilized in

[1] From the Census of Production (1949), Vol. ii, Trade J.

[2] The most common variety is (sodium) dodecyl benzene sulphonate. The usual process of manufacture starts from a suitable petroleum fraction (the 'alkyl' com-ponent). This is akin to ordinary 'kerosene' as it is popularly known in the United States of America and Australia, or common 'paraffin' as in the United Kingdom. This material is first chlorinated by treatment with chlorine gas, and the resulting 'chlorohydrocarbon' is condensed with benzene (the 'aryl' or aromatic component) using a catalyst (Friedal-Crafts). This alkyl benzene is then sulphonated by treatment with sulphuric acid, and finally converted to the sodium salt by reaction with caustic soda.

the United Kingdom until 1949,[1] it was widely adopted in the United States of America as the most suitable base for domestic soapless detergents at an early date. Thus, according to Schwartz and Perry,[2] as early as 1943 this class accounted for upwards of 55 per cent. of the aggregate output of organic detergent bases in that country. The reason for this early development in the United States of America was the ready availability of a suitable petroleum fraction as raw material in that country, despite the war. This was not only a function of plentiful crude material supplies, but also of plant. Alkylation plant in the United States for the manufacture of aviation spirit was greatly expanded during the war, so that—particularly after 1945—both plant and raw material were readily available to produce a suitable alkylate in large quantities.

During the same period the case was otherwise in the United Kingdom, and it was not until the post-war programme of oil refinery construction began to mature about 1950 that the large-scale production of the alkyl-aryl sulphonates became possible in that country. From that date, with the success of 'Tide' and its competing products in the household powder market (see the next chapter) the alkyl-aryls quickly displaced all other organic bases in the manufacture of powder products (see Table 13).

The great advantage of the alkyl-aryl sulphonates as base material for the manufacture of household soapless powder products is that the resultant powder has no tendency to be lumpy. A powder based on the secondary alkyl sulphates (e.g. 'Teepol') almost invariably was lumpy. A lumpy powder interferes with the continuous flow of the manufacturing process (at the packing stage), and in household use it will not flow freely from the packet or—when the packet is prised —too much is spilt with consequent wastage. A second advantage is that an alkyl-aryl product can be spray-dried at higher temperatures than the secondary alkyl sulphates (and also soap) which enables an increase in the throughput of the plant and consequent reduction in process costs. Third, the alkyl-aryls are superior all-round detergents to the secondary alkyl sulphates.

The principal manufacturers of alkyl-aryl detergent material in the United Kingdom are the chemical firms, Monsanto Chemicals Ltd., and Marchon Products Ltd., and rather later the Shell Petroleum Company.

[1] The alkyl-aryl sulphonates had first appeared when Hedley's changed 'Dreft' over to this material (from a primary alkyl sulphate) in August 1949.

[2] *Surface-Active Agents* (New York, 1949), p. 111.

In the case of Monsanto, supplies of the 'alkyl' component are obtained from the British Petroleum refinery at Grangemouth, and methyl-benzene from Forth Chemicals Ltd., situated adjacent to this refinery and owned jointly by Monsanto itself, the Distillers' Union, and British Petroleum. From these materials Monsanto manufactures the alkyl-aryl sulphonate at Newport (Mon.). The plant is a large one, specialized and highly instrumented, and involving (to 1957) a capital expenditure of the order of £3-4m.

At the time Hedley's launched 'Tide' in the household market Monsanto was marketing a finished alkyl-aryl sulphonate in powder form under the brand name 'Santomerse'. Hedley's purchased supplies from this source, the product being supplied to them as refined alkyl-benzene, which was then sulphonated and neutralized by Hedley's themselves so as to ensure uniform quality control. With the success of 'Tide' in the domestic market (see next chapter), production at the Monsanto plant expanded phenomenally through 1950-1 occasioning considerable comment in the financial press at the time.

In the case of Marchon Products, this company does not itself manufacture the alkyl-benzene, which is purchased from outside suppliers.[1] The company markets a finished alkyl-aryl sulphonate under the brand-name 'Nansa', and also manufactures finished blended domestic detergent products through all stages. (It has produced 'Fab' for Colgate-Palmolive, and 'Spel' for the C.W.S.)

In the case of the Shell Petroleum Company, a plant has been established for the manufacture of refined alkyl-benzene, the bulk of the output (it is understood) being taken by Unilever for the manufacture of that company's detergent products 'Surf' and 'Omo'.

(Apart from Monsanto and Shell, at least two other plants have been established in the U.K. for the manufacture of alkyl-benzene. The larger of these is Grange Chemicals Ltd., owned jointly by Distillers and the Oronite Chemical Company. The initial investment in this plant was reported to be £1m.[2])

It is impossible to be precise as to the magnitude of the total sum invested in the U.K. to date in plant to supply alkyl-aryl detergent material, but it must be of the order of £10 to 12m.[3]

---

[1] Including overseas suppliers. Indeed, until about 1953-4, a considerable proportion of the total U.K. consumption of crude alkyl-benzene was imported.

[2] *Economist*, January-March 1956, p. 318. The other plant is referred to without details in O.E.E.C., *The Chemical Industry in Europe*, 1956 volume, p. 120.

[3] Say, Monsanto and Forth, upwards of £4m.; Marchon, £2m.; Shell, £2m.; Grange and other, £2m.

ENLARGEMENT OF THE COMPETITIVE FIELD OF THE
SOAP AND DETERGENTS INDUSTRY

Thus have the organic chemical and petroleum industries become important suppliers of raw material to the 'soap' industry. And for the most part the relation of these industries to the household market for washing aids—by far the most important market, volume-wise—has remained thus, i.e. manufacturers of materials for sub-sequent processing, blending and marketing by the established soap companies. But it need not remain so, and with this the competitive field of the soap manufacturers has been significantly widened.

Thus the Marchon chemical firm[1] has produced the final blended product for retail sale through all stages. This firm, then, could itself market a soapless powder at retail if the prospects were sufficiently attractive. As Lord Heyworth, Chairman of Unilever, has said:

A new competitive element has been introduced into the detergent industry. If the soap manufacturer loses efficiency, the chemical manu-facturer can and will step into the breach. . . .[2]

Lord Heyworth added '. . . and vice versa'. Hedley's for example, as we have seen, already sulphonate the refined alkyl-benzene themselves. It would be but a relatively short step for so large a firm to go back a further stage and manufacture the refined alkyl-benzene itself, and thus enter the province of the organic chemical industry.

The truth is, of course, that the boundary line between the soap and chemical trades has never been wholly distinct, and is now even more blurred than ever.

The result of the development of the alkyl-aryl sulphonates was effectively to displace entirely the secondary alkyl sulphates as bases for domestic powder products.

Thus in 1952 it was reported that 'Teepol', for example, had been withdrawn completely as such a base. As we have seen, however, the Shell Company's stake in the market for domestic powder inter-mediates continued, as it undertook the manufacture of alkyl-benzene for Unilever. As to 'Teepol', the steady outlet in Unilever's

---

[1] The company was acquired in November 1955 by Albright and Wilson Ltd., principal U.K. manufacturer of the phosphate builders used in the manufacture of the blended household detergent powders (see below, p. 223). (Marchon had recently itself installed plant to manufacture these phosphate materials.)

[2] Annual speech to the shareholders of Unilever, June 1953, printed in *The Times*, 11 June 1953.

'Quix', the liquid dishwashing detergent, continues, and apart from this there has been an increasing orientation of the sales effort towards a fuller exploitation of the industrial market. (This indeed probably dates from the notable price reduction in the latter part of 1949[1]—though with the 'sellers' market' in this type of detergent in any event coming to an end in that year, this was in effect the fall in price typical of an emerging competitive process.) In 1950-1 'Lensex', a paste version of 'Teepol' for use by laundries, was developed and widely advertised.

All in all the prospects of a continuing expansion in the industrial consumption of the cheaper class of detergents to which the secondary alkyl sulphates ('Teepol', as well as 'Condinol', 'Iranipol', and others) belong, would appear to be good. With this a measure of stability has emerged in the detergent base materials 'industry'.

We now turn to the main task, which is to consider the impact of the soapless detergents on the development of the established soap and detergents industry from 1949-50 to the present time.

---

[1] Cf. *Economist*, July-December 1950, p. 31.

CHAPTER 11

THE POST-WAR PERIOD

II. INNOVATION AND EFFECTIVE COMPETITION IN THE SOAP AND DETERGENTS INDUSTRY

IN this chapter we take up, in effect, the threads of our narrative as it was left at the end of Chapter 9. The war and its aftermath—or the worst of it—has passed; the allocation of oils and fats to the soap-makers has been increased, and a considerable improvement in the quality of soap products effected; and after a long period during which the soap ration had not been fully taken up, soap rationing has been abandoned (September 1950). In a word, conditions in the soap trade have been restored to 'normal', more or less,[1] and the stage is set for a resumption of the competitive struggle of the 'thirties after the lapse of a decade.

That decade, however, had not been a period of inaction. In particular, as referred to in the previous chapter, in the spring of 1950 Hedley's introduced their all-purpose detergent 'Tide'. This product was vastly superior to its rival products of that date, namely Unilever's 'Wisk', the C.W.S.'s 'Cascade', and Colgate-Palmolive's 'Fab' (as of that date). The broad composition of 'Tide' was based ultimately on fundamental research by Hedley's American parent, Procter & Gamble, as far back as the war years;[2] while the actual specification of the product as marketed in Great Britain in the spring of 1950 was the outcome of product and materials development by Hedley's in this country, dating back to 1947.

(By 'materials development', I refer to the taking of the necessary steps to ensure adequate supplies of suitable raw materials. This is a not unimportant aspect of the development of a new product; not least, the final specification of the product is normally the outcome of some measure of compromise between the original design and the best that available materials will permit.)

[1] The Ministry of Food still controlled oils and fats.
[2] The American 'Tide' was first introduced in pilot areas in the U.S.A. in 1946 (nationally in 1947-8).

It may, perhaps, appear surprising that so apparently simple a product as a washing powder should involve so long a period of development. The best evidence that in the case of 'Tide' it did, is that it was not until two years later in the summer of 1952 that Unilever (with 'Surf') and C.W.S. (with 'Spel') were able to bring out products comparable to 'Tide'. In a word, 'Tide' embodied a major innovation in the character of powdered washing products: this provides the key to the understanding of the course of the development at this time.

The remainder of this chapter is divided as follows. In the first section, the nature of the innovation referred to is indicated, and in the next the manner in which it was exploited by Hedley's discussed. Thereafter the development of the industry as a whole is reviewed. Finally (from page 241) the working of the market in this period and the prospects for the future are assessed.

It may conveniently be noticed at this point that the notable success of Thomas Hedley's in this period was widely attributed in trade circles to the 'generalship'—to quote one commentator[1]—of Mr. Robert Craig Wood, managing director of Hedley's until May 1954. The military reference is not entirely inappropriate: competition in the soap and detergents industry did take on something of the character of a war in this period, and Craig Wood is a manager-entrepreneur of the first rank. Born in a small Scottish village, he graduated from Glasgow University with honours in applied chemistry, and immediately joined Hedley's in 1933. He was appointed managing director of the Company in 1947 at the age of thirty-six.[2]

INNOVATION IN THE 'SOAP' INDUSTRY, 1950

The essence of the innovation was not merely that 'Tide' was a soapless detergent; there were, as we have seen, some hundreds of soapless detergent products selling at this time. But at this remove, it is clear that 'Tide' was the first really effective general-purpose soapless detergent powder to be marketed in Great Britain—comparable in washing qualities to a first-quality soap powder, and in hard water scum-free and more efficient.

When it was introduced in 1950 the approximate composition of 'Tide' was as follows:

[1] *Economist*, May 1954, p. 732.   [2] *Scope*, December, 1948, p. 56.

	per cent.
Organic detergent base	25
(alkyl-aryl sulphonate)	
Phosphate salts	30
(sodium pyro-phosphate and some tri-polyphosphates[1])	
Sodium Sulphate	30
Sodium Silicate	5
C M C (carbyoxy-methyl-cellulose)	1

with the remainder water. (Subsequently, when increased supplies of the superior tri-polyphosphates became available, the product was improved by reducing the content of the alkyl-aryl base somewhat—to 21 per cent.—and increasing the quantity of the phosphate builders.)

Now the essence of the innovation was the combination of synthetic detergent base with phosphate builders. The fundamental experimental fact which makes possible an effective soapless detergent powder can be summed up in this equation:

	Ordinary Builders		Synthetic		Phosphate Builders
Soap +	(primarily soda ash)	=	Detergent Base	+	(preferably tri-polyphosphates)

The synthetic on its own, or the synthetic with ordinary builders, makes a poor detergent, as already noticed in the previous chapter; but the synthetic plus phosphates makes a fine detergent. Procter & Gamble in the United States of America and Thomas Hedley in Great Britain appreciated this fundamental equation early on; their principal rivals in the soap trade did not. Appreciating it, both firms set out to exploit their lead to the full.

In the case of Hedley's the motivation was very clear-cut. It has first to be recalled that during the 'thirties, the manifest long-term trend in the demand for washing aids in favour of powders and away from the traditional bar soap had been accelerated, so that by 1937 (see Table 18A, p. 238) powders (including flakes) amounted to some 35 per cent. of the total national consumption of soap products by weight and bar soap 45 per cent.—as compared with 11 and 68

[1] An explanation of the nature and commercial sources of this material is given in due sequence below.

per cent., respectively, in 1907. It was doubtless evident to Hedley's, as to any of the soap companies, that the trend would continue. The powder is relatively more expensive, but with rising living standards the price would be met and its superiority, in terms of ease of and efficiency in use is obvious. The future, then, clearly lay with the powder products.

The second point to be recalled is the hardness of so large a proportion of the British water supply. As noticed in the preceding chapter, the Water Softening Sub-committee found that the water supplied to nearly 50 per cent. of the British population may be described as 'hard' or 'very hard'. In these circumstances, if the future lay with powders, then a soapless powder—stable in hard water and in other respects as good a detergent as the best soap powder —was, if competitive in price, a better proposition still. Hedley's, with 'Tide' in the laboratory, had just such a product.

Here then was just the opportunity which the firm required if it were to push out the limit to its share of the market imposed in the late 1930's by the effective competition of its powerful rivals, Unilever and the C.W.S.[1] I am convinced that Hedley's did, in fact, seek to do this—indeed, that the situation was thought of in just these terms.

It was a matter both of prestige—of throwing off the shackles of 'number 2' position in the trade—and of long-run profitability. As to the latter, whether the prospective margin of net profit per ton of output was higher in the case of the soapless detergents than soap powders one cannot tell: in the event, I understand, the realized margin of net profit per unit has been not significantly different, though now higher and now smaller than on soap as the prices of oils and fats have fluctuated.[2] But if the prospects were only that this latter outcome could be achieved, this would be sufficient. For in so far as the firm had virtually reached the limits to further expansion (apart from normal growth) in the field of soap, as seems probable, then the investment of additional capital in this field was thereby precluded. Yet for the soap maker, investment in expanded

[1] In terms of G. L. S. Shackle's theory (*Expectation in Economics*, 1949) one might speculate that, as compared with Unilever (see next page), all this would involve a very different 'y-function' in Hedley's case—with lower y values (greater confidence) attached to favourable outcomes from an energetic exploitation of the detergents, as compared with Unilever—and hence a significantly greater 'focus gain' (and lesser 'focus loss') for such a policy, presuming similar 'ϕ-functions' for each firm.

[2] The manufacturing-cost component in the prices of the organic detergent base materials is relatively high, so that their prices, as compared with the prices of oils and fats, are relatively stable.

soap production even at only a 'normal' profit is perhaps the most profitable investment relative to the risk, open to him.[1] If then the soapless detergents promised a significant expansion in overall sales (i.e. soap plus soapless products) which was otherwise impossible (more or less), then so long as a margin of net profit of just a similar order could be anticipated on the detergent products as on the soap, investment in the former would be the most profitable and the indicated course for the soap maker to follow.

Throughout this period, then, Hedley's objective was to exploit the soapless detergents to the full, and so far as possible to replace soap products on a permanent basis. It was, in short, to 'take out' the advantage of the innovation in the form of an expanded share of the market, rather than (primarily) in the form of enhanced short-run profits. How very effectively the company succeeded in this objective will be indicated presently.

The policy of Unilever, on the other hand, was by no means so clear-cut, and in any event was bound to be more conservative in view of the magnitude of its interests in soap. There is little doubt, however, that the fundamental equation (above), which made possible the effective soapless washing powder, was not appreciated by Unilever until relatively late, by which time Hedley's had a commanding lead. Lord Heyworth, Chairman of Unilever Ltd., himself referred to 'the suspension of most research work of this kind in Europe' owing to the war, as a factor in explaining the relatively late exploitation of the discovery of combining phosphates with synthetic materials in Britain.[2] (Subsequently the lack of suitable raw materials was to hinder the Unilever concern in its efforts to counter Hedley's.) Of course, too, the decentralized management of the Unilever soap interests precluded a unidirectional policy of soap replacement on the Hedley pattern, even had it been in the company's interest.

To enlarge on this theme, the manner in which Hedley's exploited the innovation must be considered.

MODE OF EXPLOITATION OF THE INNOVATION

For the quantity production of 'Tide', it was necessary to secure adequate supplies not only of the alkyl-aryl sulphonate detergent base, but also of the key phosphate builders. Neither of these

[1] Above, p. 120,

[2] In his annual speech to the shareholders of Unilever, June 1953, printed in *The Times*, 11 June 1953.

intermediates was being produced commercially in the United Kingdom at the time.

As to the former, the alkyl-benzene for the detergent base (as we have seen) was to be supplied by the Monsanto Company, which established a major plant for this purpose.

As to the phosphate builders: phosphate products in the United Kingdom are manufactured mainly from imported supplies of phosphatic rocks, from Nauru, the United States of America, and Algeria. The dominant firm in the United Kingdom is Albright & Wilson Ltd. The problem in this connexion, therefore, in the Britain of the post-war years with its recurrent balance of payments crises, was not only that of manufacture, but of importing the necessary supplies of phosphate rock. During 1947-9 Hedley's were constantly engaged in representations to the Board of Trade in this matter. It was argued that if the Board would permit the import of the finished phosphate builders (in the short run) and of additional supplies of phosphatic rock for their manufacture in the United Kingdom (in the long run), then satisfactory synthetic washing products could be produced to reduce the nation's requirements of imported oils and fats.

In the event Hedley's were enabled to import the necessary supplies of phosphate builders during 1950, principally from Belgian and German manufacturers. Meanwhile Albright & Wilson established plant for their manufacture in the United Kingdom.

In this way Hedley's secured their supplies of the basic raw materials for 'Tide'. The risks were great[1]; but so, in the event, were the rewards of this enterprise (below, p. 248).

'Tide' was launched first in the London area in the spring of 1950, backed by a large-scale advertising campaign.

The retail price in 1950 was set at 10*d*. for the small (8 oz.) packet, and 1*s*. 7*d*. for the large (1 lb.) package, or about 19·3*d*. per pound on the average. (See Table 14.) The corresponding prices for a good-class soap powder (e.g. 'Persil') were also 10*d*. for the small

[1] Or rather, the 'uncertainty' (cf. the reference above to Shackle's theory). It is worth noticing that while Hedley's were entering into the above arrangements, opinion in some other sections of the trade was probably fairly reflected in the estimate of a contributor to the *Economist* (July 1950, pp. 31-32), obviously writing from trade information, that on the basis of U.S. experience to that date 'the possible absorption of synthetics might lie between 40,000 and 65,000 tons . . . Sales in the home market last year (1949) must have reached the lower figure; . . . the remaining 25,000 tons [may be] the measure of potential demand'. In the event sales of household detergents exceeded 150,000 tons by 1954 (Table 13, and below).

pack (about 12 oz.) and 1*s*. 5*d*. for the 'giant' pack (about 22 oz.), or approximately 12·7*d*. per pound on the average. Thus, with the introduction of 'Tide', the price of the synthetics relative to soap by weight had been reduced from the ratio of about 2 : 1 in 1948-9 (above, p. 212) to 1·5 : 1, as in the last column of Table 14. Since soap prices had fallen somewhat over this period, the reduction in the price of the detergent products was notable (in excess of 25 per cent.). Such a fall in price is typical of an emerging competitive process. In 1952 the retail prices of both the soap and detergent products were

TABLE 14

Ratio of Retail Prices, Soap Powders and Soapless Detergent Powders
(pence)

Year	Soap Powder ('Persil')			Soapless Detergent ('Tide', 'Surf')			Ratio, synthetic to soap prices per lb.
	Actual prices		Average price per lb.	Actual prices		Average price per lb.	
	'12 oz.'	'Giant' (22 oz.)		Small (8 oz.)	Large (16 oz.)		
1950	10	17	12·7	10	19	19·3	1·5 : 1
1952	12	21	15·5	12	23	23·3	1·5 : 1
1957	11·5	20	14·8	⎰ 12 ⎱ 11·5	23 22	23·3(*a*) 22·4(*b*)	1·57 : 1 1·5 : 1

(*a*) 'Tide' (and 'Daz').
(*b*) 'Surf' (and 'Omo') until July 1957; thereafter the same as 'Tide'.

increased (*pari passu* with the rise in costs and prices generally). But the ratio of prices of 1.5 : 1 was maintained. In 1957 (third row of the table), the position remained the same. Thus with some variations during the episode of price competition (discussed below), the ratio of prices of 1·5 : 1 was substantially maintained throughout the period of the exploitation of the soapless detergents. It is necessary to consider the circumstances which appear to have influenced this result.

It seems clear that the dominant consideration was that of the prospective demand for the soapless detergent powders. In this the 'hard water effect' is the important factor.

There are possibly other factors. Thus some housewives assert that there is no substitute for the 'clean, soapy smell' of clothes washed in a soap powder. But washing products can be perfumed. It is doubtful whether this consideration would exercise any systematic or permanent influence on the structure of demand.

A second factor is the comparative effect of the soap and 'synthetic' products on the skin. Any washing product by its nature tends to remove the fats of the skin to some extent. But it has been held that the soapless detergents do this to a greater extent than soaps, resulting in a dry and scaly skin.[1]

However, it is also true of blended soap products that they tend to irritate skins which have been softened by prolonged soaking.[2] It is difficult, therefore, to assess the importance of this factor as it affects the relative demands for soap and soapless detergents. Certainly it does not seem in the event to have restricted the growth of the demand for the latter.

The 'hard water effect' remains as the significant permanent factor influencing the demand structure. From the selling point of view, this has two aspects. There is, first, the possibility of exploiting the 'no scum' property *per se* of the synthetics. Housewives in hard water areas are very conscious indeed of the nuisance of scum in using soap. Second, there is the associated greater efficiency, weight for weight, of the detergents as compared with soap products— varying with the degree of hardness of the water approximately as in Fig. 14 (p. 224). It is of interest in this connexion to consider the actual strategy of the Hedley Company.

Hedley's Market Strategy. In the early advertising campaign for 'Tide', two points were stressed, first, the non-formation of scum *per se*, and second, the dirt-suspending powers of the product (from the combination of detergent base with the phosphate builders and 'C M C').[3] Only oblique reference was made to the greater weight for weight efficiency of the product in hard water.[4] This emphasis was only to be expected, because the 'no scum' property—which meant not only lack of nuisance, but in fact cleaner washing with less effort (rinsing)[5]—could appeal to users whatever the degree of

---

[1] Along with other causes. See e.g. the article 'Detergents and Skin Damage', by Prof. W. Schneider, *Soap, Perfumery and Cosmetics*, 1952, pp. 45-49.

[2] Lord Heyworth, in his address to the shareholders of Unilever, June 1953, previously referred to.

[3] Thus advertisements (e.g. *Woman*, 25 Nov. 1952) ran: 'There is *no scum* to stick in the fabrics, *Tide* never makes scum even in the hardest water . . .'; etc. As regards the second point, this was the basis of the 'no rinse' claim. Thus the advertisement referred to was headed in bold red letters: '*No rinsing*, yet wash is dazzling'.

[4] Thus on the packet it was stated: '*How much to use* . . . half of this packet [small-size] is enough for the average size family wash. *You need no more 'Tide' however hard the water.*' And further down under the heading 'the washing-up', it was stated *inter-alia* '. . . And of course, *Tide* is so economical.'

[5] Reference has already been made in the previous chapter to the 'greying' effect with white goods continually washed with soap in hard water.

hardness of the water (save in very soft water), and this, therefore, was a point of importance in launching a product ultimately to be distributed nation-wide.

Further, however, this initial procedure of the company can be seen on closer examination to fall into a clear pattern of strategy, in which the greater weight for weight efficiency of the soapless detergents in hard water has its due place.

Thus, the basic problem was to ensure the initial acceptance of the product by the housewife. This required two things. First, there should be a rough equivalence between the new detergent packs and the housewife's customary soap packs, in terms of size, appearance, and washing power. This was a matter of giving the housewife what she was familiar with: in particular, the small '12-oz.' soap pack, retailing at 10*d*. in 1949-50, had been very popular in the years after the war; it was desirable, therefore, that the new product should be presented in a similar pack (though, like the soap powders, in a large one too).

Second, it was required that the (apparent) price differential per pack, while virtually inevitable in view of the higher costs of producing the detergent product (of which more below), should not exceed 'a penny or two' at most.

If this were indeed the strategy, then on the one hand the initial emphasis on the novelty appeal of 'no scum' and on the effect of this in enabling a cleaner wash with less effort, falls readily into place: its role was to induce the housewife in the initial stages to pay the price differential as compared with the 'equivalent' soap pack, if the differential was indeed inevitable, or to swing the balance in favour of the detergents if the price pack for pack were the same, and so to get her using the product in the first instance.

On the other hand, the greater weight for weight efficiency of the soapless products entered the scheme as a factor in fixing upon the specification of a pack 'equivalent' to the corresponding conventional soap pack.

The 'equivalence' of the pack required visually a packet of about the same dimensions, and hence the same volume of powder. It required also a rough equivalence of 'washing power'. It would seem only natural at this point to look to the 'average' equivalence of soap and detergent powders for the nation as a whole, which (as discussed above p. 204) is about two-thirds of a pound of detergent to do the same work as one pound of soap. This basis being adopted, so that the 'small' detergent pack would contain 8 oz. by weight to the soap pack's 12 oz., then the equivalence of volume—to maintain the all-important requirement of similarity in appearance and hence of initial acceptability—could be effected by spray-drying to an appropriately less dense powder, yielding a greater volume per unit weight.[1]

Whether or not the company did in fact have regard to the national average equivalent of synthetic to soap powder in use, it is impossible to say. Two things, however, can be said. First, a ratio of the detergent to the soap pack of $\frac{2}{3}$: 1 by weight, and selling at the same price, was the actual position adopted in the case of the small pack,[2] and this probably meant the balance of advantage in demand in favour of the detergents. For in that section of the market served by water significantly above the average in degree of hardness, the advantage on the score of efficiency alone would be with the soapless product; in the more or less equal section served with water significantly *below* the average in hardness, the advantage would lie with the soap; while in the sector about the average where there would be indifference on this score (and even in those areas of the 'below average' section with water of an appreciable degree of hardness), the 'no scum' property would favour the detergents and would thus serve to turn the balance of advantage in the market as a whole in their favour. Such an 'equivalence' then—$\frac{2}{3}$: 1 by weight, and the same price packet for packet—bid fair to swing the powder market over to a greater consumption of the detergent than of the soap powders. The matter might thus be put, that in the neighbourhood of this 'equivalence' of price/quality the probability was that the demand for the soapless detergent powders was very elastic. Combined with the independent prestige factor—the desire to throw off the restraints of 'number 2' position in the industry—and also the certainty of eventual intense counter-competition by Unilever, Hedley's decision to take out the advantages of the innovation in terms of an enlarged share of the market is thus readily explicable.[3]

---

[1] A soap powder can always be 'blown' to give a greater or less density, and hence volume per unit weight; and the question of the right density for a powder has always been a major problem in the trade. A powder of a lighter density flows more easily and dries better; but on the other hand, the housewife does not like to be consuming 'air'.

[2] i.e. 10*d*. was the price of both the small soap (12 oz.) and the small synthetic (8 oz.), the latter being less dense to give roughly the same volume as the former.

[3] Above, Chapter 4, pp. 118-20.

Second, however, a ratio of $\frac{2}{3}$: 1 by weight and the same price would absorb a 'cost' differential per unit weight, in the production and distribution of the synthetic *vis-à-vis* the soap powders, of 1·5 : 1; and ultimately, of course, it was this—the cost factor—which governed the possibility of the foregoing, or a more, or less, favourable equivalence. It is, however, not improbable that the relative costs of the synthetic and soap powders were in fact by this time of the order of 1·5 : 1. The alkyl-aryl base itself cost perhaps twice as much as neat soap, but this would account for less than one-third of the total cost (moreover the content of soap in a soap powder is higher than the content of organic detergent base in a detergent powder); the phosphate builders were perhaps half as expensive again as the sodium carbonate of the soap powder; while other costs—packing, despatch, and distribution—would be much the same for both classes of product.

It is, unfortunately, impossible to be more precise than this. One can merely record the fact that the equivalent of $\frac{2}{3}$: 1 by weight and the same price (10*d.*) was in fact adopted for the 'small' pack; and that with this 'equivalence' maintained, a sufficient proportion of the market was won over to enable profitable production of the synthetic products at a margin of net profit per unit not significantly different (as already stated above) from that earned on the soap powder, though now larger and now smaller than the latter as the prices of oils and fats have fluctuated.

And more than that. As will be discussed in detail in the next section, so large a proportion of the market for washing powder was won over to the detergent products, and so large is the Hedley Company's share of that trade, that the Company's share of the aggregate United Kingdom market for all washing products has been more than doubled.

This enlargement of its share of the market by Hedley's is the important outcome in this connexion, and the justification of the foregoing detailed discussion of the company's market strategy. For it could have been otherwise. That the new detergent powders would in any event have captured a large proportion of the total market for washing powders, and in substantially their present form, is evidenced by parallel developments in other countries—in the United States, and later in most Western European countries.[1]

1 See the O.E.E.C. publication, *The Chemical Industry in Europe*, 3rd year (Paris, 1956), pp. 121-3.

But within this development the enlargement of Hedley's market share was by no means inevitable: it was the outcome of the early and definitive decision of the company to strive to replace soap on a permanent basis, and its shrewd assessment of the problems of winning the initial, and rapid, acceptance of the new products in the U.K. market. And the significance of this is that Hedley's early appropriation of the lion's share of the trade in the new products resulted—and to all appearances will continue to do so—in a resurgence of intense competition in the industry, as Unilever has sought to contain and to reverse this development.

THE DEVELOPMENT AS A WHOLE

(i) *1950 to 1954.*   We are now in a position to review the development of the industry from 1949 as a whole.

Hedley's introduced 'Tide' in the spring of 1950. As previously stated, there was still at this time a large number of small manufacturers producing products of varying qualities, but the principal products were the 'Teepol'-based 'Wisk' (Unilever), Colgate-Palmolive's 'Fab', and the C.W.S.'s product 'Cascade'.

The initial sales campaign for 'Tide' was concentrated in the London area, where the product was intensively advertised. (As a trial market for pilot-scale production, the London area is ideal. The concentration of one-sixth of the population there, its complex retail shop structure, and its interlocking structure of local with national newspapers reduce transportation, distribution, and advertising costs to a minimum. And, in particular, from the point of view of soapless detergents, the water supply is 'hard'—about 224 p.p.m. of hardness.) The figure of £750,000 has been mentioned for Hedley's advertising expenditure for the ensuing full year, and in the triangular contest which developed (Unilever and Colgate-Palmolive were the other contestants) similar figures were suggested for the latter also.[1] These are possibly exaggerated. The writer in the *Economist* himself goes on to state:

These figures need cautious interpretation; experienced advertisers doubt whether there would be enough press and outdoor advertising space in the areas covered on which to spend such great sums.

The estimates, however, may well include the costs of bargain and free offers, and if so, the figures could be quite accurate. The significance of the large sums spent on advertising during this period

[1] *Economist*, July-Dec., 1950, p. 31.

will be assessed presently. But in face of such intense advertising and a product so obviously superior in quality, most of the small manufacturers that remained were driven out of the market.

With the successful launching of 'Tide' in the London area, a nationwide distribution of the product was rapidly effected in the latter part of 1951.

Now it was not till the summer of 1952 that Unilever and the C.W.S. with 'Surf' and 'Spel', products strictly comparable to 'Tide', effectively joined the issue with Hedley's in soapless detergents. That meant a lag of some two years from the introduction of 'Tide'. An important reason for this was the lack of suitable raw materials, and in particular the essential phosphate builders. We have already discussed the manner in which Hedley's, apprehending the possibilities early, had secured supplies of these basic materials: theirs, therefore, was not more than a normal commercial advantage. But this lag enabled them to secure a commanding position in the market.[1]

'Surf' was marketed by Unilever first in the South, and subsequently throughout the nation. The lengths to which the company was prepared to go in its efforts to make up the leeway resulting from Hedley's early start are indicated by the initial marketing campaign: within a few days over 30,000 retailers in an area stretching from the Wash to the Isle of Wight were supplied with 'Surf' (in many cases without any prior notice, to the resentment of some), while to some millions of housewives in the area coupons were sent to enable them to buy a packet of 'Surf' at less than one-third the normal price.[2]

Hedley's met this renewed competition with characteristic vigour. A similar coupon to that for 'Surf' was promptly sent out for 'Tide', and the advertising of the latter stepped up. Then, in January 1953, the company's second string in the general-purpose detergent powder market, 'Daz', was introduced.

In fact, 'Daz' was specifically a boiling product, for 'whites', the object being to tap the large market in the United Kingdom for such a product, mainly served by Unilever's soap powder 'Persil'. The principal product refinement (minor innovation) it embodied was a bleach. 'Daz' is a blue powder—the initial sales appeal was based on this. The blue element is an improved form of the 'optical bleach',

[1] Cf. above, Chapter 2, pp. 38-40.
[2] From a report in the *Grocer*, June 1953. The number of housewives was stated to be 6,000,000.

i.e. a material which combines with fabrics to give a blue fluorescence in sunlight; it thus neutralizes the yellowish or brownish tinge fabrics show when soiled or washed repeatedly, and thereby increased the whiteness (or total amount of light reflected by a fabric) without lessening fibre strength as chlorine or peroxide bleaches may do. With this product variant, then, Hedley's sought to tap a new (product) sector of a market in which washing products are becoming increasingly specialized to particular purposes, and thus further to swing the aggregate market over to the detergent products and to maintain the firm's dominant share of this trade. At this time that share was in excess of 75 per cent. (see Table 17, p. 234).

The product variant proving successful, Unilever of necessity had to match it. Thus in June 1954, that company introduced its blue soapless powder 'Omo'. The measures adopted to launch this product surpassed even those in the case of 'Surf': a free packet was distributed to every household in the country—perhaps 15,000,000 packets.[1] Only the imperative necessity to contain, and if possible to reverse, Hedley's grip on the market for the detergent powders can account for the company going to such lengths. Nothing less than the essential 'connexion' of the Unilever business, in a sizeable sector of the total market for washing products, was at stake.

These measures, however, met with only indifferent success; and in November 1954, in the absence of any new product development, Unilever had resort to the only remaining weapon, namely, price competition.[2] The episode is of great interest and merits rather detailed discussion.

(ii) *Price Competition in the Detergents Industry, 1954-7*

The key outcome of events to 1954 is brought out by the data in the two right-hand columns of Table 15, and graphed in Fig. 14. These data express (approximately) the respective shares *by value* of Unilever and Thomas Hedley, in the total U.K. trade in household washing powders.[3]

Thus in 1950 Unilever held more than 50 per cent. of this market, and Hedley's just short of 30 per cent. But with the massive success of 'Tide', the Hedley share increased rapidly, so that by 1952 it actually exceeded that of Unilever by a few percentage points. In

---

[1] *Economist*, April-June, 1954, p. 322.

[2] Cf. Chapter 2, pp. 32-33 above.

[3] It is held that the shares by value, rather than by weight, is the relevant basis for the argument, since (as stated above) the profit margin per unit sale of the soap and detergent products has been much the same taking the period as a whole.

TABLE 15

Shares of Global (i.e. Soap plus Soapless Detergents)
Washing Powder Market: Unilever Ltd. and Thomas Hedley Ltd.

	Weight Basis*		'Soap Equivalent'† (approx. Value Basis)	
	Unilever %	Hedley %	Unilever %	Hedley %
1950	53·5	26	51·5	29·5
1951	54·5	35	50	39
1952	50	39·5	43	45·5
1953	49	42	44	47·5
1954	51	43	45·5	49
1955	57	39	51·5	44
1956	60	35	55	40
1957	57·5	38·5	53·5	42·5

* These estimates derived from annual data (from trade sources) compare very closely with P. A. R. Puplett's extremely variable figures recorded in the first two columns of his Table XVI, *Synthetic Detergents* (London, 1957), p. 129, relating to selected dates in the years shown. (The estimates for 1950 are less soundly based than for the other years.)

† In these columns the detergent component (physical output) in each firm's sales, and in the total of sales, is multiplied by the factor 1·5, before the percentages are taken. Cf. above, p. 204, and below, p. 237, n.3.

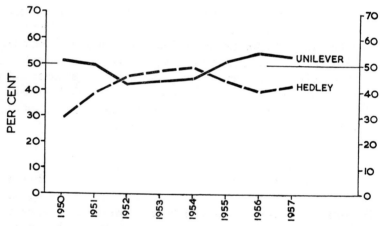

Fig. 14: Shares of Global Washing Powder Market (approx. Value Basis) 1950-57

1953 through 1954, both firms increased their share of the market (at the expense of other producers); but by the latter year, Hedley's share was just short of 50 per cent. of the market and the margin between its own and the Unilever share persisted.

It is scarcely surprising then that Unilever should adopt the strongest measures in the attempt to reverse this trend. In November 1954, the price of 'Surf' and 'Omo' was cut by 3d.—from 1s. 11d. to 1s. 8d. ('giant' pack).[1] Hedley's response was twofold: the price of 'Tide' and 'Daz' was reduced by only 1*d*. to 1*s*. 10*d*.; but—attacking the sector of the market (soap) wherein Unilever was dominant, just as Unilever had attacked the sector (detergents) in which Hedley was dominant—the price of 'Oxydol' soap powder ('giant' pack) was cut by the full 3*d*., from 1*s*. 8*d*. to 1*s*. 5*d*. This Unilever met by reducing the price of the corresponding 'Persil' pack to 1*s*. 6*d*.[2]

TABLE 16

Retail Prices, Soap and Soapless Detergent Powders: U.K. 1952-7

| | Soap Powder | | | | Detergent Powder | | | |
| | Unilever ('Persil') | | Hedley ('Oxydol') | | Unilever ('Surf', 'Omo') | | Hedley ('Tide', 'Daz') | |
	'Giant'	'Large'	'Giant'	'Large'	'Giant'	'Large'	'Giant'	'Large'
1952	1/9	1/-	1/9	1/-	1/11	1/-	1/11	1/-
Oct. 1954	1/8	11*d*.	1/8	11*d*.	1/11	1/-	1/11	1/-
Nov. 1954	1/6	10*d*.	1/5	9*d*.	1/8	10½*d*.	1/10	11*d*.
April 1955	1/6	10*d*.	1/6	10*d*.	1/8	10½*d*.	1/10	11*d*.
Nov. 1955	1/7	10½*d*.	1/7	10½*d*.	1/8	10½*d*.	1/10	11*d*.
June 1956	1/8	11*d*.	1/8	11*d*.	1/10	11½*d*.	1/10	11½*d*.
Dec. 1956	1/8	11*d*.	1/8	11*d*.	1/10	11½*d*.	1/11	1/-
July 1957	1/9	11½*d*.	1/9	11½*d*.	1/11	1/-	1/11	1/-

Source: Unilever Ltd. and Thomas Hedley Ltd.

The resulting price differential of 1*d*. between the competing soap powder brands was maintained for only five months, to April 1955 when Hedley's raised their prices to match Unilever's. But the differential of 2*d*. ('giant' pack) in the prices of the two firms' detergent powders was maintained for fully eighteen months, to June 1956, when Unilever raised their prices to match Hedley's.

[1] This represents a reduction of some 13 per cent. Presumably distributors' margins were not reduced, and these amount to about 15 per cent. of the selling price, i.e. 3½*d*. in the retail price of 1*s*. 11*d*. The price cut of 3*d*., therefore, borne by the manufacturer would amount to 15·4 per cent. of the 'normal' net manufacturer's price of 1*s*. 7½*d*. (i.e. 1*s*. 11*d*. less 3½*d*.). With a net profit rate of (say) 25 per cent. on capital, and a ratio of annual turnover (total revenue from sales) to capital of the order of 3 to 1, the net profit rate in ratio of the manufacturer's price (i.e. unit turnover) would be of the order of 8-9 per cent. It would appear therefore that a price cut of 15·4 per cent. involved selling below cost.

The magnitude of the cut was thus such as to raise the question of 'fair competition'. For the Unilever share of the U.K. trade in soapless detergents represented only a minute fraction of its total business (indeed its trade in 'soap and other detergents' both at home and overseas accounted for only 14·8 per cent. of total turnover in 1954-5—see Unilever Ltd., Annual Report, 1956). In Hedley's case, on the other hand, their trade in the soapless detergents in the U.K. represented upwards of 70 per cent. of their total business.

However, in this battle of 'giants' it would, no doubt, be wrong to make too much of this question of 'fair' or 'unfair' competition. After all, Hedley's are backed by the resources of the U.S. parent firm, Procter & Gamble—as dominant in the U.S.A. as Unilever is in the United Kingdom. This question apart then, the resort to price competition is indeed refreshing, and the final consumer has received the benefit.

[2] Hedley's also reduced the price of the firm's household bar soap 'Fairy' by 1*d*., which cut was fully matched by Unilever ('Sunlight').

Prices were then maintained level until the following December when the price of 'Tide' and 'Daz' (Hedley) was restored to the 1954 level (1s. 11d.), 'Surf' and 'Omo' (Unilever) continuing at 1s. 10d. This differential of 1d. was then maintained for six months, until in July 1957 Unilever raised its prices to match Hedley's, since when parity of prices has been maintained.

Now in my opinion it is impossible to doubt that these price differentials in favour of Unilever—2d. (9·1 per cent.) for eighteen months, and later 1d. (4·3 per cent.) for six months—contributed significantly towards enlarging the market share of Unilever and cutting back that of Hedley.[1] Thus the respective shares of Unilever and Hedley in the total sales of the detergent powders only, are shown in Table 17 and illustrated in Fig. 15. These data clearly

TABLE 17

Shares of Soapless Detergent Powder Market: Unilever Ltd. and Thomas Hedley Ltd. (Per cent.)

	Unilever ('Wisk', 'Surf', 'Omo')	Hedley ('Dreft', 'Tide', 'Daz')
1951	10	79·5
1952	9	81
1953	19·5	74
1954	25	71·5
1955	32	65
1956	36·5	60·5
1957	38	59·5
1958	n.a.	n.a.
1959	41·5	57·5

* Based on annual data from trade sources.

suggest an approach to stability in the pattern of this market divided as between Hedley and Unilever in the ratio 60 : 40. But it is, I think,[2] reasonable to speculate that the pattern might well have worked out less favourably for Unilever in the absence of that firm's aggressive price competition. For while the Hedley share

[1] Mr. P. A. R. Puplett's account of these same events tends in some places to suggest the opposite conclusion: see *Synthetic Detergents*, pp. 152-3. However, among other points, Mr. Puplett relies dangerously on estimates of market shares at particular dates, which can be extremely variable: thus (e.g.) conclusions are drawn from a comparison of shares in May 1955 with those in October 1954, although it is evident from his data recorded elsewhere (e.g. see row 1 for 'Tide', Table XIII, op. cit., p. 119) that for some reason May figures are frequently and systematically higher than October figures of the previous year even with a declining (year to year) trend. With this 'seasonal' removed, it appears that 'Tide'—a 'dearer powder' (op. cit., p. 225)—barely maintained its position in the market in 1955, despite the momentum of its very long start; and 'Daz' (another dearer powder) certainly lost considerable ground.

[2] One recognizes the danger of too fine shades of interpretation with data which are only rough in the nature of the case.

in 1951-2—dominating because 'Tide' was virtually alone in the field—was bound to be eroded somewhat with the subsequent competition of so powerful a rival as Unilever; yet it is evident that its rate of decrease—and, correspondingly, the rate of increase in the Unilever share—was declining in 1954, so that the situation may (circumstances remaining the same) have stabilized with a division of the market, say, in the ratio 70 : 30, as indicated in Fig. 15 by the dotted lines.

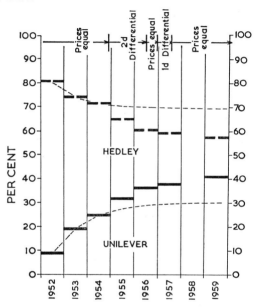

Fig. 15: Shares of Soapless Detergent Powder Market, 1952-9

In fact, however, the rate of decrease (increase) started to rise again in 1955-6; and the evident new factor in the situation was the Unilever price cut not fully matched by Hedley's.[1]

1 It might be objected that the issue is not that the Unilever price-cuts were without effect, but rather that in view of the assertions of our own analysis (above, Chapter 2, pp. 47-49), the effect of a price differential of the order of 9 per cent. maintained for eighteen months was not even larger than that here detected. A number of factors are relevant in this connexion. First Hedley's, following a very early start, were 'riding' a strong upward trend in the demand for the detergent powders. Second, there is an essential unity in the global (soap plus detergents) washing powder market, and the issue was confused (a) during the initial period, by the cut and counter cut—Unilever initiating with the detergents, and Hedley with the soap products; and (b) throughout the whole period, by bargain (coupon) offers by both firms superimposed on the cuts in nominal prices. Third, quite apart from 'irrational' preferences for the long-established Hedley products (especially 'Tide'), the principal Unilever product 'Surf'

Meanwhile Unilever maintained, indeed increased somewhat, its share of soap powder sales. (The price differential of 1*d.* in favour of Hedley was, as already stated, maintained only for a brief period, and was in any event obscured by simultaneous coupon bargain offers.) The overall effect therefore in the global powder market (i.e. soap plus detergent powders) was abruptly to reverse the trend to 1954 previously discussed: the Unilever share increasing in 1955 to more than 50 per cent. of the market, with Hedley's falling back to 44 per cent. (Table 15 and Fig. 14, above). And in 1956 Unilever moved even further ahead.[1] Looking at the matter from the Unilever point of view, the company had indeed succeeded in 'stopping the rot'.

In concluding this discussion, it might be remarked that the changing pattern of shares in the U.K. washing powder market from 1950-1, including the episode of price competition, is quite consistent with the generalizations advanced in Part I, above: namely, that with major innovation a decisive alteration in the pattern of shares of a market may be effected; that at the same price for similar size/quality of product and in the absence of innovation, the tendency is for the division of the market established as the outcome of the particular historical development (typically, an unequal division) to persist—perhaps the 'normal', the situation in most industries at most times; but that in the event of a price differential from whatever

was in fact a denser product than 'Tide'. (See also P. A. R. Puplett, op. cit., p. 132 n.). Since 'Tide' had been in use for some years when 'Surf' appeared, it would tend to have established housewives' habits in respect of such products, and in particular the *volume* of powder necessary for a given washing task. Using the same volume of the more dense 'Surf', therefore, the effect would be more (though superfluous) lather and washing power, but a greater consumption by weight of the product. Since the 'Surf' and 'Tide' packs contained the same weight of product, 'Surf' at the same price per pack would thus work out more expensive to use. This then would provide a partial rational basis for a housewife-consumer continuing an established brand preference for 'Tide', at the price differential of 2*d.* above 'Surf'.

[1] In 1957 Hedley's succeeded in again reversing the trend, to a limited degree. This resulted mainly from the successful introduction (in July 1957) of the company's new soap powder 'Fairy Snow'. The powder was flecked with green, in order—along with the name—to establish the association with Hedley's own (green) household bar soap, 'Fairy'; and the green packet was not dissimilar to the 'Persil' packet, against which product it was undoubtedly primarily directed. The introduction of this powder may be interpreted as an aggressive 're-entry' by Hedley's into the soap powder market, the force of the company's early policy to replace soap with the detergent powders on a permanent basis, having been spent by this date. And throughout the period, Unilever's 'Persil' had continued strong and had always been something of a 'nigger in the woodpile'.

cause,[1] with the dominant firm charging the higher price, that firm will lose ground and market shares will tend to equality, setting up pressures towards the restoration of parity of prices.

(iii) *Growth of Sales of the Soapless Detergent Powders*

Under the pressure of this intense competition, the total consumption of the soapless detergent powders in the United Kingdom increased rapidly until the beginning of 1954 (see column 2 of Table 13, p. 209). From 22,000 tons in 1949 and 32,000 tons in 1950, the sales of these products grew to the order of 127,000 tons in 1953 and 150,000 tons in 1954. Then the rate of growth slackened noticeably (and the resort to price competition by Unilever is thus the more readily explicable); so that in 1955 the total consumption of the household detergent powders approached stability at an annual rate somewhat in excess of 150,000 tons. This rate, however, was within an aggregate consumption of washing products, soap and detergents, notably enlarged as compared with the levels of 1950-1 (see Table 20, below, p. 243).

On the basis of the calculations of the previous chapter (where it was concluded that 'on the average 1 lb. of the soapless detergent powders displaces in use about 1·5 lb. of soap powder'),[2] the soap equivalents of the consumption of the soapless detergents in the census years 1951 and 1954 were, respectively, about 74,000 tons and 225,000 tons.[3] Thus, as indicated in the second column of the data relating to 1951 and 1954 in Table 18A, the aggregate consumption of washing powders (excluding flakes) in 'soap equivalent' in those years was about 268,500 tons and 380,500 tons respectively. It is evident that the soapless detergent powders had

---

[1] The price differential emerged and persisted in the present case of the soapless detergent powders, because as previously suggested if Hedley's had fully matched the Unilever price cuts, this would virtually have eliminated the firm's net profit altogether. Even so the effect of the limited reduction in Hedley's prices which was made (combined with the maintenance of the firm's massive advertising expenditures) was very apparent in Hedley's reported profits, which amounted to £2·4m. in 1952-3 and £2·2m. in 1953-4, and then fell abruptly to £565,000 in 1954-5 and £1·4m. in 1955-6. (See Appendix 2.)

[2] Above, p. 204.

[3] It is to be emphasized again that in the circumstances of the time these indicate (approximately) both *value* and *volume* equivalences.

That is to say, the value of 150,000 tons of synthetic powder at retail was approximately equal to the value of 225,000 tons of soap powder—since the 8-oz. packet of synthetic retailed at the same (or a higher) price as the 12-oz. soap powder product.

And the volume of 150,000 tons of synthetic as marketed was roughly equivalent to the volume of 225,000 tons of soap powder—since the volume of the (less dense) 8-oz. synthetic pack was roughly the same as the 12-oz. soap powder pack.

TABLE 18A

Aggregate (a) U.K. Consumption of 'Soap' Products by Product Classes, 1907-54 (000 tons)
(Source: Censuses of Production, and Table 13)

Product Class	Year	1907	1924	1930	1937	1951 Actual Tonnage	Do. in 'Soap' Equiv.'	1954 Actual Tonnage	Do. in 'Soap' Equiv.'
Hard Soap, in Bars	Tons	239·0	264·3	239·5	225·7	141·0	141·0	117·0	117·0
	%	67·7	64·0	57·0	45·0		22·1		16·3
Powders	Tons	40·0	72·0	98·8	122·3	Soap 195·0 / Non soap (b) 49·0 / Total 244·0	268·5	Soap 155·5 / Non soap (b) 150·0 / Total 305·5	380·5
	%	11·3	17·5	23·5	24·4		42·1		53·1
Flakes and Chips	Tons				52·7	30·0	30·0	28·0	28·0
	%				10·6		4·7		3·9
Toilet (incl. shaving)	Tons	12·5	24·7	20·0	38·2	58·0	58·0	64·5	64·5
	%	3·5	6·0	4·7	7·6		9·1		9·0
Scouring and Abrasive	Tons	..	32·0	33·5	36·4	Soap (c) 58·0 / Other 8·0 / Total 66·0	66·0	Soap (c) 20·5 / Other 31·0 / Total 51·5	51·5
	%		7·8	8·0	7·3		10·3		7·2
Soft	Tons	61·5	16·0	17·1	18·9	12·0	12·0	8·0	8·0
	%	17·5	3·9	4·2	3·8		1·9		1·1
Other	Tons	..	3·0	11·1	5·8	Soap 7·0 / Non soap 37·0 / Total 44·0	62·5	Soap 4·5 / Non soap 42·0 / Total 46·5	67·5
	%		·8	2·6	1·3		9·8		9·4
Total	Tons	353·0	412·0	420·0	500·0	595·0	638·0	621·0	717·0
	%	100·0	100·0	100·0	100·0		100·0		100·0

Notes: (a) I.e. sum of 'Household' plus 'Industrial' Consumption. See Table 18B for breakdown for 1954.

(b) 'Household' Consumption only. All 'Industrial' is included in 'Other—Non soap'.

(c) There is some ambiguity in the available statistics in respect of 'Scouring and Abrasive Products'. During the period 1952-5, the major soap companies progressively changed the (active) base material in such products as 'Vim', 'Ajax', 'Mirro', etc., from soap to synthetic detergent materials. However, the output of these products is variously recorded as 'soap' or 'other than soap'. The 20,500 tons recorded above as 'soap' is the quantity included in the Board of Trade figures for aggregate consumption of soap products in Table 20 below (398,000 in 1954: i.e. the sum of 117·0, 183·5, 64·5, 20·5, 8·0, 4·5). The balance of the estimated consumption of 51,500 (i.e. 56,000 from the 1954 Census, less 4,500 tons exported) is recorded as 'Other'. The quantity of active

exploited—and undoubtedly in turn promoted—the pre-war trend away from the traditional bar soap and towards an increasing use of powder products.

This trend is brought out by the lower figures in each row of Table 18A expressing the various product classes as percentages of the total consumption. Thus the total of powder and flake products (in 'soap equivalent') amounted to 46·8 per cent. of the aggregate consumption of all washing products in 1951,[1] and nearly 60 per cent. in 1954; as compared with 35 per cent. in 1937 and 17·5 per cent. in 1924. On the other hand, the consumption of household bar soap amounted to but 22 per cent. of the aggregate consumption in 1951 and 16 per cent. in 1954; as compared with 45 per cent. in 1937, 64 per cent. in 1924, and nearly 70 per cent. in 1907. These changes reflect in large part the rising levels of real income in the United Kingdom over the period in view.

And within the aggregate consumption of washing powders, the detergent powders had indeed appropriated a half, or somewhat larger, share of the market by 1954—as presaged above (pp. 227-8). In this context the reference is to the aggregate household consumption of these products, which is indicated in Table 18B. In 1954 the total household consumption of powders (excluding flakes) amounted to 295,000 tons. The consumption of the soapless detergent powders, at 150,000 tons, thus represented a little more than 50 per cent. of the total. In 'soap-powder equivalent' the consumption of the detergent powders would be 225,000 tons (as previously stated), or 60 per cent. of the corresponding total consumption of 370,000 tons.

Within this development, as referred to earlier, Thomas Hedley's achieved a significant expansion in their share of the general United Kingdom market for washing products. In the immediate pre-war year 1938-9, the company's share of the aggregate household market was of the order of 15 per cent., and as suggested above that seemed to represent the limit to the expansion of its market position in the conditions of that time. But with the rapid growth in the consumption of the soapless detergents and the appropriation by Hedley's of so large a proportion of that trade, the company succeeded by 1954 in expanding its share of the aggregate U.K.

---

[1] i.e. the aggregate including the synthetic detergents, and expressed in 'soap equivalent', namely, 638,000 tons.

household market to the order of 35 per cent. (in 'soap equivalents', i.e. rough value basis.)[1] Excluding toilet soap, in which sector of the market Hedley's do not market a product, the percentage is nearer 40 per cent.

Meanwhile Unilever, by retaining its grip on the market for soap products, maintained its share at just in excess of 50 per cent.[1] The C.W.S. on the other hand had by this date lost considerable ground, with a share of the market of the order of only 6 per cent.[1] With this the combined share of the 'big three' amounted to upwards of 90 per cent. of the market as compared with 75-80 per cent. in the immediate pre-war period (Table 8, p. 183), so that other soap makers, too, had lost ground: this trend one would expect with the intense competition of the period. But so far as the two dominant firms in the industry are concerned, the outcome of the process of exploiting the major innovation of the soapless detergent was a significant 'evening up' in their relative market positions.

[1] These results are estimated as follows:

Shares in the U.K. Household Market 1954

Product group	Thomas Hedley Ltd.			Unilever Ltd.			C.W.S.	
	Share %	Sales (000 tons) Actual	'Soap Equivalent'	Share %	Sales (000 tons) Actual	'Soap Equivalent'	Actual	Sales (000 tons) 'Soap Equivalent'
Household Bar	20, say	17·0	17·0	70, say	59·5	59·5	⎫	
Powders and Flakes	13	21·0	21·0	79	129·5	129·5	⎬ 25·0	25·0
Toilet	Nil.	Nil.		40, say	21·5	21·5		
Scouring	15	7·5	7·5	54	27·0	27·0	⎭	
Detergent Powders	71·5	107·5	161·5	25	37·5	56·0	⎫	
Liquid detergents	Nil.	Nil.		30	2·5	3·5	⎬ 6·0	9·0
Total			207·0			297·0		34·0
Aggregate Consumption	⎰ inc. Toilet — 590·0 ⎱ exc. Toilet — 536·0					590·0		590·0
Hedley share	⎰ inc. Toilet — 35·0 ⎱ exc. Toilet — 38·6			Unilever share		50·5	C.W.S. share	6·0

Sources: Total consumption in each product group—Table 18B; shares in each sector (Hedley and Unilever)—Table 17, and estimates from trade sources; in case of C.W.S., direct information as to volume of sales kindly supplied by the Secretary, C.W.S., Manchester.

TABLE 18B

'Household' Consumption (1951 and 1954) and 'Industrial' Consumption and Exports (1954 only)

	1951	1954				
	Household Con-sumption	*Household Con-sumption*	*Industrial Con-sumption*	*Total U.K. Con-sumption*	*Export (f)*	*Total U.K. Produc-tion*
Hard Soap, in Bars	116·0	85·0	32·0	117·0	39·5	156·5
Powders:						
Soap	170·0	145·0	10·5	155·5	3·5	159·0
Non soap	49·0	150·0	(c)	150·0	(c)	150·0
Flakes	21·0	19·0	9·0	28·0	·5	28·5
Toilet (incl. shaving)	48·0(g)	54·0(g)	10·5(d)	64·5	11·5	76·0
Scouring and Abrasive	56·0 {	(e) 20·0	·5	20·5 }	4·5 {	(e) 25·0
		30·0	1·0	31·0		31·0
Other:						
Soap	(a)	(a)	12·5	12·5	·5	13·0
Non soap	18·0 (b)	8·0(b)	34·0	42·0	31·0	73·0
Total Soap	411	323·0	75·0	398·0	60·0	458·0
Total Soapless Detergents	67	158·0	34·0	192·0	31·0	223·0
Do. in 'soap equiv.'	100	237·0	51·0	288·0	46·0	334·0
Other Non soap (scour)	—	30·0	1·0	31·0	—	31·0
Grand Total (soap equiv.)	511	590·0	127·0	717·0	106·0	823·0

(a) Negligible: attributed to 'Industrial'.
(b) Liquid Soapless Detergents.
(c) Included in 'Other Non soap'
(d) Mainly Government and Municipal Contract Sales.
(e) Top figure 'Soap' and bottom figure 'Other, Non soap', abrasive products. (See note (c) Table 18A.)
(f) Source: *Abstract of the Overseas Trade of Great Britain*.
(g) Includes all 'Shaving' (from Census) as well as household Toilet.

ASSESSMENT: EFFECTIVE COMPETITION IN THE SOAP AND DETERGENTS INDUSTRY

It is necessary now to consider the question of how effective the working of competition in this period has been. As stated in the opening paragraph of this chapter, conditions of more or less 'free competition' were restored in the industry during 1950; this year therefore may be taken as an appropriate base year for the present discussion.

The question may be discussed with reference to the following dimensions of industry performance: prices, output, productivity, profits, and advertising.

(i) *Prices*

In Table 19 the course of retail prices generally, and the prices of soap and soapless detergent products from 1950 are compared.

TABLE 19

Price Index Numbers, Soap and Detergent Products: 1950-7

	General Retail price index 1	Soap		Soapless Detergents	
		Powder, retail ('Persil') 2	B.O.T. Wholesale price index, all products 3	Powders, retail 4	B.O.T. wholesale price index, all products 5
1950	100	100	100	100	100
1	109	109·5	109	108	107·5
2	119	120·5	116·5	120·5	116
3	123	118·5	110	120·5	117
4	127	113	106·5	119	116·5
5	132·5	105	104	110·5	108
6	139	112	114·5	113	112·5
7	143	118·5	123	119·5	119

Sources: Col. 1.—Interim Index of Retail Prices.
Cols. 2, 4, 5.—Retail Price data supplied by Unilever Ltd. and Thomas Hedley Ltd.
Cols. 3, 6.—Board of Trade Wholesale Indexes.

It will be seen that the prices of washing products have fallen notably since 1952 relative to prices generally. Indeed, in the case of the detergent powders, the nominal retail prices at the end of 1957 were identical with prices in 1952 (as we have seen), whereas retail prices generally increased steadily between these dates by about 17 per cent.

The prices of soap products (Board of Trade index) have of course been influenced, apart from the Unilever-Hedley price competition, by fluctuations in the prices of oils and fats. (A notable rise in the prices of oils and fats occurred in 1956 and has continued; this is reflected in the sharp increase in the index in that year.) In the case of the household soap powders ('Persil', 'Oxydol'), however —which are directly competitive with the detergent powders—the retail price in 1957 stood at 118·5 in relation to 1950, as compared with 120·5 in 1952.

(ii) *Consumption and Output*

With the prices of soap and detergent products thus maintained low in relation to prices generally; with continued high levels of aggregate employment and real national income (apart from the minor recession of 1952); and in face of the intense selling pressure throughout the period, a notable expansion in the overall consumption of washing products in the U.K. has taken place. The pre-war consumption per head was re-attained sometime in 1949; and the total consumption in 1949-50—both soap and detergent products (in 'soap equivalent')—was 639,000 tons. In 1955 (see Table 20) the aggregate consumption expressed in this way was 736,000 tons—an increase of 15 per cent.[1] The rate of growth in the total consumption over the period was thus of an even higher order—about $2\frac{1}{2}$ per cent. per annum—than in the decade of the 'thirties (see Table 10, p. 193).

TABLE 20

Aggregate Consumption (Household and Industrial) of All Washing Products: U.K. 1949-50 to 1955
(000 tons)

	Aggregate, all soap products (a) 1	Aggregate, non-soap products		Total	
		Soapless detergents (b) 2	Other (c) 3	By weight (sum cols. 1+2+3) 4	'Soap equivalent' (cols. 1+ 2×1·5+3) 5
Av. 1949-50	531	72	—	603	639
1951	501	86	8	595	638
2	437	124	18	579	641
3	413	166	25	604	687
4	398	192	31	621	717
5	406	200	30	636	736

Sources: (a) Data provided by Board of Trade. For reconciliation with Census of Production Reports, 1951 and 1954, see Table 18A above.
(b) From Table 13 above.
(c) Scourers, detergent based, n.e.i. (See note (c) to Table 18A.)

(In this connexion, one can reasonably speculate that the total consumption would have been less, and if not, that the output consumed would have been produced and sold at higher prices, had the soapless detergents not been exploited in this period—first in North America and Britain, and later in most European countries. Lord Heyworth has estimated that in 1952, the additional world requirements of oils and fats to supply the same total demand for washing products by soap only, would have been $2\frac{1}{2}$ per cent. of the then world production:[2] this would have resulted in a somewhat higher level of market prices for oils and fats. Since then the production of

[1] This result based on 'soap equivalents' (i.e. production 'value-weighted', and an approximate indication of effective 'washing-power' consumed) is identical with that of Mr. P. A. R. Puplett based on weight of products consumed with reference to the household market only (*Synthetic Detergents*, p. 65).
[2] Speech to the shareholders of Unilever, June 1953, previously referred to above.

soapless detergents in all countries taken together doubled (to 1955-6), and notwithstanding this the prices of oils and fats rose sharply in 1956. Soap prices, therefore, would inevitably have been higher but for the development of the soapless detergents. For the same reasons, of course, the competitive position of soap products *vis-à-vis* the detergents is enhanced to some extent by the very development of the latter.)

In addition to the increased production for consumption at home, the industry in this period also achieved a considerable expansion in the volume of exports. In 1951 exports of soap and detergent products totalled 78,000 tons by weight (soap, 66,000; detergents 12,000), or 84,000 tons approximately in 'soap equivalent': in 1955 the corresponding figures were a total of 114,000 tons by weight (soap, 61,000; detergents, 53,000), or 140,500 tons in 'soap equivalent'.

In the normal pre-war year 1937, exports of soap products totalled 41,400 tons: the expansion to 1955 was thus of the order of 3 to $3\frac{1}{2}$-fold. (Imports in recent years have been negligible, e.g. a mere 116 tons in 1955.)

The total production of soap and detergents products in Great Britain in 1955 was thus 750,000 tons by weight, or 876,000 tons in 'soap equivalent'. In 1938-9 it was about 570,000 tons, and in 1949-50 it was 651,500 tons by weight[1] or 689,000 tons in 'soap equivalent'. The increase from the latter date to 1955 in soap equivalent (the relevant unit of comparison) was thus of the order of 27 per cent., as compared with the increase over the period in the general index of industrial production of 21 per cent.

(iii) *Productivity*

Moreover this expanded output was produced with a significant increase in efficiency. The data in Table 21 continue for this later period the crude productivity comparisons for the inter-war period essayed in Chapter 9 (Table 11 above, p. 199).

It will be seen from the table that the number of employees (operatives and salaried employees) in the soap and detergents industry proper decreased by 1,730 from 1951 to 1954, and by nearly 3,000 from the former year to 1955. Production per employee thus increased at the rate of nearly 4 per cent. per annum on a weight

[1] U.K. consumption, 603,000 (Table 20); exports—soap products, 45,000, detergents, 3,500 (Table 13).

basis (6 per cent. expressing the outputs in 'soap equivalent') from 1951 to 1954, or nearly 5 per cent. per annum (7 per cent. in 'soap equivalents') taking the period 1951 to 1955. The latter period probably provides the better indication, as it would permit of the very large capital investments in the development period of the soapless detergents' manufacture (to 1953-4) to show their full effects. In any case it is evident that the increase in the efficiency of production over the period was substantial.

TABLE 21

Production per Employee: Selected Years to 1955
Soaps and Detergents Industry: U.K.

	Total production (a) (tons)	Number of Employees (d)	Production per employee
1937	523,100	22,920	22·8
1951	631,000(b)	23,202	27·2
	662,000(c)		28·5
1954	653,000(b)	21,472	30·4
	738,000(c)		34·3
1955	672,000(b)	20,392	32·9
	763,000(c)		37·4

(a) Includes net exports, but excludes output by firms classified in the Census of Production to other industries (principally the chemical and petroleum industries), as follows (weight basis):

	(000 tons)		
	Soap	Detergent	Total
1951	7	35	42
1954	7	52	59
1955	7	71	78

(b) Actual tonnage: weight basis.
(c) 'Soap Equivalent': i.e. rough adjustment for increasing proportion of more efficient and expensive soapless detergent powders.
(d) From Censuses of Production.

It is of interest in this connexion to notice that wages paid per 'operative' employed[1] increased in real terms by 12·8 per cent. from 1951 to 1954,[2] or about $4\frac{1}{4}$ per cent. per annum. It would appear therefore that manual employees in the soap and detergents industry shared appropriately, more or less, in the gains associated with the increase in efficiency in the industry. In a recent article Messrs. Reddaway and Smith found, for the industrial division 'Chemicals' over the period from 1948 to 1954, that whereas the increase in

[1] 'Operative' is the term used in the Census of Production to indicate employees other than administrative, technical and clerical employees, i.e. 'broadly speaking, all manual workers'.
[2] Years of full Censuses of Production. (Reliable data not available for other years.)
  Wages paid per operative amounted to £323 in 1951, and £424 in 1954. The 1951 figure would be £376 expressed in 1954 prices (the retail price index increased by 16·5 per cent. from 1951 to 1954). Thus the increase over the period was £48 in 1954 prices—about $4\frac{1}{4}$ per cent. per annum on the average.

crude (or gross) labour productivity was 42·2 per cent., the increase in overall efficiency (i.e. roughly speaking, output per unit input of capital-and-labour—or, productivity adjusted for additional capital inputs) was 22·2 per cent.,[1] that is, about 52 per cent. of the crude productivity increase. Although detailed information is lacking, it is very probable that the incidence of capital expenditure in the soap and detergents industry was much the same as in the chemical industry generally. Then taking the increase, above, in gross labour productivity on the 'soap equivalent' basis (approximate value basis), namely, 6 to 7 per cent. per annum, as the appropriate measure for the soap and detergents industry in the present context, one can reasonably judge that the increase in real wages of 4¼ per cent. per annum represents a proper sharing by labour in the gains from the increase in efficiency in the industry.

To this point then, the general picture for the industry is of an expanding production for home consumption and export, substantially increased efficiency, and virtually unchanged prices despite the rise in general prices and costs over the period.

(iv) *Profits*

Nevertheless the foregoing does not indicate any definitive answer to the important question of the relation over the period of the prices of soap and detergent products to the 'cost of production'. In previous chapters the calculations of the Government Committee of Inquiry in 1920 provided a basis from which this question could be approached (working backwards in Chapter 6, and forwards in Chapter 8 and 9).[2] But that objective basis is quite inappropriate to the changed conditions of the production and sale of soap products in the present period, and *a fortiori* in the case of the soapless detergents where the structure of costs is essentially different from soap. It is necessary therefore to adopt a somewhat different approach.

This may begin with a survey of the level of profits earned in the industry over the period. Fortunately data are available from the annual statements of accounts lodged under the Companies Act of 1948. In Table 22 the level of profits in the soap and detergents industry is compared with some other industries and with 'All Manufacturing Industries'. (The nature and sources of the figures in the table are discussed in Appendix 2 to this Part.)

---

[1] W. B. Reddaway and A. D. Smith, 'Progress in British Manufacturing Industries in the Period 1948-1954', *E. J.* 1960, Tables I and II, pp. 27-28.

[2] Above, Fig. 10 and 12, Appendix 2 to Chapter 6, and Appendix to Chapter 8.

TABLE 22

Profits in Relation to 'Capital Employed', 1949-56, British Soap and Detergents Industry, with some other Industries

	Unilever Ltd. (four companies)	Thomas Hedley Ltd.	Industry average, soap and detergents	Food and confectionery	Tobacco	Clothing and footwear	Chemicals and paint	All manufacturing
1949	13·4	21·0	14·9					
1950	12·0	24·6	15·1					
1951	18·1	17·3	17·9	18	20	18	14	19·4
1952	15·9	20·4	17·4	14	17	14	10	15·4
1953	16·2	32·2	21·5	18	17	17	12	16·6
1954	10·3	19·1	13·2	19	18	17	13	17·2
1955	13·9	11·7	13·2					
1956	15·6	18·7	16·6					
Average, years shown:	14·4	20·6	16·2	17·2	18	16·5	12·2	17·2

Sources: Data in cols. 1, 2 and 3 calculated from balance-sheets and appropriation accounts submitted by companies under the Companies Act of 1948. For details, see Appendix 2. Other data from the Monopolies Commission, *Report on the supply of Certain Industrial and Medical Gases* (H.M.S.O.), Appendix 16, p. 133.

Prima facie the picture is one of only a 'reasonable' level of earnings in the soap and detergents industry. Over the period 1949-56 as a whole, the realized annual rate of profit before tax was of the order of 16·2 per cent. for the industry, as compared with 17·2 per cent. for 'All Manufacturing Industries'.[1] As between the two leading firms in the industry, however, there is a notable difference in the level of profits earned. In the case of Thomas Hedley's the rate of profit is consistently above that for the Unilever soap companies, rising to a maximum of 32·2 per cent. in 1953.[2] This pattern we should expect: the year 1953 was the year of 'full flood' (so to speak) in Hedley's exploitation of the major innovation of the soapless detergents, and this high level of profits indicates the rewards of this enterprise. Subsequently, with the intense counter-competition of the Unilever group, the rate has fallen: in the Hedley financial year ended 30 June 1955, to as low as 7·3 per cent., but recovering in the following year to 16·1 per cent.

In assessing the significance of the observed industry rate of profit, with respect to the all-important question of the relation of prices to costs, it is first necessary to observe that for its American counterpart (which is structurally similar to the British industry), Mr. J. S. Bain has estimated the goodwill or 'product differentiation' barrier to new entry as bordering between his 'Moderate' and 'Great' categories,[3] that is, equal approximately to 5 per cent. of the unit cost of production including 'normal' profit. Now the ratio of the annual turnover (total receipts from sales) to capital employed is of the order of 3 to 1 in this industry.[4] Therefore if the

[1] The figure for 'All Manufacturing Industries' relates to the years 1951-4 inclusive only. During this period the average for the soap and detergents industry was rather higher (17·5 per cent.). But whereas the figure for 'All Manufacturing Industries' may be accepted as a reasonable 'normal', the rate of return in the soap and detergents industry in these years reflects the gains associated with the exploitation of a major innovation. It seems proper therefore to base the comparison on the longer period for the soap and detergents industry.

[2] Estimated calendar year rate—see Appendix 2. For the Hedley financial year ended 30 June 1953, the rate was 33·5 per cent.

[3] Table 1, above, p. 93.

[4] It is impossible to be more precise because figures as to the total turnover are not required to be supplied under the 1948 Act. However, the total receipts from sales of Thomas Hedley Ltd. for both the years 1953 and 1954 can be estimated with reasonable accuracy at £23-25m., while the capital employed was £7·25m. and £7·1m. respectively in these years (Appendix 2). This suggests a ratio of between 3·2 and 3·5 to 1.

In the case of the Unilever business as a whole (its interests apart from soap are in related industries where the ratio is probably similar), the total turnover in 1956 was £1,671m. and the 'capital employed' £497.5m., giving a ratio of 3·35. (From Unilever Ltd., *Annual Report and Statement of Accounts*, 1956).

potential entry gap of 5 per cent. were fully exploited to return excess profits, such profits would amount to 15 per cent. in ratio of capital employed. If a normal rate of profit, additional to this, is put at 17 per cent. on the capital employed (the reported profit rate for 'All Manufacturing Industries', as noted above), then the total return would amount to 32 per cent. in relation to capital employed (or about $10\frac{2}{3}$ per cent. in ratio of the annual turnover, or unit price). In fact, however, the realized rate of profit over the period was just in excess of 16 per cent., as above.

While thus the realized rate of profits suggests *prima facie* that competition has been effective in maintaining the prices of soap and detergent products in close relation to the 'cost of production', this is nevertheless not conclusive. There remains the possibility referred to above[1] that the potential excess of price over cost has in fact been realized, but that it has been absorbed in 'excess' expenditure on advertising.

(v) *Advertising*

The available information bearing on this vital question of advertising expenditure is assembled in Table 23. In part the figures are securely-founded on published data; in part they are no more than speculative estimates, for no information is more jealously guarded by the firms concerned than the magnitude of their expenditure on advertising.[2]

It will be seen from the table (cols. 8 and 9) that the expenditure on advertising the household detergent powders, including bargain and coupon offers. varied in different years from nearly 5 per cent. of the total manufacturers' receipts from the sale of these products to upwards of 11 per cent. This incidence of advertising expenditure is indeed high relative to manufacturing industry generally, but it is not uncharacteristic of the 'soap' industry: as we have seen (above, Chapter 6) W. H. Lever's expenditure on advertising during the first twenty years of the business amounted to some $12\frac{1}{2}$ per cent. of the total revenue from sales.

But, of course, in whatever manner the expenditure on advertising particular products is formally accounted within a firm, the funds are ultimately derived from all the firm's activities. For our present purposes therefore a more relevant measure of the incidence of advertising expenditure for the industry is the total advertising

[1] p. 95.   [2] The nature and sources of the figures are described in Appendix 3.

expenditure for all products, soap and detergents, in ratio of the total manufacturers' receipts from sales of all washing products. For the two full Census of Production years 1951 and 1954, which provide accurate data for the total of manufacturers' receipts, this ratio is 5·5 per cent. and 9·1 per cent. respectively (col. 12 of the table).[1]

It would appear then that even if one were to assume that advertising expenditures were as much as 50 per cent. in excess of a 'normal' or 'reasonable' level, this would still involve an effective profit rate for the industry below the rate consistent with maximum exploitation of the entry barrier—and, correspondingly, a price structure below the no-entry ceiling level. For with advertising at the high figure of 9·1 per cent. of total receipts, an 'excess' expenditure of 50 per cent. would imply that a sum equivalent to 3 per cent. of receipts, or about 9 per cent. in ratio of capital employed, should properly be regarded as net profit, additional to the recorded (average) profit rate of 16·2 per cent. This would suggest an effective profit rate of 25 per cent.—still significantly below the rate (32 per cent.) suggested above as consistent with maximum exploitation of the entry barrier. Expressed in ratio of turnover (total receipts), the comparison is between an apparent margin of net profit of about 8·4 per cent. as compared with a potential 10⅔ per cent.

The difference of 2-2½ percentage points may appear rather fine on which to base a definitive conclusion. But this is very probably a minimum figure, rather than the reverse. In particular, the assumption that the excess of advertising expenditure has been of the order of 50 per cent., is rather strong and especially as applied to the whole period to 1955.[2] The sums involved have indeed been

---

[1] In relation to the entire output of the 'industry' (as defined for Census purposes) the ratios are as follows:

	'Gross output' £m	Total advertising as percentage %
1951	88·3	4·2
1954	91·2	7·2

The principal outputs other than soap and detergent products were glycerine, fatty acids, and candles, and since such products are not significantly advertised these latter ratios perhaps provide the better indication of the incidence of advertising expenditure in the industry.

[2] Some (rather slight) grounds are noticed in Appendix 3 for putting the 'excess' at about 50 per cent. in the case of the detergents for the latter years of the period (below, p. 263). But the detergents accounted for rather less than half of the total advertising expenditure; moreover during 1954 and 1955 in particular (and indeed, in part just because of the enlarged advertising expenditure), the recorded profit rate for the

large in absolute magnitude, but they are bound to have been so with the process of establishing new products on a national market. And they have undoubtedly resulted in (offsetting) economies elsewhere, namely, in other distribution costs,[1] and in enabling a speedier determination of the extent and division of the market for the detergent products, with a relatively steady volume of sales of the few dominant brands resulting in full utilization of large plant installations at all stages of production. What requires to be borne in mind is the important point noticed above,[2] that in the context of exploiting a major innovation in product (a 'new' product) advertising expenditures in large part must be regarded as in the nature of capital or investment expenditure: the money is to be seen as invested in the creation of the essential 'connexion' in the market as the assured (more or less) outlet for the product of large-scale manufacture, and the more quickly this object is achieved the better. It is evident that the firms concerned have viewed their expenditure in this period in this way. Thus Lord Heyworth has stated in the speech previously referred to:

Introductory advertising, the cost of which is undoubtedly heavy, has to be regarded as a kind of capital investment, which will have a beneficial effect on manufacturing costs in the long run, because the blenders and suppliers of ingredients can plan with greater certainty the required outputs.

Again a statement issued by Hedley in early 1954 attributed the low profit in 1951-2 (7·3 per cent., in relation to capital employed:

industry was significantly less, namely, 13·2 per cent., than the average of 16·2 per cent. for the whole period used in arriving at the above result. Again, the figure of 9 per cent. for total advertising in ratio of turnover is assumed to apply over the whole period, but this is probably a maximum figure: the comparable estimate for 1951 is in fact (as above) only 5·5 per cent.

It may well, therefore, be nearer the mark to envisage a ratio of advertising expenditure to turnover of 5·5 per cent. for (say) 1950 to 1952, with 9 per cent. for 1953 to 1955; and to suppose the 'excess' during the earlier period to be smaller, say, 25 per cent. For the entire period this would mean an effective profit rate in relation to turnover of 6·7 per cent. (i.e. average industry profit rate of 16·8 per cent., or approximately 5·6 per cent. on turnover, plus 1·1 points for the 'excess'). This would suggest for the whole period an average effective profit rate in relation to turnover of the order of 7½ per cent. (average of 6·7 and 8·4 per cent.)—rather more than 3 percentage points below the potential maximum. It is not desirable, however, to press such a calculation too finely.

[1] Particularly stockholding and other retailing costs. Initially retailers were offered incentive margins on the soapless detergents, but by 1954 margins had been brought down to the relatively low level (about 15 per cent., on average) characteristic of highly advertised 'soap' products. (Cf. P. A. R. Puplett, op. cit., pp. 159-61.)

[2] p. 91, n.

TABLE 23

Advertising Expenditure, Soap and Soapless Detergent Products: United Kingdom, 1950-5*

(£000)

Year	All soap products				Soapless detergent products					Total advertising, all soap and detergent products £m	Recorded value of Sales (Manufacturers' Net), all soap and detergent products	Total advertising as percentage %
	Press	Outdoor and cinema	Other (includes window, coupon schemes, etc.)	Total	Press, outdoor, and cinema	Other (includes window, coupon schemes, etc.)	Total	Total value, manufacturers' sales, household products £m	S.D. Advertising as percentage %			
	1	2	3	4	5	6	7	8	9	10	11	12
1950	1,765	387	430	2,582	843	170	1,013	8·8	11·5	3·6	—	—
1951	1,976	434	480	2,890	672	135	807	10·6	7·6	3·7	66·7	5·5
1952	1,750	384	425	2,559	625	235	860	17·7	4·9	3·4	—	—
1953	2,269	498	550	3,317	1,695	340	2,035	24·9	8·2	5·4	—	—
1954	2,567	563	625	3,755	2,355	470	2,825	28·0	10·1	6·6	72·5	9·1
1955	2,745	603	670	4,018	2,584	515	3,099	28·3	10·9	7·1	—	—

* Notes and Sources: Appendix 3.

see Appendix 2) to 'a deliberate decision to spend heavily on the company's development', and in reporting this the commentator in the *Economist* inferred that 'the "development" mentioned here includes [apart from new plant] the very heavy costs of initial sales promotion to launch its new products on a mass market'.[1]

With these qualifications to the above argument, the conclusion that competition has been effective in maintaining the prices of soap and detergent products in a reasonable relation to the 'cost of production', remains a valid inference.

One final point should be made in connexion with the advertising expenditures of this period. The reasonableness of such expenditures is sometimes tested by an arbitrary comparison with the total of investment in fixed plant over the corresponding period. In the case of Thomas Hedley Ltd., the total of expenditure on 'new buildings, plant and vehicles, less retirements' for the seven years 1949 to 1955 was £3·5m.[2] as against a total expenditure on advertising of about £7-8m. mainly concentrated on the soapless detergents.[3] In this sort of case, however, it is important that account should be taken of investment outside the soap companies themselves.[4] In respect of the detergents, one may speculate that the prospect of Hedley purchases 'underwrote', in effect, the initial investments by Monsanto and Albright & Wilson in setting up the complex plants for the manufacture of the organic detergent base materials and the phosphate builders used in the soapless detergents.[5] These investments would now amount to the order of £4-5m.; while the total investment in plant for the manufacture of such materials has probably been in excess of £15m. The essential market outlets of these investments, as well as the investment within the soap companies themselves, were at stake; so that the former are surely no less relevant than the latter to a comparison with advertising expenditures at the final stage of production and sale.

[1] *Economist*, April-June 1954, p. 732.

[2] Extracted from the annual statements submitted under the 1948 Act. Similar data not available for Unilever Ltd.

[3] Estimated as follows: press, cinema, and outdoor advertising, detergent products ('Dreft', 'Tide', 'Daz')—£5·3m. (from Puplett, op. cit., Table XXVI, p. 209); other advertising, detergent products, say 50 per cent. of amounts in col. 6 of Table 23, above—£932,000; soap products, say 5-10 per cent. of 'Total, all soap products', col. 4 of Table 23, plus £100,000 for 1949—£1·1m. to £2·0m.: grand total, 1949 to 1955—£7·3 to £8·2m.

[4] In general, as stated elsewhere, the ratio of the annual turnover to capital in the case of mass-produced consumer goods is of the order of 3 : 1. But if account is taken of the capital employed in the production of materials and components, the ratio is reversed—to the order of 1 : 2.   [5] Above, p. 223.

Overall the general picture which emerges is one of effective or 'workable' competition in the soap and detergents industry. At least during the period reviewed, there have been reasonable profits, expanded output, a progressive technology, improved products, and prices in reasonable relation to the cost of production.

What are the prospects for the continuance of this performance in the future? Within the 'soap' industry as such, two conditions are obviously of key importance: first, that the non-collusive rivalry of the two dominant firms in the industry should continue; and second, that new discoveries should be made in the laboratories from time to time to permit of new product and process developments which ultimately are the only effective bases of dynamic variations in the balance of market power of the dominant firms (or again, the only effective basis of a challenge to the positions of the latter by a new competitor).

As to this second condition opinion in the industry itself is that the prospects are not unfavourable. One may again quote Lord Heyworth:

The new detergents, as might be expected, have stimulated scientific thought on detergency and the washing process. There has been a marked re-emphasis of the more fundamental chemical aspects of the industry. The work involved in determining new analytical procedures is con-siderable. Soap analysis has been a subject for the textbook for many years; now each new synthetic substance presents a fresh problem that has to be dealt with on its own merits.

The change in emphasis in the laboratory is of special importance to the industry. The chemistry of washing products seemed to have been so thoroughly explored that the scientist appeared to have relatively little future scope. It was the salesmen and the advertising experts who seemed to play the decisive roles. While the latter are no less important today, the new products have introduced a more balanced perspective to the industry and the scientist can look forward to a future as absorbing and exciting as can be found anywhere in the chemical trade.

As we have seen, the 'synthetic' detergents, on the one hand, have led to a new emphasis on the development of a wider range of washing products 'tailored' to a variety of particular purposes; and on the other hand, they allow of recourse to a large and increasing variety of raw materials. With the increased emphasis on research into detergency and detergent materials referred to by Lord Hey-worth (both in the 'soap' and the chemical trades proper), therefore, the prospects of new product and process developments in the future would appear to be good. The development of an effective (and cheap) 'synthetic' toilet soap is one such possibility which springs readily to mind.

There is perhaps, however, a difficulty in this connexion. The exploiting of new products in this industry is bound to involve a recurrent resurgence of advertising expenditures to very high levels in absolute terms. Yet even the large sums expended in this way in recent years have been lower, in relation to the massive turnovers of the two dominant firms, than were the amounts spent on advertising by the larger number of smaller firms in the industry in the early nineteen-hundreds (Chapter 6 above). Moreover, I believe it is beyond question that other types of distribution costs (distributors' margins, and the sales overhead within the soap companies) are lower than they would be if the present structure of the industry were in some way replaced by a larger number of smaller firms.[1] That in an interregnum between new product developments some pressure to avoid excesses of advertising expenditure should be brought to bear by an appropriate public authority, might be salutary; the existence of but two dominant firms in the industry would facilitate this. But beyond this I would myself hesitate to go.

As to the first of the above conditions, the non-collusive rivalry of the two dominant firms—sharpened as it is by its international flavour—shows no sign of abating. Indeed some seventy years after W. H. Lever first disturbed the comparative peace of the nine-teenth-century soap industry, competition in the industry (in the ordinary sense of the word) is more intense than ever, with the active aggressive leadership of the industry assumed now by the one, and now by the other, of the two principal competitors, one of whom is the erstwhile 'monopolist' of the early 'twenties.

Moreover, 'outside' the industry the competitive field is now wider than ever before. As emphasized in the previous chapter, firms in the petroleum and organic chemical industries have become

[1] Distributors' margins would tend to be higher both because real costs due to larger stocks and storage space, etc., are higher (above, p. 31), and also because point-of-sale display and distributor preference would be more important, with retailers assuming the active selling functions of earlier years which services have to be paid for.

It is relevant to point out that a comparison with the present margins on the soap products of such small companies as survive today would shed no light on this point: because on the one hand, in so far as they are higher, this represents primarily an attempt to buy distributor preference; while on the other hand, they would probably be higher still if they did not have access to a distributive network increasingly geared to the selling of a small number of leading brands in most industries.

potential competitors to the industry in a very real sense. New discoveries are more or less equally likely to originate in the laboratories of the latter, as in those of the soap industry. And already (as we have seen) there are chemical manufacturers who produce finished detergent products for retail sale—just as the soap manufacturers now produce in part their requirements of the organic detergent materials.

As I see it, therefore, there is every prospect that the performance of the industry in the 'fifties will continue. On the whole, our study suggests that national competitive oligopoly in the soap industry, in the decade of the 'thirties and in the post-war period, has served the consumer well. Subject, perhaps, to the minimal pressure with regard to excesses of advertising referred to above, I believe it will continue to do so.

APPENDIXES TO PART II

1. PRODUCTION AND USE OF SOAPLESS DETERGENTS

(Table 13)

1. The table is in two parts:
    (*a*) Columns 1-7: U.K. Production, Consumption and Exports of Soapless Detergents.
    (*b*) Columns 8-12: Output Consumed in U.K. by type of Organic Detergent Base.

The data in columns 1 to 7 refer to tonnages (thousands of tons) of finished detergent products as marketed.

The data in columns 8 to 12 provide an approximate breakdown by the type of organic detergent base material embodied in finished products, in respect of output consumed in the U.K. These data therefore are not actual production figures for the various types of base material as if marketed in the form of intermediate products. They may, however, be taken as providing an approximate indication of such output trends (increased appropriately to include supplies embodied in export production) inasmuch as the detergent base materials are frequently supplied in 20-25 per cent. (approximately) active form, while the proportion by weight of active detergent in finished products is, on the average, of the same order of magnitude. Considered as such the table conveys some impression— a more detailed classification would be necessary to bring this out adequately—of the growth and supersession of different products characteristic of such a dynamic developing industrial process.

2. The classification of the organic detergent base materials as 'Anionic', 'Cationic' or 'Non-Ionic'—columns 8 to 12—is well established; see for example J. L. Moilliet and B. Collie, *Surface Activity* (1951), p. 9 and

passim. It is suggested in the first instance by the electro-chemical properties of the materials, but also corresponds to many of the properties of detergents.

Thus anionic and non-ionic compounds are more suitable as general-purpose detergents than cationic compounds, because the latter tend to promote (or at lease fail to inhibit) the re-depositing of dirt on the washed article—due in part to the positive electrokinetic potentials imparted at surfaces by the cation (+ ve ion) of the molecule. The relatively small commercial production of cationic detergents indicated in column 10 of the table consists mainly of quaternary ammonium compounds, which are important because they combine both detergent and germicidal properties. They are used as a bactericidal rinse in food and drink establishments, for washing milk-cans and general dairy equipment, and so on. The British Hydrological Corporation, Ltd., is a leading manufacturer of such detergents.

Detergent materials of the third class have important industrial applications because, being non-ionizing, they are stable and sufficiently soluble in acid and alkaline solutions, as well as in water. Imperial Chemical Industries Ltd.'s 'Lissapol' accounts for the bulk of the production of non-ionic detergents indicated in column 11. Apart from its manifold industrial uses, 'Lissapol' is used as the active agent in the household liquid detergent 'Stergene'. It is, however, inherently non-foaming which reduces its acceptability as a household detergent.

It is the anionic detergent compounds, manufactured for the most part (as outlined above) from available petroleum fractions, which are used as the active material in the bulk of commercial detergent production. The electro-chemical properties of the principal anionic materials are such as to promote most phases of the normal washing process. Alkyl-aryl sulphonate materials predominate: they were used as the active detergent base in upwards of 75 per cent. of detergent production consumed in the U.K. in 1955 (column 9 of the table). A variety of products of the alkyl sulphate type (column 8) make up the balance of the anionic class, with the Shell Petroleum Co.'s pioneer product 'Teepol' accounting for most of the production.

3. Sources

(*a*) Columns 1 to 7. Estimates based on information from trade sources by P. A. R. Puplett, op. cit., pp. 27 (columns 1, 6), 95 (columns 2, 3, 4), 167 (column 5).

During 1952-3 the present author compiled a set of estimates by the same categories for the period 1939-51, which was circularized within the trade. Subsequently the estimates were brought up to 1955, working from a large number of published, but fragmentary, sources. This independent set of estimates differed by less than 0-2 per cent. from the above. It seemed unwise therefore to present a second set of estimates for which no greater accuracy could be claimed.

(*b*) Columns 8 to 12. The data (all columns) for the end-year, 1955, are based on estimates quoted by Mr. F. Courtney Harwood, in a lecture entitled 'Modern Detergents' published in the *Chemical Trade Journal and Chemical Engineer*, 22 February 1957, p. 432.

Column 8.—Ultimately the series in this column is equal to the total consumption (column 12) less columns 9, 10, and 11. In fact, and particularly for the early years of the period, this series and the series for non-ionics (column 11: see below) were estimated together essentially as production data, on the basis of fragmentary information as to capacity and output. Thus it was stated (*Economist*, July-December 1950, p. 31) that the initial Stanlow plant for the production of 'Teepol' had 'an annual capacity of 11,000 tons' (i.e. 21 per cent. active material) and that 'subsequent extensions [to 1950] increased this initial capacity some six or seven times'. Assuming an initial utilization of about one-third, with a steady rate of growth to 1949-50 when 'Teepol' was rapidly replaced as an intermediate for domestic powder products, and allowing for an output of the primary alkyl sulphates of from 1-2,000 tons per annum, this is consistent with the series entered in the column.

Column 9.—Estimated from output data for alkyl-aryl-sulphonate-based powder products. Mainly household products, but small industrial use also (about 1,000 tons in 1955).

Column 10.—Estimate of 1,000 tons in 1955 from Courtney Harwood, loc. cit. Assumed to be the same in 1954. For 1950-3 production assumed small, and not entered.

Column 11.—The Report of the Census of Production, 1948, for the General Chemicals Trade (Vol. 2, Trade E) states that the production of 'Washing materials other than soap' in the trade amounted to 11,160 tons. It is reasonable to assume that this is predominantly 'Lissapol', supplied commercially at 25 per cent. active content. Increased to express as 20 per cent. active, and allowing an additional 5 per cent. (say) for other products, yields the estimate of 15,000 tons entered in the table for 1948. (As a check, it was stated in the trade that 'Lissapol' at this time accounted for about 25 per cent. of the total production of detergent base material which amounted to 62,000 tons in 1948—column 1). The series entered was then estimated (in conjunction with the estimate in Column 8) by interpolation assuming a steady rate of growth from an output of the order of 1-2,000 tons in 1942-3, through to about 18,000 tons in 1949; falling to about 14,000 tons in 1950 in proportion to the major decline in the usage of domestic liquid detergents at that time (column 3 of the table); thereafter stabilizing at about that figure, as reported by Courtney Harwood (loc. cit.) for 1955.

APPENDIX 2

PROFITS IN RELATION TO CAPITAL EMPLOYED, 1949-56

(Table 22)

1. In Table 22 'profits' and 'capital employed' are defined as follows:

'*Capital employed*'—Fixed assets less depreciation *plus* current assets (excluding outside investments and goodwill items), *less* current liabilities (excluding bank loans and provision for future taxation).

The effect of excluding the latter from current liabilities to be subtracted from the sum of assets is to *include* these items—i.e. bank loans, provision for future taxation—in 'capital'.

On this definition capital employed '. . . is represented not only by share capital but all forms of borrowing (including bank overdrafts) and also capital and revenue reserves (including provision for future taxation)'. The quotation is a statement of their own procedure by the Monopolies Commission (*Report on the Supply of Certain Industrial and Medical Gases*, 1956, p. 134), which is thus identical to that adopted here.

'*Profits*'—Reported profit after subtraction of directors' fees, etc., and depreciation, and (i) before deduction of taxation; (ii) before payment of interest on loans and overdrafts, since the latter are treated as capital employed; and (iii) after deducting non-trading profits.

The adjustment under (ii) has been effected, following the Monopolies Commission, by estimating this interest at a rate of 4 per cent. of total loans as at the balance sheet date, and *adding this* to the reported profit.

The concept of profit thus corresponds to that adopted by the Monopolies Commission (see reference above).

The foregoing are the only practicable definitions to adopt. In general, however, they involve that the rates of profit shown *overstate* the (so-called) 'true' profit in relation to capital, because (*a*) fixed capital less depreciation refers to 'historical' values, and (*b*) the recorded profits in some years at least include significant elements of stock appreciation (inevitable with FIFO accounting).

2. The data on which the figures of the first three columns of Table 22 are based have been extracted from the balance sheets and appropriation accounts submitted annually to the Registrar of Companies at Somerset House, London, under the Companies Act of 1948. (Since 1953 Thomas Hedley's have published annually a *Financial Statement* in the form of a handsome company report.) The figures for profits and capital, as defined above, and accordingly the rate of profit on capital, are set out in Table 24 herewith.

3. In the case of *Thomas Hedley & Co. Ltd.* (Somerset House File, No. 83758), the accounts run from 1 July to 30 June of the following year. Thus in column 7 of the table, an average of the profit rates for the years ended 30 June 1949 and 1950 is taken as relating to the calendar year 1949; and so on for subsequent years. It is these estimates which are entered in column 2 of Table 22.

4. In the case of *Unilever Ltd.*: the published *Annual Reports* do not, of course, separate out the results of trading either by product group, or by particular countries, and thus are of no help in the present connexion.

I have therefore taken out data from the accounts submitted to the Registrar of Companies, for the following Unilever soap and detergents companies:

(1) Lever Bros., Port Sunlight, Ltd.
(2) Joseph Watson & Sons Ltd.
(3) Crosfields (CWG) Ltd.
(4) Hudson & Knight Ltd.

The first two are manufacturing and distributing companies, the last two (I suspect) distributing companies only. The figures in column 1 of Table 24 give the sum of profits for the four companies, and in column 2 the sum of capital employed. Thus column 3 gives a weighted average ratio of profit to capital employed for these four companies and is here accepted as providing a reasonable indication of the rate of profit earned by the whole complex of Unilever soap and detergents companies in the United Kingdom. It is entered in column 1 of Table 22.

TABLE 24
Profits, Capital, and Profit Rates

Cal-endar Yrs.	Unilever Ltd.			Thomas Hedley & Co. Ltd.			
	Profits £000 1	Capital £000 2	Rate of profit on capital % 3	Profits (Year ended 30 June) £000 4	Capital £000 5	Rate of profit on capital % 6	Do. (Calen-dar years) % 7
				808	4,017	20·1	
1949	991	7,419	13·4				21·0
				1,057	4,855	21·8	
1950	905	7,544	12·0				24·6
				1,748	6,373	27·4	
1951	1,437	7,940	18·1				17·3
				414	5,664	7·3	
1952	1,339	8,423	15·9				20·4
				2,439	7,255	33·5	
1953	1,615	9,981	16·2				32·2
				2,203	7,106	31·0	
1954	1,047	10,174	10·3				19·1
				565	7,765	7·3	
1955	1,520	10,943	13·9				11·7
				1,415	8,801	16·1	
1956	1,807	11,605	15·6				18·7
				1,920	9,203	21·3	
1957							

5. *The Industry as a Whole.* Since Unilever and Hedley together account for upwards of 75 per cent. of the total sales of soap products in the U.K., it is presumed that an appropriate average of the profit rates of these two companies provides an adequate indication of the profit rate of the industry as a whole.

TABLE 25
Industry Profit Rate

Year	Unilever rate % 1	Weight 2	Hedley rate % 3	Weight 4	Industry rate: Weighted average $=\text{Cols} \dfrac{(1 \times 2 + 3 \times 4)}{2+4}$ 5
1949	13·4	4	21·0	1	14·9
1950	12·0	3	24·6	1	15·1
1951	18·1	3	17·3	1	17·9
1952	15·9	2	20·4	1	17·4
1953	16·2	2	32·2	1	21·5
1954	10·3	2	19·1	1	13·2
1955	13·9	2	11·7	1	13·2
1956	15·6	2	18·7	1	16·6

It is probable that the rate of profit earned by other companies (with the C.W.S., a rather special case in this connexion, principal among them) was less than the average of Hedley and Unilever. If this were so then the 'industry' profit rate would in fact be somewhat lower than that entered in column 3 of Table 22.

The weights used in taking the average of the Unilever and Hedley profit rates were based on the approximate shares in the U.K. market of the two companies over the period, as indicated in Table 25.

APPENDIX 3

ADVERTISING EXPENDITURES

(Table 23)

1. No direct information on advertising expenditures was provided by individual firms.

2. The nature and sources of the data in Table 23 are as follows:

The total of 'Press Display' advertising of soap and detergent products, based on data published in the *Statistical Review of Press Advertising* (Legion Publishing Company), as recorded by P. A. R. Puplett, op. cit., p. 193, is shown in column 1 of the following table:

Year	Total expenditure (£000) 1	Expenditure on soapless detergents (£000) 2
1950	2355	590
1951	2446	470
1952	2190	440
1953	3459	1190
1954	4447	1880
1955	4815	2070

Now the total of 'press, outdoor, and cinema' advertising expenditure on the soapless detergents is estimated by Puplett (op. cit. p. 209), as in column 5 of Table 23.

The ratio of press to outdoor-and-cinema in case of the soapless detergents during this period is estimated at 70 : 30 to 1953, and higher at 80 : 20 for 1954 and 1955. Thus the expenditure on press advertising of the soapless detergents is estimated—column 2 of the table above—by applying these ratios to the total of 'press, outdoor and cinema' spending.

Reverting to Table 23:

Column 1.—Press advertising of soap products other than soapless detergents, is the difference between columns 1 and 2 of the above table.

Column 2.—'Outdoor and cinema' advertising is derived by assuming that the ratio of press to outdoor-and-cinema advertising for 'soap

SBSI

products other than the soapless detergents', is the same as for All United Kingdom advertising, which is estimated at 82 : 18 for the period.

In *Column 3* an allowance is made for forms of advertising expenditure other than press, outdoor, and cinema. These include window display, free samples and coupon offers, catalogues, exhibitions, and 'administration'. The ratio of press, etc., to these latter forms, for total U.K. advertising expenditure in 1952, has been estimated at approximately 70 : 30 (*Advertiser's Weekly*, 18 March 1954—quoted by Puplett, op. cit., p. 210). However, in the case of soap products, expenditure on catalogues and exhibitions (together accounting for 16 of the 30 points) would be negligible, and window display (7·9 points) small. Samples and coupon offers (2 points) would, however, be higher than for advertising generally. A ratio of 70 to, say, 12-15 for soap products would, therefore, seem to be reasonable. Accordingly a figure equal to 20 per cent. of the sum of columns 1 and 2 is entered in column 3. (In respect of 1955 this represents a figure of some £670,000, which—it has been suggested to me—more likely overestimates than underestimates spending under the present heads.)

Column 5. As noted above.

Column 6.—Again a figure equal to 20 per cent. of press, outdoor, and cinema advertising (column 5) was calculated as a first basis of estimate. This yields the series entered, save for the year 1952 which on this basis would read £125,000. However, in the period 1951 through 1953, sales of the soapless detergent powders expanded rapidly—from 49,000 tons in 1951, to 84,000 tons in 1952 and 127,000 tons in 1953; this would suggest that the figure of £125,000 for 1952 is rather out of line. The cost of coupon schemes, for example, would be roughly proportional to the volume of sales. Now the estimates of £135,000 and £340,000 for 1951 and 1953, respectively, each represent about £2·8 per ton. Applying the same expenditure per ton to the 1952 volume of sales suggests a figure of £235,000 for that year, which would appear more reasonable. Accordingly this sum is entered in the table for 1952.

In *Column 8* manufacturers' returns are estimated by valuing recorded sales at retail prices less an average distributors' margin of 15 per cent.

Column 10.—Sum of Columns 4 and 7.

Column 11.—From *Report* of the Census of Production for 1954: Soap Candles and Glycerine (Volume 2, Industry J.), pp. 4-5.

3. Mr. Puplett (op. cit., p. 209) records the following estimates of spending on 'press, outdoor, and cinema' advertising for the principal detergent powder brands of Unilever and Thomas Hedley Ltd.:

	1950	1951	1952	(£000) 1953	1954	1955
'White' powders:						
Tide (Hedley)	174	234	400	634	637	666
Surf (Unilever)			128	507	550	582
'Blue' powders:						
Daz (Hedley)			1	483	582	610
Omo (Unilever)					457	626

These data are of great interest. Two points in particular may be noticed.

First, by 1955 when the competitive struggle had been fully joined for some time, the absolute level of expenditure on each product whether 'white' or 'blue' *was of much the same order of magnitude* (£600,000), *and very large*; whereas the actual volumes of sales in that year were 60,000 tons for 'Tide' as against 20,000 tons for 'Surf', while for the blue powders sales were 39,000 tons for 'Daz' as against 27,000 tons for 'Omo'. Subject to some qualification these data may be interpreted as illustrating the proposition argued above (Chapter 2, p. 30n. and Appendix) that in a context of large-scale advertising the necessary level of advertising expenditure is large in absolute amount and to a large degree independent of the actual volume of sales achieved.

Second, in the cases of both the white and the blue powders the appearance of the directly competitive brand from the dominant rival involved a 'build-up' in expenditure per brand of the order of 30 to 60 per cent. Thus the expenditure for Hedley's 'Tide', at £174,000 with sales of 10,000 tons in 1950 and £234,000 with sales 29,000 tons in 1951, rose to £400,000 with sales of 62,000 tons in 1952. In that year Unilever's 'Surf' was introduced. In the following year the advertising expenditure for 'Tide' jumped to £634,000, and in 1954 and 1955 with sales at 58,000 tons and 60,000 tons respectively—about the same volume as 1952—spending was £637,000 and £666,000 respectively.

Again in its first full year on the market (1953) spending on 'Daz' (Hedley) amounted to £483,000. With the advent of 'Omo' (Unilever) in 1954 it increased to £582,000 and to £610,000 in 1955. (The volume of sales increased from 22,000 tons to 39,000 tons.)

It is tempting, and not at all unreasonable, to suggest that in this context the *necessary minimum* level of expenditure (in the sense of the Appendix to Chapter 2, above) was of the order of £400,000 for the individual product; with a 'build-up' (excess) of expenditure of the order of £200,000 or 50 per cent., emerging with the development of fierce competition.

INDEX OF AUTHORS

INDEX OF TRADE PRODUCTS

(One reference only, in general the first, is given. In case of Unilever companies, product is attributed to Unilever)

GENERAL INDEX

Advertising, 33–36; heavy initial, as investment expenditure, 91 n, 251; as barrier to entry, 13, 91; 'necessary minimum, in a market, 29 n, 55–57, 195–6, 263; excess profits appropriated as, 95, 249; 'build-up' in competition to excessive levels, 13, 101, 153; as itself innovation, 34 n, 146–9; W. H. Lever's, 149, 154–5; soapless detergents, 249–53, 261–3; comparison with expenditure on capital equipment, 253.

Albright & Wilson, Ltd., 216 n, 223.

alkali, caustic, as raw material, 127–8, 133–4, 167–8.

anti-monopoly policy, 81, 114, 116 n, 122.

antitrust, U.S., 115 n, 116 n, 121.

Barriers to new competition, 15, 23, 77 ff; artificial, 22 n; goodwill (or product differentiation) as, 88–94; economies of scale as, 81–87; systematic cost differences as, 79–81; capital requirements as, 78–79.

Bibby, J., & Sons, Ltd. (Liverpool), 173, 176, 181.

British Hydrological Corporation, Ltd., 179 n, 257.

British Monopolies Commission, 68 n, 80 n, 115.

British Petroleum, Ltd., 79 n, 215.

British Soap Company (of B.O.C.M., Ltd.), 176–7, 181, 186.

Brunner Mond & Co. Ltd., 167–8.

butter industry, Australian, 99 n.

Chevreul, 133–4.

classes, three broad, of manufacturing industry, 28 n, 93–94.

Colgate-Palmolive Ltd., 175, 178–9, 181, 191, 213, 229.

collusion, 6, 14, 22 n, 33 n, 73, 115, 137; and excess capacity, 96–100; in soap industry, 138, 142.

Committee, Standing, on Trusts, 169 n, 170 n, 171, 172 n, 174; and cost of production, 131, 155.

competition, 4–5; potential, 5, 68 ff; actual, or intra-industry, 22, 76, 111 ff (and innovation —see Innovation); price competition, 13, 32–33, 51–52, 99 n, 117, 121, 137–8, 231–7; other means of competition, 13, 33–37, 55; 'effective' in soap industry, 241 ff.

conscious parallel action, oligopolists, 115 n.

Co-operative Wholesale Society, Ltd., 139 n, 163–5, 171, 180, 181–3, 185, 189, 197, 218, 229, 230, 240.

cost conditions: short-period, 61–4; long-period, 64–68, 107; in relation to long-term demand, 27, 63–64; inter-firm variations in unit costs, 68 n, 105; 'the' cost of production, 111; distribution costs, 31, 251 n, 255 n; cost of production, soap, 155 and see also Prices, in relation to Costs; soap-synthetics, cost ratio, 212–13, 228.

cost controversy, 18 n, 19.

Craig Wood, Mr. R., 219.

criteria of evaluation, 7 ff.

Daily Mail and soap 'trust' episode, 162–3.

demand conditions: individual firm, 43, 59–61, 72; market demand, 54–55, 59; of soap products, 128–9.

demand-transfer period, 42.

Differentiated Competition, 'pure' model, 94.

discretion, margin of, in setting prices, 8, 52, 60, 94.

Distillers' Union, Ltd., 79 n, 215.